A Strange Proximity

What happens in the relationship between audience and performer? What choices are made in the space of performance about how we attend to others?

A Strange Proximity examines stage presence as key to thinking about performance and ethics. It is the first phenomenological account of ethics generated from, rather than applied to, contemporary theatrical productions.

The ethical possibilities of the stage, argues Jon Foley Sherman, rest not so much in its objects—the performers and the show itself—as in the "how" of attending to others. *A Strange Proximity* is a unique perspective on the implications of attention in performance.

Jon Foley Sherman is a teacher, scholar, performer, and director. He is co-editor of *Performance and Phenomenology* (Routledge 2015). An award-winning actor and deviser, he has performed in Chicago, New York, Philadelphia, Switzerland, and Washington, DC.

A Strange Proximity

Stage presence, failure, and the ethics of attention

Jon Foley Sherman

Routledge
Taylor & Francis Group

LONDON AND NEW YORK

First published 2016
by Routledge
2 Park Square, Milton Park, Abingdon, Oxon OX14 4RN

and by Routledge
711 Third Avenue, New York, NY 10017

Routledge is an imprint of the Taylor & Francis Group, an informa business

© 2016 Jon Foley Sherman

British Library Cataloging-in-Publication Data
A catalogue record for this book is available from the British Library

Library of Congress Cataloging-in-Publication Data
Sherman, Jon Foley, 1972-
A strange proximity : stage presence, failure, and the ethics of attention / Jon Foley Sherman.
pages cm
Includes bibliographical references and index.
ISBN 978-1-138-90776-8 (hardback) -- ISBN 978-1-138-90777-5 (pbk.) -- ISBN 978-1-315-69490-0 (ebook) 1. Acting--Psychological aspects. 2. Stage presence.
I. Title.
PN2058.S53 2016
792.02'8019--dc23
2015036214

ISBN: 978-1-138-90776-8 (hbk)
ISBN: 978-1-138-90777-5 (pbk)
ISBN: 978-1-315-69490-0 (ebk)

Typeset in Sabon LT Std
by GreenGate Publishing Services, Tonbridge, Kent
Printed by Ashford Colour Press Ltd.

For Richard

Contents

Figures

Acknowledgments

On a train ride back from a visit to my mother with Linda Hasunuma and my son Lazlo, a stranger sitting behind us waves to get my attention. He says he's a writer and that he's been observing me and Lazlo and he'd like to share what he wrote. He hands me his laptop and I read the passage to Lazlo. And it's all about how Lazlo is a great teacher because everything he was doing—his exploring, play-acting, ways of talking with me—was done in complete wonder and joy. For teaching me daily about the power of astonishment and the wonder of any part of the world I attend to, I thank my son. Linda is a profound artist, a committed activist and scholar, an inspiring and attentive teacher, a deeply loving mother, and an unstintingly helpful and understanding partner. I am grateful and proud to be her husband and I will never stop thanking her for everything she means to me, her daughter Emily, and Lazlo. Our family, like the one I came from, is scarred by separation and distance. Our love for each other is no less intimate or astonishing because of it.

I have had the great good fortune to enjoy the guidance of established scholars, some of whom I can call friends, others of whom simply helped me because that is how they live their lives. Harvey Young has since my dissertation defense been as staunch a supporter, as patient a reader of proposals, and as tireless an answerer of random and panicked questions as I could have ever imagined. This book would not exist without his help. David Krasner stepped in at a delicate moment to offer detailed and generous advice that changed the way I was thinking about the book's style. Andrew Sofer gave gentle course corrections beyond his duties as a writing seminar leader at the Mellon School for Theater and Performance Research at Harvard. Philipa Rothfield provided exactly the feedback I needed for a chapter drafted later in the process. D. Soyini Madison introduced me to the work of Kelly Oliver, whose thoughts on witnessing proved so important to this book.

Among my peers there are few who did not offer the slow-burning support and encouragement without which projects like this one can hardly be expected to survive. I owe special gratitude to my dearest friend from graduate school, Chlöe Johnston, as well as to other classmates from Northwestern University, including Oona Kersey Hatton, Sam O'Connell, and Ann Folino White. They all offered feedback and support at key moments.

Several institutions and organizations provided support for this project in part and in whole. The American Society for Theatre Research has been the site of many productive conversations about issues in this book. The Mellon School of Theater and Performance Research at Harvard planted me in the midst of a lively discussion with lovely scholars thinking about philosophy and performance while also granting me the time to workshop what would become Chapter 4. The German Academic Exchange Service (DAAD) invited me to a summer seminar at the University of Chicago and first put me into contact with the pungent and unfailingly provocative work of Jacques Rancière. I owe great thanks to Soren West and Lydia Henry at ATOMIC for seeing to it that I had the time to focus on this book both while and after I worked there. Chapters 2 and 3 include content that also appears in my chapter from *The Routledge Companion to Jacques Lecoq* (2016). Chapter 5 includes content first published in *Performance Research*, 16.4 (2011): 52–61.

This book has benefited from the patience and generosity of readers who tackled drafts early and late, and usually under unfair deadlines. In addition to Connor Kalista, who read most of this book more than once, Molly Shanahan, Philipa Rothfield, Kerry Whiteside, Linda Hasunuma, Ginger Farley, Heath Massey, and my artistic partner Julie Beauvais are what any optimistic writer hopes colleagues will be. They have all waded through earlier versions of these pages and given me the opportunity to make them better.

I could not have written this book without the support of many teachers. Richard Romagnoli, to whom this book is dedicated, first taught me to take seriously the ethical and political possibilities of theatre. We have made art together, always stay up too late, and I have cherished his friendship and mentorship for over 20 years. My father made it possible for me to study with Jacques Lecoq and Thomas Prattki in Paris; they transformed my artistic practice and encouraged me to look between rather than at, introducing me to a spatial awareness that has nourished me ever since. Dermot Moran agreed to lead an independent study with me at Northwestern University despite having never met me before; our work laid the foundation for how I have sought to elaborate on Merleau-Ponty's thoughts on space. My thoughts on generosity can be traced to a sermon my mother Samayadevi gave in which she introduced me to the concept of "radical receptivity." The rest of what she has taught and given me could never be enumerated. I have been inspired by students at Northwestern, Beloit College, and Franklin & Marshall College. Among these I want to single out the students in my Devising New Work course at Beloit; they provided me with the most rewarding and exciting teaching experience of my life, in addition to presenting me with an important problem for my research discussed in Chapter 5.

Lastly, I want to acknowledge Talia Rodgers at Routledge. Our first conversation took place over several hours and locations, and from then on she has been a warm advocate of this work. I hope these pages reward her patience and encouragement.

Preface

A Strange Proximity operates as a kind of manifesto. I describe the world and recommend a way of encountering it differently. I forgo conclusions and embrace speculation, aiming at the enhancement of experience rather than its confirmation. Verifiable explanations and falsifiable theories serve engineers and physicians but they are of little use to the practice of theatre that this book seeks to honor. By the nature of its practitioners theatre addresses human experience, and human experience cannot be proven for (at least) two reasons: no one can appraise it apart from participation in it, and because of its fundamental and inexhaustible strangeness. I aim to evade the rule of positivism that waits for performance around the corner of the cognitive turn pursued so ardently in the humanities at present. With *A Strange Proximity* I want to enlarge rather than reduce the world's wonder.

Wonder does not suppose a comfortable place in which to recline and take in the show, however. On the contrary, it demands and unmoors. Astonishment is taxing, but without wonder the world empties. Wonder initiates and sustains encounters with others in a way that allows them to remain beyond me, outside of what I can circumscribe. To suggest a preference for this kind of encounter amounts to making an ethical claim, namely that walking into wonder involves an orientation around how I should engage with others. In a word, without wonder an encounter with others tethers them to the known, reduces them to the not-I, and constitutes an aesthetic and ethical affront. Delimiting others within my own sphere of experience ties their being to my own limitations instead of to their possibilities, it impoverishes their capacity for expression, and it diminishes them to beings incapable of existence outside of my recognition.

And yet everyone lives this failure constantly. It is, I will argue, inevitable. The perpetual failure to meet wonder's demands might generate mounting despair, but it might also establish the grounds for ethical decision-making. When and with and by whom I wonder are not simply questions of convenience or privilege, they are questions that concern the ability of other people, everyone, to exist in the bottomless mystery of experience. How to live among others depends on the answers.

In searching for these answers I pursue a phenomenological exploration of stage presence. Phenomenology, or the very specific tradition of it modeled after Maurice Merleau-Ponty's work that I follow here, shares key characteristics with performance, chief among them the acceptance of impermanence and partiality and the insistence on embodied encounters. Like performance, phenomenology also holds an often hidden conflation of the descriptive and the normative—what appears first as a description of a perceptual phenomenon or attending a production conveys strong assessments of how things should be in the world. Unlike the preponderance of work on performance and ethics that places artists and their work center stage, I take phenomenology's cue and focus on perceivers, or, as I call them here, attendants. Phenomenology precisely emphasizes the central role of experience in any attempt to reflect on life and so I look for the ethical possibilities of performance not simply in its objects—the shows and artists—but also in the how of attending to it.

More specifically, I consider the particularly pleasurable experiences of attending to others popularly called stage presence. Understood as a dynamic perceptual relationship rather than the inevitable outcome of performance techniques, stage presence offers up a great many possibilities for ethical reflection. Descriptions of stage presence carry with them very specific implications and foundational problems for ethics that involve how I encounter other people, what kinds of agency I retain or release in these encounters, and the kinds of responsibilities that arise as a result. Despite its function as a preposition, the "stage" in stage presence concerns more than a particular location for presence. It puts into the foreground of experience how I relate to other people in moments of wonder or astonishment. It suggests that this relation involves more than a single perceiver and perceived. A Strange Proximity does not identify stage presence as it "is" or has been, nor do I seek to "emancipate" the spectator or claim a communal experience. Rather, a phenomenological account of stage presence points to the ongoing and particular experiences of astonishment and care. An ethics of attention founded on the shared, problematic task of perception will be an ethics founded on specific possibilities as well as radical failures. It will lack the stability of imperatives while infusing the ambiguity of experience with astonishment.

Chapter 1

May I have your attention

Paula and the classic question

And then the Russian Empress Alexandra entered upstage right. The room, both the stage and the brick-walled auditorium, seemed jolted alive. Something was *happening*. Previously, the actresses playing her daughters had allowed the appearance of assorted furniture and the scenic flats to do the work of conveying where they were—under guard awaiting certain execution by their captors. But when Paula Gruskiewicz as the Tsarina arrived she seemed to bring that situation into the room. The other actresses seemed to sense it, too. Where just the moment before there had been the same beds, chairs, window, and assorted props, now a dank cottage of grungy upholstery leeched danger into the fabric of a family on the verge of extermination. When Gruskiewicz entered, she seemed immediately to invest each inch of the room with threat, discomfort, and constraint.[1]

At the time the experience thrilled me, but as the years passed I grew increasingly puzzled by it. Paula's entrance seemed a classic example of stage presence. Things got more interesting with her around. I felt swept up in the world of the play and forgot my previous qualms, forgot myself a little. Nonetheless, something about it never lined up. If asked, I would have said that Paula "had" stage presence. But I began to question what this actually meant. It wasn't that *she* became more fascinating; it was that she had seemed to make what was happening on stage more interesting without *herself* occupying the center of my attention. Rather than someone who became the focus of my attention or who excited me, here was someone who changed my relationship to the room and to the other actors; the excitement I felt extended to the stage area and the space between Paula and her surroundings.

My focus on her surroundings indicated a departure from the traditional model of stage presence in which performers, not their surroundings, take focus. In the classic model of stage presence performers are more than—more powerful/interesting/exciting than other people on stage with them and certainly than the attendants imagine themselves to be. Such performers, by definition remarkably different than others, take on proportions larger than their bodies; they tower, they command, fascinate, and compel, and they do so by virtue of something intrinsic to themselves. Such qualities capture attendants and yoke them to the performer as an object of attention. This kind of stage presence is often described in quantitative terms: actors have a lot of it, they have enough of it, they could do with more of it. Movie stars that show up on Broadway stages are frequently assessed in this manner. Here Howard Kissel goes after Julia Roberts: "As mesmerizing as she is onscreen, she has surprisingly little stage presence." Roberts' co-star in that production, Bradley Cooper, would later become an A-list Hollywood celebrity and Oscar nominee himself. In the *Daily Mail* preview article on Cooper's London premiere in the title role of *The Elephant Man*, columnist Quentin Letts writes:

> Stage presence [...] perhaps stems in part from a combination of physical beauty and self-confidence. Bradley Cooper certainly has those two things in *The Elephant Man*, but the paradox with his performance is that he is playing a character who is notoriously ugly.

Tellingly, stage presence is something the actor has, not the character. Actors may be born with it, they may study to acquire more of it, but actors are the ones who have it and "it" is "of" the actors. Which is also to say that in some way it relates to them as persons; "their" stage presence is a function of their specific being placed in front of other beings. Thus this description of two actresses who exchanged roles during the run of the 2013 West End revival of *Old Times* by Harold Pinter: "No matter which role they play, the inwardly centered Ms Scott Thomas and the more visibly anxious Ms Williams project almost opposite stage presences" (Brantley, "London Theater Journal"). So the classic version of stage presence concerns not simply an excess, but an excess connected to the sense of perceiving something about the performer, a unique truth about the performer magnified by the stage. Curiously, this trait can, over time, "trap" an actor whom critics describe as always playing a version of themselves: after the initial introduction, intoxication can give way to familiarity and impatience. My father enjoyed telling the story of how, over the course of attending several productions starring legendary stage actor Sir Laurence Olivier, he took less and less pleasure in them. He had come to expect carefully detailed performances and Olivier always gave them. For my father, Olivier had normalized astonishment and effectively destroyed it in the process. As Bernhard Waldenfels notes, "a methodologically produced amazement [would] not master wonder but rather abolish it" ("Strangeness, Hospitality, and Enmity" 93).

For there to be something about performers that makes attendants react with fascination and attraction, the quality of themselves that performers exhibit must be singular, impressive, and seemingly unrepeatable. This classic sense of stage presence fits Max Weber's description of charisma as "a certain quality of an individual personality by virtue of which he is set apart from ordinary men and treated as endowed with supernatural, super-human, or at least specifically exceptional powers or qualities" (358–9). In Weber's definition, charisma operates almost independent of charis-matic people—something they have, a quality of their personality, does the work of singling them out. They are the possessors if not the owners of charisma—it eludes their control because it resides in them and not in their actions. Similarly, this understanding of charisma does not grant any agency to people who recognize charismatic people. A quality appears in someone and results in a certain treatment. Those affected do not choose to behave in any particular way, they simply do, and, Weber implies, they are correct to do so.

The idea that an actor has "a" presence to offer on stage has been sub-ject to convincing criticism for some time. Scholars writing about video art, Internet performance, and other forms that involve the heavy use of digital mediating technologies have recognized that a *sense* of presence may be had in more than one place. The possibility of projecting an actor's—or audience member's—image across multiple locations puts pressure on the idea that stage presence remains strictly local to bodies. For example, in *Performing Presence: Between the Live and the Simulated* (2011), Gabriella Giannachi and Nick Kaye examine the work of Lynn Hershman Leeson, Gary Hill, and Paul Sermon and find the possibility of presence "across divi-sions, differences, and multiplications" (241).[2] Many of these pieces offer "live" performances where performers are separated from each other as well as from the attendants by monitors and screens; Giannachi and Kaye argue that they nonetheless achieve a feeling of proximity, often as a result of rupturing the sense of place. Such performances threaten traditional notions of stage presence that presume it to be a part of the actor. Nonetheless the phenomenon is still *done to* attendants, if not by the actors then by the tech-nologies of the performance.

Another common model does not require possession or singular loca-tion, but action. Sometimes this action concerns temporality: actors "are present," "in the present," or "in the moment." Perhaps by diving into the depths of the present tense actors provide immediate contact between themselves and the world, and thus make direct contact with those in the auditorium. Or perhaps their mastery of time involves the ability to com-press the past (rehearsal) and the future (the foregone conclusion of the performance script or score) into the present moment (Erickson, "Tension/ Release and the Production of Time in Performance" 92–3). Achieving stage presence amounts again to a kind of "being present" in which some-thing essential—belonging to the actor or perhaps to time itself—becomes available to attendants. These descriptions convey a dual nature of stage presence: materiality and atemporality. Thus Suzanne Jaeger's claims that to *do* stage presence or *be* present, one must be bodily with another while also so embedded in the present as to be freed from the experience of passing time (123, 129).

Acting teachers from Zeami in fifteenth-century Japan to Anne Bogart in twenty-first-century America have elaborated on this version of stage presence by proposing that an actor's interest on stage may be understood in terms of specific techniques related to balance, weight, and tension. At the same time that actors "with" stage presence might exist as a "higher form of being with great spiritual vitality," there are *means* of achieving presence that can be taught. The actor can practice these means "through [the] manipulation of space and materials, including his [sic] own body and posture" (Power 49). Phillip B. Zarrilli explores many of these exercises involving breath and movement in his recent work on psychophysical acting, the most recent of which positions his own practice and performances as models of these methods ("An Enactive Approach," "'...Presence ...,'" "The Actor's Work on Attention").

All of these renderings of stage presence, whether formulated as a quality, a possession, a state, or an action, obscure a crucial element: the attendants. More precisely, these theories imagine attendants without agency.

Whether stage presence is described as a kind of personal intensity or as a learned practice, the performer occupies a position of power. A cursory observation of the terms used in reference to stage presence reveals the force at play: attendants are "taken," "compelled," and "captured" by performers who "are" "magnetic," "mesmerizing," and "electric" (Goodall). The name of a 2000 colloquium on "the presence of the actor" makes explicit the violence inherent in these descriptions: *Burn the Boards, Shatter the Screen* (Farcy and Prédal).[3] This violence may yet produce something pleasing, as Erika Fischer-Lichte argues in her accounts of stage presence. All the same, she deploys the language of dominance in exemplary fashion: through a "mastery of certain techniques and practices," a performer can "occupy and command space" and is capable of exerting "a vice-like grip on [spectators'] attention" (Fischer-Lichte, *The Transformative Power of Performance* 96, 108, 109). The experience definitively begins with the actions of performers through which "they appear as embodied mind" (99). It is enough to perceive this appearance in order to have one's own experience as an embodied mind. Although part of "the nature of human beings," this state is elusive, and "the actor who grants us such an experience, rare in everyday life, will quite understandably be celebrated" (Fischer-Lichte, "Appearing as Embodied Mind" 116).

Through submission, chosen or not, the attendants' wills are shaped by the performers before them. In its neat inversion of Michel Foucault's regulating gaze, the classic model of stage presence conceals the attendants' participation because it describes something that happens to them. Placing all the action in the performer—or the performance—also forces the hand of anyone analyzing stage presence because it prompts the question of why anyone would submit to the performers. This risks queuing up any number of consoling but over-determined explanations whose packaged responses precede the question itself, for example the unconscious desires, impulses, and transfer of psychoanalysis or the rigorous economic structure of will in Marxism and cultural materialism. These explanations carry the risk— or precisely emphasize the inevitability—of securing the attendants' lack of agency and enforcing their submission.

Despite efforts to explain it, stage presence has proven remarkably resistant to scholarship. Perhaps because of its inherent involvement with what feels like the unknown and unknowable of human attraction and fascination, stage presence remains or *should* remain just beyond reach. Hence the French expression for an unnamable charm, "un certain je ne sais quoi." Literally, "a certain I don't know what," the phrase indicates that within the inability to articulate an idea there lies an irresistible appeal. It might be that this appeal simply repeats the standardized allure of what cannot be possessed. The failure to explain precisely what it is about someone that appears so peculiarly engaging might also speak to something enduringly mysterious, strange, and fundamental to experience.

Of course, as far as stage presence is concerned, it turns out that you can actually pinpoint the market rate plus $20 convenience fee for basking in the reflected glory of movie stars appearing on stage together. When Ian McKellen's Gogo and Patrick Stewart's Didi embraced each other the first time in the show, the audience responded with appreciative applause and cooing that spoke more to how the attendants imagined the two actors to be "in real life" than to what that embrace meant in the context of yet another star-studded *Waiting for Godot*.[4] But the price of admission can't describe how McKellen's Gogo broke my heart when, standing in a hole in the stage, he looked to Didi and croaked, "We are happy ... What do we do now, now that we are happy?" To dive into that moment, to describe how the smallest gestures can disorient in the largest ways, means trading in the repeatability of cultural materialism or psychology, the falsifiability demanded by scientific inquiry, and taking up in their place the precision and ambiguity of poetry, of speculation.

Which is where stage presence belongs. What could be more deflating than to conclude that my attention fell to this or that performer because she reminded me of The Virgin, or because as a member of the bourgeoisie I am arranged to consume spectacle, or because the performer enacted a series of bodily shifts to which I as a biped am destined to respond with curiosity, or because the latest science says that human brains operate in such and such a way? These interpretations might *explain* stage presence, but they do not seem able to *describe* it, because a successful description of stage presence will leave something to the imagination. One need not wheel out portmanteaux like "energy" or "feeling," or confine stage presence to an island of cultural luxury as a result. What might be unknowable, thrilling, and astonishing could still be *necessary*.

As a heightened experience of others, stage presence concerns and foregrounds how I attend to others and what it means to be with other people. It suggests a variety of possible relations between attendants and performers and yet other attendants. My sense of attachment to and distance from others arises amidst these possibilities. Thinking about stage presence means thinking about how attending to some people differently than others, perhaps more than others, transforms all those involved. Thinking about stage presence, then, means thinking about the configuration of responsibility between others and myself. In other words, stage presence is an ethical matter.

It becomes one by posing questions of perception, of *how* I attend to other people. Locating stage presence *in* or *with* the performer pushes towards a particular model of perception in which objects simply *are* and I take in their manifestations like a recording device. Perception becomes passive, more like *reception*. And, just like the classic model of stage presence, it happens to the perceiver.

But perception doesn't *happen* to anyone. It is something people do. It's how people *are*. Or so phenomenology would have us believe.

A plunge into the world

Phenomenology operates as a poetics of experience. It seeks organizing principles to be sure, but these serve to further open the horizons of perception. Instead of ratifying what is perceived, a poetics of experience describes the strangeness of perception. As such, it offers a model of embodied—and embodying—analysis ideally suited for reflecting on performance.[5]

Phenomenology has since its formalization in the early twentieth century by philosopher Edmund Husserl (1859–1938) insisted on the irreducible connection between understanding the world and experiences of it. Rather than seeking the truth of human experience in abstract concepts, phenomenology has, broadly speaking, argued that corporeal involvement with the world forms the linchpin to understanding that world. For French philosopher Maurice Merleau-Ponty (1908–1961), this branch of philosophy "is not the reflection of a prior truth, but rather, like art, the actualization of a truth" (Merleau-Ponty, *Phenomenology of Perception* lxxxiv).[6] Phenomenology does not take for granted that "laws" exist to which I might gain access either through reason or experiment. On the contrary, it suggests that I can only *achieve* truth, which means that it will never exist independently of me.

This "radical, anti-traditional style of philosophizing" (Moran, *Introduction to Phenomenology* 4) proposes that everything in the world, from my thoughts of it to the materials I sit on while having those thoughts,

must all be embodied in the world of perception to exist in any meaningful way. Bridging the gap between strict empiricism—the world is exterior
to me and I only witness it—and intellectualism—I can only be sure that
I imagine the world—phenomenology insists that perception of the world
both constitutes that world and adheres to a place in it. "The relations
between things have always our body as their vehicle" and, as such, "all
knowledge is established within the horizons opened up by perception"
(Merleau-Ponty, *Phenomenology* 320, 215). Perception does not *contain*
the world—those horizons open to something beyond the perceptible. But
it makes the world possible through bodies that secure the appearance of
things by engaging with them. However, the world is not simply what I
think of it either—there is more to perception than an idea of the world:
"The world is not what I think, but what I live through" (Merleau-Ponty,
Phenomenology lxxx). I can be sure there is a world but only because I participate in it.

Husserl defined the discipline's central intellectual operation as the *epoché*,
or bracketing of experience. He meant to short-circuit assumptions handed
down by tradition, science, and culture through the suspension of a "natural
attitude" that accepted appearances; this in turn was intended to provide an
approach to the "things themselves" through embodied engagement with
phenomena (Husserl, *Ideas* §90, §2). By shaking off my accustomed manner
of working through the world, I might hope to encounter it afresh and touch
on the essence of things. As Bert O. States, who popularized the phenomenological approach in theatre studies, would claim, "it is only the moment
of absorption that counts; what conditions the moment and what follows it
are somebody else's business" ("The Phenomenological Attitude" 370).

Husserl's *epoché*, however, cannot address the multitude of bodies whose
varied histories are necessarily excluded by the transcendental subject that
came to occupy the center of his phenomenology. Merleau-Ponty—in
many ways deeply and openly indebted to Husserl—argued that a total
epoché, a complete "phenomenological reduction," was impossible: embodied existence requires an involvement with the world and this guarantees
that individual histories and other people will always shape perception
(*Phenomenology* lxxvi, 364–83). Rather than imagining a withdrawal from
the conditions that frame it, the "moment of absorption" has come to represent their extension and expression. Instead of "the" body there is an endless
host of them, all socially constituted and subject to the pull of materiality.
There is neither a moment separable from others that remains a part of lived
experience, nor any way to abstract the world from an abstract position.

Rather than observe from on high, phenomenology "must plunge into
the world" (Merleau-Ponty, *The Visible and the Invisible* 38/60). In doing
so, Merleau-Ponty's phenomenology will establish two claims about perception crucial to this book: it is always incomplete and it is social. As an
embodied being, I am involved with the world around me—I can neither be

separate from it, as empiricism requires, nor its source, as intellectualists would recommend. Merleau-Ponty further expanded on Husserl's empiricism by noting that no one can shed embodiment enough to comprehend, even over time, the fullness of any object.

The very nature of phenomenology's object—embodied experience—leaves completion out of the question. Perception itself is not comprehensive. No one can see or feel or smell or touch or taste all of anything, and I move through my days without attempting to complete my experience of things. Even when I try, the effort is hopeless: "I am open to the world, I unquestionably communicate with it, but I do not possess it, it is inexhaustible" (Merleau-Ponty, *Phenomenology* lxxx–lxxxi). There will always be more of anything, of everyone, than I can perceive or know.

Bodies are always in the process of becoming, of altering their organization by how they are seated, standing, running, sleeping, eating. They do not stop, even at death. Marc Richir explains Merleau-Ponty's appraisal of bodily integrity by noting that "every being, of whatever sort, is always and in principle *unfinished*, repeatedly open to horizons of completion which are themselves penetrated with incompletion" (36).[7] Merleau-Ponty's horizons cannot be crossed—they are not occluding edges but the constantly shifting limits of each object; objects are not only incompletely perceived, they are themselves essentially incomplete. The work of perception never finishes; I am situated, and my bodily existence among others guarantees perception's inability to present the world entire.

In Merleau-Ponty's invocation of Paul Valéry, "perception is the 'flaw' in this 'great diamond'" and, as a result, "the picture of the world will always include this lacuna that we are and by which the world itself comes to exist for someone" (*Phenomenology* 215). Embodiment casts a shadow on the center of knowledge. The knowable will always be *local* in the sense that it appears through specific acts of perception that occupy a place in the world. Similarly, the pervasive unknowable appears *as such* through each person's particular acts of perception. Rather than being a hidden part of knowledge, it is what *cannot* be known, cannot be captured. The only way to complete the picture of the world or of anything would be to remove me from a lived experience of it.

This failure of perception serves as a reminder that "embodiment" does not solely concern bodies. A common misperception plaguing phenomenology supposes that it refers simply to the physicality of experiences. Phenomenology starts from the recognition of corporeality but it also characterizes this corporeal being as one determined largely by its *relationships* with a corporeal world. Approaching and retreating from others establishes my material existence. My body does not simply operate on the world in the act of perceiving it, nor does the world simply act upon me in the act of being perceived. Rather, an unending engagement defines them and binds them.

"For I see these other glances too"

In addition to its endlessly receding horizon, Merleau-Ponty's phenomenology characterizes perception by its sociality. The social nature of perception helps fuel the radical incompleteness of any perceiver's experience of things in several ways. To begin with, embodiment, the corporeal relationships with the world that allow perception at all, depends on others. All people are born of and borne by bodies; the world everyone enters has already been formed by others. As Merleau-Ponty puts it, "with our first oriented gesture, *someone*'s infinite relationship to his [sic] situation has invaded our mediocre planet and opened an inexhaustible field to our behavior" (*Signs* 67/108). I employ "[sic]" here not simply to correct for the tendency of male philosophers through most of history to tuck women into observations about men. Rather, I want to emphasize that, so far at least, all human life grows inside a woman. *Her* situation, everything about it from her socio-economic class to her race and sexuality and geographic location, operates on the child's perceptual abilities at their very formation. After birth all caregivers, all the others the child encounters, continue this molding work: "before I see the Other, the Other was there teaching me how to see, eliciting and structuring my look and my voice" (Burke, "The Moral Power of the Face of the Child" 294). Although perception isn't exactly given to me by others, it arrives with them.

It does so in part because they help secure a world with which I can be involved. The habit of exclaiming "Did you see that?!" after something astonishing happens speaks to a desire to validate perceptions through their confirmation by others. Even when I harbor an experience within myself, the pleasure I derive from it involves others to the extent that their ignorance warms my appreciation of the experience. Merleau-Ponty goes so far as to claim that the things perceived "would really only be being if I learned that they are seen by others, that they are visible to every viewer who warrants the name" (*Signs* 168/273). Without others perceiving—according to their own situations—what I perceive, I cannot be sure that I perceive at all.

Performance events in particular reinforce my reliance on other people's perceptions by the nature of attendants standing or sitting amongst each other. The experience of attending a performance with others heightens some reactions and dampens others—tears flow easily to join the snuffling in the next row or laughter sputters guiltily to avoid disturbing a somber mood. Fischer-Lichte describes a positively Rabelaisian scene of attendants who

> laugh, cheer, sigh, groan, sob, cry, scuff their feet, or hold their breath, they yawn, fall asleep, and begin to snore, they cough and sneeze, eat and drink, crimple wrapping paper, whisper, or shout comments, call "bravo" and "encore," applaud, jeer and boo, get up, leave the theatre, and bang the door on their way out.
>
> (*Transformative Power* 38)

Even in more orderly auditoria, responses emerging with an awareness of their contexts result from the sharing of perception with others. Being in an audience foregrounds the combined actions that found the world of perception. This is a world defined by "the sense that shines forth at the intersection of my experiences and at the intersection of my experiences with those of others through a sort of gearing into each other" (Merleau-Ponty, *Phenomenology* lxxxiv).

Of course, I do not perceive the same things exactly as others do. Anyone who has argued over the merits of a performance knows this. "Did we even go to the same show?" But far from suggesting that perceptions are my own, separate from others, the divergence of experiences establishes above all the possibility that what I perceive does not belong to me or I to it. In a passage to which I will return, Merleau-Ponty notes that

> the perceptible is precisely that which can haunt more than one body without budging from its place. No one will see that table which now meets my eye; only I can do that. And yet I know that at the same moment it presses upon every glance in exactly the same way. For I see these other glances too.
>
> (*Signs* 15–16/29)

A complex world of perception presents itself here, in which I find myself close to others both because of and in spite of my seeing (hearing, smelling, etc.) nothing the same way. It starts from how the perceptible world possesses me. My body is haunted by the perceived—I am altered not by things themselves but by their shades. Residues, vestiges move me in a way uniquely resonant with my body, *just as they do others*. Seeing the table does not mean it emanates from me or is subject to me. Instead, it can meet others in the same manner in which it meets me. And yet I am inevitably rooted in situations whose involvement with others is specific; I can no more overcome the particularity of my experience than I can escape its participation in the common world of perception. Which is to say, the table might meet others in the same way and mean something to each one, but it will never mean the same thing. All that can be guaranteed is that these differences are what make it possible for me to exist in a perceptible world.

A phenomenon presses on me and on others in the same way not because they and I perceive it as the same thing, but because they and I perceive it at all. Each act of perception establishes specific histories and concerns while simultaneously affirming shared participation in a world accessible through perception. Perception is always social in this way—I must at least imagine the possible others who can have their own experience of what I perceive.

And I can feel myself doing this. Attendants at a performance function as hives of perspective even within the most conditioned and supposedly monolithic responses. Walking into a performance venue indoors or out, taking a seat or assuming a position amidst other walkers, plugging into an MP3 player before heading out to a guided tour of a city neighborhood, all of these entrances stage the blending of my perspective with others. This blending happens all the time of course, but simply attending a performance event can foreground the experience; all of these other people have made an effort to come to this place to experience something during the same time. Before, during, and after performances I "see these other glances too."

In between, during performances, my supposedly individual perspective comes into being amidst others. Nicholas Ridout and Susan Manning among others have written about how performance audiences themselves disrupt the convergence of meanings. Manning describes how different social positions conditioned spectatorship among attendants at mid-twentieth-century performances, noting that sexuality molds movement on stage into very different experiences in the auditorium ("Looking from a Different Place"). And yet, other attendants can also perceive these differences, as Manning elaborates in a later study of raced bodies in, and segregated auditoria at, American concert dance performance (*Modern Dance, Negro Dance*). Thus one portion of the audience might follow the lead of another to rise and move along with the dancers during Alvin Ailey's *Revelations* (Manning, *Modern Dance, Negro Dance* 217–20). As much as I am perhaps *supposed* to forget that I attend performance among others, I can very rarely ignore them, which means I am always learning from and regulating myself according to what others perceive.

Even my failure to do so binds me to the other attendants in perception, as Ridout suggests when he notes that getting it wrong can help install playgoers in a community of many voices. He describes the phenomenon of the "mis-spectator" whose experience of a performance fails to recognize, much less honor, the metrics preferred by "expert" spectators (Ridout, "Mis-Spectatorship"). Simply by unapologetically missing the point—of a line of dialogue, of a line of movement—attendants can render themselves and those near them aware that the "consensus that masquerades as collectivity" suppresses the unique strains of experience within it (Ridout, "Mis-Spectatorship" 182). Not getting it in public demonstrates as well as anything that performance does not so much reveal meaning as present opportunities to make it with other people. In an audience I will always shape meanings alongside others working with materials encountered in the same place. Sometimes I'm pleased with what I've made, sometimes not, but as an attendant I cannot make anything without being influenced by the work of my neighbors. In terms of stage presence, performers do not simply require attendants to receive their brilliance; performers need attendants to engage in multiple acts of perception and alteration. Which is to say, performers need attention.

Economies of attention

Attendants do more than attend performances—they attend *to* them. Even when sense differs from person to person, attending to a performance suggests perception's shared effort. For Merleau-Ponty, attention had to be something more than the simple narrowing of the perceptual field or a kind of focus within it; such a description presupposed an abstract world that lay *outside* of perception, a world to which attention was applied.

> To pay attention does more than further clarify some preexisting givens; rather, it is to realize in them a new articulation [...] they are only preformed *horizons*, they truly constitute new regions in the total world [...] attention is the active constitution of a new object that develops and thematizes what was until then only offered as an indeterminate horizon.
>
> (Merleau-Ponty, *Phenomenology* 32, 33)[8]

Merleau-Ponty would discard the separation of consciousness and the world implied here. What remained, however, was his belief that the world of perception arose between perceivers and the horizons that surround them. My experience of the world does not come about because I pay attention to the world, but through the combined attention of others and myself. By addressing myself to an object (or another person, or a landscape) I neither imagine nor acknowledge its appearance. Attention thematizes the work of perception. It describes my awareness of a process "that creates, all at once, out of the constellation of givens, the sense that ties them together. Perception does not merely discover the sense *they have*, but, rather, sees to it *that they have a sense*" (Merleau-Ponty, *Phenomenology* 38).[9] Performance foregrounds this bedrock dynamic of perception because "the" performance does not exist before attendants so much as through them; performance comes to being through their different kinds of attention. In this sense, attention is not only an action, but also a medium, a means of achieving an experience. Attendants experience a performance through the medium of attention.

Bringing attention to attention during performance reveals an economy at play. Waldenfels describes the economization of attention when he notes that "the selection inherent in all attention [...] turns attention into a rare good" (*Phenomenology of the Alien* 68). "Selection" indicates the value of attention on the basis of the economic theory of supply and demand. I can hold attention and I can give it. "Do I have your attention?" But it is limited. I never perceive as much as I fail to notice and I am always missing something; thus the ceaseless demand for more attention.

Rather than a good that must be made, however, attention operates more like a currency. The English language certainly arranges this meaning: I "pay" attention. During performance, attention is paid in order to gain an experience. Performers of course hope for attention to be given—if not to them individually, then to the production as a whole. For attendants, it costs something more than money to participate in the experiences of the performance; it even makes sense to say that paying a lot of attention takes something out of me. Consider the different amounts—and kinds—of attention asked for by Samuel Beckett's *Not I* (1972) and *The House with the Ocean View* (2002) by celebrity performance artist Marina Abramović. In the former, an onslaught of language pours from a spotlit mouth hovering eight feet over a stage with a hooded figure nearby; the entire play lasts between 9 and 14 minutes, depending on the actress.[10] In *Ocean View*, attendants meander as they like in a gallery housing the raised boxes where Abramović spent 12 days.

All performances propose hierarchies of attention whether they intend to or not: how actions are lit, timed, and placed all contribute to—without entirely determining—where and how attendants engage a performance. The elements of these systems can be managed with everything from mind-boggling precision to clear emphasis on some rather than others to a potentially disturbing lack of coherent pattern. In each case, however, attention's distribution in performance deeply concerns all participants, especially because they can never pay enough of it. Describing its exchange, its movement, concentration, and dispersal traces different performances and also suggests implicit social arrangements.

Certainly during stage presence I attend more to ... *something* than to others. Whatever else it may be, stage presence is not equitable. Within any system of attention managed by perceivers and perceived, stage presence foregrounds an unequal distribution that characterizes *all* attending and perceiving. As a relationship, stage presence involves not only attendants but also other performers potentially excluded from this relationship. Indeed, without the relegation of other actors to the background, stage presence might not even exist as a phenomenon. As Waldenfels puts it, "Turning-toward and turning-away occur at the same time" (*Phenomenology of the Alien* 64). On stage or off, there is only so much attention to go around.

While it might seem far-fetched to suggest that a production operates with a "free market" or a "socialist" economy of attention, these terms might still indicate how attention is distributed: does it aggregate around one or two performers, around the scenography, roughly evenly across a range of performers, or randomly between performers, setting, sound, and costume? Actors as individuals are hardly the only elements of attention during performance: the different rhythms of movement, sound, and form—for starters—all might constitute attention's work. Even more broadly, philosopher P. Sven Arvidson identifies three concentric "regions" of attention: "theme, thematic context, margin" (101–2). Each region or level addresses a kind of attention even as the levels form a kind of hierarchy. During performance these levels proliferate prodigiously as bodies, movement, and sound multiply attentive possibilities. In short, attendants cannot attend to everything, but they can attend to anything.

The formality or looseness of the economy depends not only on the work of the artists but also on the willingness of attendants to adhere to the signs of that economy offered by the performance. For one thing, the action of perception that underwrites attention involves the developed and developing priorities and habits of each perceiver. And no matter how much a production's *mise-en-scène* directs attention, attendants may always resist its indications or follow their own interests in spite of it. This might be the most ethical approach to some performances.

The classic model of stage presence does not allow for such resistance. As noted above, the discourse on stage presence brims with verbs that speak to a uni-directional power: attendants are "compelled," "commanded," "captured," and "struck" by performers. Consider the exclamation, "I couldn't take my eyes off her!" At first, this seems to describe an ocularcentric understanding of perception—as if I was *only* seeing someone, as if seeing someone did not also involve the other senses, and as if those other senses might not more productively account for an experience of that relationship. The phrase also contains an indication of the haptic nature of vision through its implication that to see someone is to touch her. Ultimately, however, the phrase is transparently hyperbolic because attendants *can* take their eyes "off" the performer. Perhaps the very exaggeration of the loss of will precisely describes the phenomenon of stage presence. "Sure, I normally decide where I look, but she *took* that control from me!"

But such claims are dangerous. At the very least they slide uncomfortably close to the familiar refrain of the sexual predator whose excuse is that a woman's clothes rendered him unable to deny violent "instincts." Performances may indeed be capable of directing my attention, but they are not able to remove me from the action of perception, from my responsibility for perception. Associating stage presence with a loss of control on the part of attendants divests attendants of responsibility for the theatrical exchange and invokes a more serious violence. It also obscures how and what attention adds to perception, in particular the varied suite of experiences invested in the verb "to attend."[11]

Attending to others involves more than awareness. To begin with, I am also *there* for them, in the sense of occupying a place directed towards another. This might be a seat in a black box theatre, a corner of a warehouse, or a spot on a beach—in each case, to attend requires and even foregrounds a place to do it. The nature of my relationship to the place will determine in part both what and how I attend to what happens there. I'm sick to death of conventional theatres; I love walking into the lobby of the Paris Opéra at the Palais Garnier; I like sitting close by; I'm unnerved by finding the audience on stage; I'm bored by yet another repurposed industrial site; I'm keen to discover the relationship between a factory's former products and the cultural product under construction. Place *matters* to attendants. And no matter what place one has, attending means directing it towards others.

I am there *for* them. Attention formalizes the work of perception that directs me towards something or someone else. In this way attention raises a host of questions associated with *presence*, itself an extremely loaded term, as seen above. Can I attend to those who are not with me? Do I attend performers onscreen the same way I do performers who share space with me, performers whose alteration by me can be perceived just as they alter me? Can I attend to an idea? Not all of these questions will be fully answered in what follows, but they point to how, insofar as "being there" for someone has to do with presence, it also has to do with the nature of my relationship to others. When I attend to people, I can be there for them as a doctor attending a patient or a parent attending to a child. This solicitousness emphasizes what strikes me as a core value of attention and what it adds to perception: care.

Care, astonishment

Attention arranges perception so that what I feel, need, desire, and think forms the background to someone or something else that concerns me. Attention thematizes perception and moves it away from its source. To attend is to care for.[12] Hence, "you're not paying attention" means "I want you to care." I want you to care because placing something—say, a vulnerable person—in the midst of care assigns importance in that moment. Asking others to care for me means asking them to place concern for me, if only momentarily, above concern for themselves. They do not—cannot—disappear as perceivers, but their alteration by perception becomes the ground from which they address my experience. Caring for another does not diminish caring persons so much as it displaces them from the center of their own attention.

Life requires care. No infant can survive without care of some kind. That care might be limited and cursory, but survival under even the most debased circumstances requires being cared for. The limits of that care shape a more or less expansive understanding of care just as they mold an understanding of self. It requires little imagination to conceive of the different worlds made for someone surrounded with care and someone for whom care arrives in the most meager portions. Too much care can smother, too little can poison, but without it life diminishes, ceases. In Virginia Held's words, "Without the actual practice of care, there cannot be human life at all" ("Liberalism and the Ethics of Care" 302). Through its direction, its placement, its address to another, attention expresses—and produces—care. And to the extent that care *should* be about others, it will involve a presumptive ethics.

Carol Gilligan's ground-breaking *In a Different Voice: Psychological Theory and Women's Development* (1982) helped launch a passionate discussion about the role of care in ethical theory. Having identified the rigidly masculinist perspective of widespread and supposedly neutral tools for measuring moral development, Gilligan observed that girls and women had learned to make moral decisions based on relationships and affect as much as on purportedly autonomous reason. Maurice Hamington writes that "Gilligan's 'care ethics' is a relational approach to morality that avoids generalization in favor of particularity and connection" (*Embodied Care* 14). Gilligan's work invited bold binary conclusions based on sex and an opposition between universalist and particularist ethical models. These models refer to three of the dominant genealogies of Western thinking on ethics, those of Immanuel Kant, virtue ethics, and utilitarianism. Kant understood that ethics were derived from rational, universal principles that autonomous agents could then apply in fulfillment of a categorical imperative. These ethics are sometimes called "deontological" in reference to their insistence on one's duty to a principle. Virtue ethics are most closely associated with Aristotle, who supposed that the virtuous action was that which best expressed the nature of its doer. "Care ethics," which insist on the centrality of care to human experience, are often associated with virtue ethics. A third strain of ethical thinking qualifies actions as "good" if they produce good results—the utilitarianism of Jeremy Bentham and John Stuart Mill being the chief examples of a tradition whose adherents often disagreed over whether a group or an individual could be the benefactor of a good result.

Among these traditions Virginia Held argues that Gilligan's real contribution can best be understood as a layering of different perspectives on moral decision-making. The universalizing "'justice perspective'" of Kantian ethics might be adapted to specific cases, while a "'care perspective'" could focus on relations between people and prioritize "narrative and sensitivity to context in arriving at moral judgments" (Held, *The Ethics of Care* 27–8). Instead of *replacing* situation-agnostic imperatives or utilitarian calculations, an ethics of care could precede them and direct their application in any particular context.[13]

Joan Tronto and Berenice Fisher identified four elements of care:

> caring about, noticing the need to care in the first place; taking care of, assuming responsibility for care; care-giving, the actual work of care that needs to be done; and care-receiving, the response of that which is cared for to the care.
>
> (Tronto 252)

From these, Tronto derives four elements of an ethic of care: "attentiveness, responsibility, competence, and responsiveness" (252). These elements will help steer an ethic of care through the difficulties it engenders, including partiality/parochialism, paternalism, and privileging the care of those with the greatest means to achieve it (Tronto 258). For Tronto, an ethic of care cannot answer all problems, but neither has any preceding theory of ethics been able to do so—even the supposed "rights of man" enshrined in Western ethical and political discourse has "allowed exceptions around many forms of difference" (259). The shortcomings of an ethic of care are, for Tronto, as worthy of engagement as those of any universalist ethics.

Hamington notes how Merleau-Ponty enriches the concept of care, claiming in particular that his "philosophy of the body provides an epistemological foundation for an embodied notion of care" ("Resources for Feminist Care Ethics" 216). Care arises from embodied interactions, through proximity, touch, and bodily knowledge. Describing how he taught his daughter how to ride a bike without training wheels, Hamington argues that his care for her progress as well as his care for her well-being translate directly into her motor habits and responses (*Embodied Care* 59).

In order to account for how care can ever be more than intensely local, Hamington identifies the "caring imagination" as central to the practice of care. The caring imagination's chief tenet roughly corresponds to empathy: "affective responses to an 'other' that integrates knowledge and emotions to better apprehend their situation and feelings" (Hamington, *Embodied Care* 62). It transports caring persons beyond their spatio-socio-temporal boundaries and completes a picture of others that allows for care that reaches across time and social context (Hamington, *Embodied Care* 64–5). The caring imagination not only allows me to reflect critically on possible consequences of caring action, it supposedly allows me to think about action and context from another's place. In short, the caring imagination functions as another kind of knowledge. For Hamington, "knowledge is necessary for care," even if one is only working from "a presumption of knowledge" (*Embodied Care* 43; "Resources for Feminist Care Ethics" 216). Although he celebrates Merleau-Ponty's expansion of knowledge to include learned bodily comportment, Hamington believes that "we cannot care for that for [sic] which we have no knowledge" ("Resources for Feminist Care Ethics" 216; *Embodied Care* 44–5).

This marks the point at which a Merleau-Ponty-inspired ethics of attention will adopt a different trajectory. More than providing for multiple forms of knowledge through embodied intersubjectivity, phenomenology offers the possibility of *finding* care among others, of caring for that which I do not know, of learning to care. If care is to be, as Held argues, a practice as well as a value (*The Ethics of Care* 42), then *learning* must be integral to it. Attention brings care to perception, and care orients me in a world that transforms me in the act of attending to it.[14] The process of adaptability, more than the attitude that might inspire it, occupies a central role in the work of attention and distinguishes it from an ethic of care. Tronto assigns to "attentiveness" the task of noticing the manifestation of need—in others but also in oneself. However, attention as I am describing it concerns more than locating another in a perceptual field—it concerns astonishment.

I can never take in all of other people, and part of them will always elude me. I might *sense* a side of something but I do not know it. When I allow these mysteries to remain in place I stoke a sense of wonder that arises from the unknowable aspect of another. For Merleau-Ponty, "phenomenology's task was to reveal the mystery of the world and the mystery of reason" (*Phenomenology* lxxxv). Reveal, not solve. Knowledge can be had and can be necessary, but phenomenology does not seek it. "All forms of knowledge are supported by a 'ground' of postulations, and ultimately upon our communication with the world as the first establishing of rationality. Philosophy, as radical reflection, abstains in principle from this resource" (Merleau-Ponty, *Phenomenology* lxxxv). There will be no edifice of knowledge produced by the care of attention. Instead, it will involve attending to how the explainable rests on the unknowable. The care of attention will not draw a roadmap. It will instead lead to wonder.

If Merleau-Ponty's phenomenology has a zero point, this is it: the mystery and wonder of the world. Renaud Barbaras notes that, for Merleau-Ponty, "the mystery is not solely my opening before the presence of the world, it is that I can astonish myself, which is to say, disrupt my familiarity with myself and begin to think" (*Merleau-Ponty* 10).[15] Astonishment infuses—or *can* infuse—my engagement with the world and with myself as an element of that world. My experience of wonder in the world begins with my capacity to be a stranger to myself. This is "an astonishment that gathers the incontestable and strange possibility instead of considering it as coming from the self, which is to say, instead of backing it into the intelligible world" (Barbaras, *Merleau-Ponty* 10).[16] The known may surprise, may soothe, may wound, may disappoint, but it cannot astonish.

In aiming towards mystery, phenomenological questioning of the world supposes an unknown that cannot be converted into the known. Philosophy is precisely not "an awakening of consciousness." Instead, "the object of philosophy will never come to fill in the philosophical question, since this obturation would take from it the depth and the distance that are essential to it" (Merleau-Ponty, *The Visible and the Invisible* 101/136). If I cannot perceive everything, and if my experience of the world arises through perception, then any philosophical examination must do two things: posit a limit to what is knowable and operate according to a respect for that limit. "The task of philosophy should be to describe this labyrinth, to elaborate a concept of being such that its contradictions, neither accepted nor 'transcended,' still have their place" (Merleau-Ponty, "The Concept of Nature, II" 158). A philosophical engagement with things and people requires that I assume the attitude of someone who "wishes not to have them but to see them, not to hold them as with forceps, or to immobilize them as under the objective of a microscope, but to let them be and to witness their continued being" (Merleau-Ponty, *The Visible and the Invisible* 101/136). In doing so I admit that I cannot be completed by knowledge of things or others. There is no existential gap that knowledge—or another person—can fill. In adopting a phenomenological approach, I address the world as a question that provokes not an answer but "a confirmation of its astonishment" (Merleau-Ponty, *The Visible and the Invisible* 102/136).

Stage presence and attention taken together can elaborate an ethics based on the wonder at the heart of the phenomenological enterprise. After all, Merleau-Ponty infamously promised but never delivered on an ethics derived from his philosophical investigations. In a mid-1950s résumé of his scholarship Merleau-Ponty cast doubt on his previous work and made a tantalizing suggestion:

> The study of perception could only teach us a "bad ambiguity," a mixture of finitude and universality, of interiority and exteriority. But there is a "good ambiguity" in the phenomenon of expression, a spontaneity which accomplishes what appears to be impossible when we observed only the separate elements, a spontaneity which gathers together the plurality of monads, the past and the present, nature and culture. To establish this wonder would be metaphysics itself and would at the same time give us the principle of an ethics.
>
> ("An Unpublished Text" 11/409)

What this principle is, Merleau-Ponty never clarified; the passage above concludes the document of which it is a part and his subsequent work never explicitly addressed the question of ethics. Indeed, it has been a serious question as to whether any phenomenology can provide a basis for ethics at all. Waldenfels poses the question this way: Is the goal a "phenomenology of morals" that reflects on the embodied codes of values undertaken in particular circumstances, or a "moralizing phenomenology [that] not only invokes the values with which its research starts but also ends up recommending them" (Waldenfels, "Responsivity of the Body" 92)? The latter would from the beginning be compromised by its determination to arrive at conclusions about actions. Further, Mary Rawlinson notes that the very act of deriving a principle from life, which is to say, the act of abstracting a question (for example, "is X wrong?"), risks separating it from lived experience (72). No embodied ethics can afford this kind of separation.

The alternative seems equally problematic. A "phenomenology of morals" could no more "recommend" kinds of conduct than it could recommend touch or space. Phenomenology promises that *how* I attend to others might be described along with its consequences for my relationships and responsibilities to others. But as a descriptive practice, phenomenology, the argument goes, cannot also be prescriptive without suffering from the is/ought fallacy in which a description of behavior/phenomena assumes that this is the way things *should* be. In its grappling with experience, phenomenology would seem to have no means of producing a principle outside of experience by which to determine how experience should proceed.[17]

Performance, however, both describes and prescribes the world. Any given production describes available material and imaginative resources while also proposing that they should be assembled as they have been. Every show is a should. The principle of particular creative responses to the world could hardly provide the guidance required of even the most adaptable ethics. For his part, Merleau-Ponty did not believe theatre could offer much to ethics. He claims that, in comparison to theatre, in life "we cannot restrict our responsibilities as we do in aesthetic activity [...] in the theater, one can always start again, in life everything one does is absolute" (Merleau-Ponty, "The Experience of Others" 56). But he misunderstands theatre here: starting again in the theatre is (also) starting differently. The local and historical formations of creative expression that constitute stage presence might be turned back to phenomenology and provide detail to Merleau-Ponty's "principle of an ethics."

In particular, thinking about stage presence spatially moves away from reflecting on binarized power in performance and towards reflecting on the shifting codes of responsibility enacted by relations to others. Stage presence formalizes the choices people make—within constraints not entirely of their own making—about how to attend to others. Now, I do not seek to "emancipate" the spectator by elevating agency to the highest ethical-political good. Indeed, the ability of an individual to accomplish anything as an act of solitary will attracts one of its most rigorous critiques in the study of perception sketched above. Nonetheless, attendants—emancipated or not—act in several important ways. And attendants—disciplined or not—bring with them myriad complexes of experience and socialization that (help) determine not just *what* they perceive but *how*. The intersection of phenomenology and stage presence nourishes astonishment between people. And the "ought" derived from astonishment will call for a lived practice of opening to what I do not know and transforming into something new.

A Strange Proximity thus joins two lineages: one that seeks to develop an ethics from Merleau-Ponty's unfinished writing and one that proceeds from Laura Cull's inaugural work on "performance philosophy" with her book *Theatres of Immanence: Deleuze and the Ethics of Performance* (2012). In the latter case, Cull looks to performance as a means of generating an ethics applicable outside of it. She hopes to avoid simply identifying the reflection of an extant moral philosophy in particular performances as does much theatre scholarship. Instead, Cull describes how performances themselves propose ways of understanding what it means to participate in the whole of Being through particular acts. These are meant to promote the play of immanence and transcendence that characterizes life, at least life as Deleuze and his interpreters saw it. Beyond noting their consonance with Deleuzian readings of avant-garde performance, Cull proposes that these performances establish in their doing an "'attentive respect'" (237). But like Merleau-Ponty, she concludes her work with this promising phrase, leaving to others the task of engaging what "respect" might mean apart from and alongside attention.[18] Without attempting to improve on Cull's rich analyses, I hope to add to her treatment of attention a specifically phenomenological ethics derived from performance.

Phenomenological doubts

Phenomenology and performance make especially strong partners but they also make for especially tempting targets, perhaps no more so than when taken together. In the leadoff article to a special edition of one of the most prominent journals in theatre studies, Bruce McConachie inveighed against theatre scholarship that relied too much on phenomenology or any "a-scientific" methodology or theory. In their place he embraced the positivist impulses in scientific discourse and argued passionately for reorienting theatre studies around them. Among his complaints against phenomenology are that it and semiotics "divide the viewing experience between subjects and objects" and that phenomenology cannot tolerate the idea of people as "embodied, imaginative creatures" (McConachie 565, 566).[19] To be sure, he is quite wrong on these counts. And yet he articulates for many others a larger concern that theatre scholars are beholden to "master theorists" and that the affinity for "a-scientific theories" inevitably sets up a losing conflict with science. "What happens, though, when theories deriving from good science come into conflict with critical theories that have no basis in scientific evidence or logic? Which theories should we trust?" (McConachie 555). McConachie frames the questions so that their answers are meant to be obvious, but he completely misses the *other* obvious answer: whichever ones make for the best experiences of theatre.

As a performer and scholar and attendant, I want good theatre more than I want assessments of events that coincide with the popular science of the day. Whatever "good" theatre is, it won't necessarily prompt good scholarship or the concentration of established knowledge; and "bad" theatre certainly can result in great writing about it. For that matter, aping the customs of the sciences won't necessarily produce bad theatre or bad scholarship, either.[20] It may even be that "the credibility of our discipline" depends on mimicking another discipline's priorities, even if only to arrive at the same conclusions as Aristotle (in his writings on theatre, not his writings on science, which were of course once considered as ground-breaking as mirror neuron theory is today). But the anxiety about resolving conflicting perspectives in theatre is misplaced and the dismissal of "a-scientific" thinking unearned. For practitioners of theatre, surely the more pressing concern is making the best theatre possible within one's present constraints. And for "theorists" of theatre, surely the most pressing concern is enriching readers' experience of theatrical events. If a theoretical disagreement cannot be resolved because it turns out not to be "responsible to and refutable by a network of studies and theories with which it remains in dialogue" (Cook 580), I am not the worse for it. Perhaps "good science [...] encourages the resolution of such differences and may lead to the accumulation of knowledge" (McConachie 574), but theatre is not good science. And neither is phenomenology.

It so happens that the disparate practices under the term "cognitive science" have been catching up with Merleau-Ponty's observations.[21] A recent article in the *Journal of Personality and Social Psychology*, for example, suggests that experiences of awe can promote generosity and strengthen collective living (Piff et al.). However, turning to studies such as these to validate the poetic reflections of phenomenology and performance undermines the confidence required by artistic creation and expressive attention. I might need to appeal to the hard sciences in order to secure a repeatable result derived from an experiment (or simply to secure funding), and for historians it remains imperative to be able to defend claims about past events. But theatre does not need to prove anything. This hardly disqualifies it from any utilitarian claims that might be made for (or against!) it. In any case, the purpose of theatre can be described the same way Yvanka Raynova describes the purpose of phenomenology: bringing the attendant into a "reintegration within experience" (241). Rather than establish empirical truths, theatre asserts lived experience as the primary mode of being, one that ultimately escapes total comprehension. A performance may or may not be true, but it will always be *experienced*. In Merleau-Ponty's gracious words, philosophy asks of science, "whether science does, or ever could, present us with a picture of the world which is complete, self-sufficient and somehow closed in upon itself, such that there could no longer be any meaningful questions outside this picture." He goes on to note that the "modern" approach of science itself prompts this question; it also encourages a negative response (Merleau-Ponty, *The World of Perception* 34–5).

Another concern that attaches to phenomenology is that, because phenomenology operates through a rigorous description of experience, written accounts of embodied experience tend to assume unwarranted authority. Those of us working within phenomenology must remain vigilant of false and often unspoken claims to universality and stay loyal instead to the profound contingency of all experience. Embodiment as Merleau-Ponty understood it (and contrary to several critics' misreading) also demands attention to cultural and historical specificity.[22] "Experience occurs in a body which is thoroughly marked by history," Philipa Rothfield notes, which means that it is "not a pure zone whose analysis can reveal the [...] essence" of the phenomena in question (47). Rothfield goes on to caution against "thick description," amassing copious detail in a simultaneously overt yet obscured act of interpretation (43, 51 n.1).[23] Ultimately, descriptions, like the different applications and forms of phenomenology, are useful insofar as they provoke the imagination of a reader and encourage interrogation of one's own experience. They are dangerous insofar as they might stifle it, and in some ways the most convincing descriptions might achieve precisely that.

Nonetheless, as a phenomenological investigation, the study that follows must rely extensively on my own experiences as an attendant and a performer, experiences that I will describe in detail. It would be very difficult indeed to propose a phenomenology of anything without drawing explicitly on the author's experiences.[24] These are neither offered as "proof" of anything nor are they to mean that I am a model participant in performances, though this is certainly a familiar criticism of first person accounts. Another criticism charges that, if phenomenology presupposes embodied experience, then it will ultimately prove incapable of honoring anything utterly "other" because everything perceived arrives through recognition. The course of phenomenological description risks implying, if not directly asserting, that the author's experience *must* be that of the reader.

The fact that these criticisms apply to all expression, certainly to any kind of literary analysis, is beside the point: these are far from inevitable outcomes of a phenomenological methodology. My personal experiences are indeed wielded as a kind of evidence—just like any published review of a performance. They are presented as the edited artifacts from which a scholar derives an understanding of the world. In this case, those artifacts include my experiences attending and performing in theatre, dance, and performance art. Reviews, monographs, conversations, journal entries, and unverified recollections all serve as different kinds of evidence in support of a project that binds an ethics to the enrichment of experience.

The extensive use of personal experience must also raise the shadows of "bias" and validation. How much of this is what I "really" remember and how much of it is what I want to remember to make my point? Alas, there is no answer to these questions, quite simply because they signify the inherent ambiguity of any writing that acknowledges the author's embodiment.[25] In this kind of a project, which does not aim to prove the existence of an event or a person or a document, questions of source, authenticity, and validation diminish in comparison to their place in assessing other kinds of scholarship. It need hardly be added that when reading *any* work the reader understands there to have been a prior process of selecting material presented as evidence. All histories are acts of interpretation crafted to depict a particular vision of the world. The evergreen scholarly scandals of research misconduct speak to the fragility of all scholarly validation, from repeatable experiments in a lab to psychoanalytic interpretation of texts.[26]

My choice of performances to write about has been driven in part by consideration of these potential problems. The first criterion was that I had attended or performed in them; I make one notable and self-conscious exception to this rule in Chapter 5. Beyond that, while widely recognized artists made some of the performances examined here, some of the artists discussed have achieved only local recognition. This choice reflects the concerns of an emerging scholar and mid-career performer all too aware of the role academics play in extending the reach of performers' work. Rather than simply solidifying the pervasive academic appreciation of the usual suspects, I also hope to introduce the work of those lesser known. Describing performances both familiar and unfamiliar also allows me to range across different contexts for these performances, from well within the orbit of notoriety to far outside it. The particular space of stage presence proposed here, while certainly possible with a well-known performer, describes a kind of relationship quite distinct from that of the fan and the star. Indeed, one of the chief concerns of this phenomenology will be to describe an experience of stage presence that does not bolster the barriers erected by celebrity.

Further, much of the performance analyses that follow, from both sides of the curtain, focus on minute moments—intakes of breath and shifts of shoulders. I stand ready to accept the accusation that I make mountains out of molehills—that is what artists often do when they look at molehills. A phenomenological study and a performance-based speculation on attention require nothing less than observations of the embodied responses to others, and these can best be understood, perhaps may *only* be understood, in their slightest variations. Similarly, because phenomenology and performance both posit that language not only reflects but also actively *constitutes* what I perceive, turns of phrase will take on unusual importance. For example, I use "attendant" rather than "audience" or "spectator" or "observer" to identify someone at a performance not formally recognized as a performer. The hidden sensory biases of these latter terms obscure the active work of perception, work that never engages only one sense at a time.

In keeping with the "a-scientific" character of this project, the text that follows will shift, sometimes abruptly, sometimes gradually, between recounting personal experience and analysis of theoretical and philosophic texts. I have chosen to write this way for two reasons: first, the abrupt shifts will hopefully serve as a kind of uneven paving stone. Tripping over it might briefly render surroundings strange, produce a flash of heat in the body, and require some work to "right" the reader. Which is to say, the discomfort provided by some of these shifts might provoke readers to try to reorganize themselves and in so doing bring themselves to the work of the argument. This reorganization is a response to a sort of disorientation, and that is the second reason for this stylistic choice: it mimics the core thesis about stage presence, namely that it involves a kind of disorientation.

Four kinds of failure

The following chapters each address moments of failure and seek within them generative possibilities that might constitute the basis for an ethics of attention. Chapter 2 takes up the construction of difference at the heart of stage presence, a phenomenon that, if nothing else, distinguishes some from others. I approach the arrival of difference by considering efforts to be the same, namely acting pedagogies that explicitly emphasize mimicry. The two schools analyzed at greatest length are, or were, led by Eugenio Barba and Jacques Lecoq. Both men, it turns out, have been described as having the kind of charisma Weber identified. Without attempting to explain their "own" appeal or possible participation in stage presence, I describe how their approaches to mimicry both formalize habits of perception and indirectly advocate particular concepts of difference. Barba's confidence that mimicry of others was possible produces the actor as master of others and leads to questions of cultural appropriation. Lecoq's conviction that mimicry inevitably fails precedes a belief that this failure produces a new way of being entirely specific to the student involved. Merleau-Ponty's theories of "the flesh" and the reversibility of perceiver and perceived provide the setting for thinking about Lecoq's neutral mask training, in which students attempt to mimic imagined environments without judgment. The failure to mimic others leads, for Lecoq, away from codifying them as "other" and towards what lies between them and myself. Which is to say, it leads to space.

Chapter 3 expands into an analysis of space during performance, in particular the promenade performances *Song* (2007) and *Sleep No More* (2003/2011) that enmesh attendants and performers. Jacques Rancière's critique of participatory and activist art and Renaud Barbaras's phenomenology of distance provide perspectives on the ethical questions stirred up by performing different kinds of proximity. By linking physical and political encroachment, Rancière stands up for attendants pushed around—sometimes physically—by performance, and suggests maintaining a distance between art and "emancipated spectators." As he puts it, "we do not have to transform spectators into actors, and ignoramuses into scholars. We have to recognize the knowledge at work in the ignoramus and the activity peculiar to the spectator" (Rancière, "The Emancipated Spectator" 17). From his position I take up the possibilities of responsibility found in distance rather than in proximity. These reflections are informed by Barbaras's proposal that desire generates rather than dissipates distance between perceivers and perceived. As a phenomenon staked on its continual displacement, desire becomes for Barbaras the central dynamic of perception, propelling perceivers from one object to the next. I critique the ethical implications of this position by elaborating on the phenomenology of space proposed by Merleau-Ponty. To his argument that space concerns the "I can" of bodily comportment, I add the element of imagination, the combination of past and present constraints into possibilities not yet realized or realizable. With space as an embodied, imaginative relationship with others, I replace Barbaras's desire with Merleau-Ponty's astonishment as the central characteristic of perception.

I begin Chapter 4 by describing a technical miscue in performance. During the 2010 tour of *Moon Water* by Cloud Gate Dance Theatre of Taiwan, the music began skipping and was finally silenced. With eyebrow-raising sang-froid, the dancers steeled themselves to continue without musical accompaniment and did so until, much to more than one attendant's regret, the problem was rectified. From the experience of disorientation provoked by this performance, I propose a phenomenology of theatrical failure that draws from Bernhard Waldenfels's phenomenology of *fremde* or the "strange." Waldenfels argues that the strange can only be experienced through acts of creative expression in response to it. These responses in turn embody temporal and spatial paradoxes such as how the call of another finds expression in my simultaneous response. The strange displaces responsibility for stage presence from performers, and I propose different kinds of space initiated by attempts to grasp my own and others' possible actions. Two dance theatre performances, *I Want to Dance Better at Parties* (2007) by Chunky Move and *My Fellow Americans* (2009) by Peter Carpenter Performance, provide the means for examining modes of attention that support these spaces, in particular the centrifugal space of stage presence. I argue that this space involves a failure to stay oriented, a loss of certainty regarding the center of my own system of possible actions. The pleasures of this kind of disorientation depend in turn on cultural and societal formations of possibility, and the chapter concludes by examining the various privileges assumed by experiencing failure as generative.

Chapter 5 starts by considering the ethics of withholding attention from problematic performance. The reactions to Brett Bailey and Third World Bunfight's heavily protested and occasionally shutdown performance about legacies of European colonialism, *Exhibit B* (held from 2010–2015), provide the basis for weighing the possibility that turning away might constitute an ethical response to a work of art. I position Kelly Oliver's work on the ethical imperative to witness others as a challenge to this idea. Oliver contends that each person comes into subjecthood through the acts of witnessing and being witnessed by others. Relying on the imperative impartiality of philosophers such as Emmanuel Lévinas, she places the dual action of witnessing at the heart of my responsibility to others. From Oliver's embodied account of witnessing, I return to Merleau-Ponty in order to describe the problems of presuming to make everything and everyone "seen." For Oliver, eradicating "blind spots" is the central work of ethical witnessing, but for Merleau-Ponty blind spots are what make perception possible. They cannot be removed—they can only be displaced.

I take this to signal a fundamental crisis in an ethics of attention and suggest that in place of seeking to attend to as much as possible we aim instead at increasing the astonishment of the world. I cannot attend to everything and so must choose to whom and to what I pursue an ethical relationship of astonishment. These choices I make, and I always make them alongside others and within constraints that are not my own, these choices concerning how I contribute to the distribution of attention play a crucial role in determining the kinds of relationships I have with others. After all, not all attention is wanted, and I might even actively try to avoid it. As Waldenfels warns, "Any attention can easily become harassment" (Waldenfels, *Phenomenology of the Alien* 64).[27] My well-being can depend on escaping it, just as my well-being might feel staked to achieving the attention that involves me in an expansive and creative relation with another. Instead of the defensive posture of witnessing—forever vigilant against possible violations of subjectivity and forever thrusting subjects into the light—the work of ethical attention adds to the world of perception. And what it adds is astonishment. Through this experience the strangeness of shared perception can express the compromises and failures, and the choices and possibilities, that characterize an ethics of attention.

Notes

1 Norman Allen's *Waiting in Tobolsk: Children of the Last Tsar* premiered in June of 1997 at the Church Street Theater in Washington, DC. Performers: John Benoit, Rachel Gardner, Paula Gruskiewicz, Roger Krauss, Lenora Pritchard, Sarah Schnadig, Christine Tivel. Director: Dwayne Nitz.
2 See also Auslander, *Liveness*; Giannachi et al., *Archaeologies of Presence*; Kaye, *Multi-Media*; Weber and Cholodenko, especially Chapter 5. Weber, and Kaye after him, relies heavily on Walter Benjamin's notion of "aura," a concept explored further in Chapter 3.
3 "Brûler les Planches, Crever l'écran."
4 The response to these two movie stars "in the flesh" partly explains why I have chosen not to write about actors on film or video. The main reason is that my understanding of stage presence hinges on a relationship of mutual alteration. Although the debate on the "liveness" of broadcast performances remains as robust as ever, I am not yet willing to argue that performers in these media are able to participate in the changes available to actors and attendants during (most) theatrical performance, however "live" or "mediated" one or the other might be.
5 See, for example, Garner, *Bodied Spaces*; Jones; Zarrilli, "Towards a Phenomenological Model of the Actor's Embodied Modes of Experience"; Kozel. The trajectory of phenomenology both outside and within theatre studies has been detailed elsewhere and what follows will be an outline of one branch of the phenomenological tradition. For summaries of the field from within theatre studies, Stanton Garner's work remains the most thorough: see *Bodied Spaces* and "Theater and Phenomenology." For an overview of the interaction between phenomenology and performance studies, see Maaike Bleeker et al., *Performance and Phenomenology: Traditions and Transformations* (London: Routledge, 2015).
6 There are two English translations of *Phenomenology of Perception* in three editions: the Colin Smith translation of 1962, rereleased with different pagination in 2002, and the Donald A. Landes translation of 2012. Almost the entirety of Merleau-Ponty scholarship in English references the 1962 edition's pagination, but Smith's translation has long been considered uneven and Landes's superior

2012 translation was met with both praise and relief. This edition's many merits include not only the annotation of Merleau-Ponty's footnotes, but also the pagination of the 2006 French edition. Landes has chosen the most recent and accessible edition in French, but, of course, this is not the edition most widely cited in either French or English commentary, which remains the original release, or at least its pagination. Despite the difficulty this may cause scholars engaged in deep research of Merleau-Ponty's work, I have chosen to cite the 2012 edition. I hope to honor the work of those who have come before me, but I also hope to speak to future scholars, and there can be little doubt that the Landes translation will become the standard. Further parenthetical citations from *Phenomenology of Perception* will use *Phenomenology* to designate the book instead of its full name. Although citations of *Phenomenology of Perception* do not require it, citations from other works by Merleau-Ponty will include the page number for the French edition.

7   See also Barbaras, "Perception and Movement" 86.

8   In the excellent *Suspensions of Perception: Attention, Spectacle, and Modern Culture* (1999), Jonathan Crary amply demonstrates the historical and geographical formation of the concept of attention. Through a rigorous reading of a dizzying array of source materials, he tracks the emergence of the term's alignment with economic, technological, medical, and artistic developments around the turn of the twentieth century. His reading of Merleau-Ponty, however, falls prey to the temptation of reading Merleau-Ponty's lengthy exegeses of other authors as an endorsement of their perspectives. As such, Crary writes of the "devaluation of attention as a problem" in *Phenomenology of Perception* (33 n.59). But Merleau-Ponty does nothing of the kind—instead he criticizes prior approaches to attention as part of an argument for phenomenology's superior perspective. When he writes that attention "does not exist as a general and formal activity," he refers to the unintended consequences of early psychological theories. He then follows these with his own, which include the claim that attention was "thought itself" (Merleau-Ponty, *Phenomenology* 33). Merleau-Ponty even goes so far as to use quotation marks, "scare quotes," around the term attention in the title of the chapter in question: "'Attention' and 'Judgment.'"

9   Original emphasis.

10 Roslyn Sulcas's profile of Lisa Dwan noted how much faster her interpretation was than others'.

11 Working from dictionary definitions, especially those from the supposedly authoritative *Oxford English Dictionary*, mimics some of the positivist tendencies I want to avoid with this book. Defining words does not prove that the objects, actions, or concepts described by those words definitively *are* that way. I have drawn inspiration from the *OED* less as a repository of conclusive knowledge than as a field of resources. For more detail, see in particular definitions 1, 4, 5 in *Oxford English Dictionary* 85.

12 Even attending to myself suggests this distance—how else could "I" attend to "myself" other than to imagine a separation between the one attending to and the one attended to?

13 Michael Slote, for one, *does* suggest such a replacement, arguing that the reach of deontological ethics and the adaptability of utilitarian ethics are both housed in the ethics of care when appropriate emphasis is placed on empathy.

14 Responding to Allan Kaprow's view that paying attention to something changes it, Laura Cull adds, "But it also alters the attender in a reciprocal determination" (150).

15 My translation.

16 My translation.

17 Diane Perpich makes just this critique of Waldenfels's own work (127).

18 Cull does offer Howard Caygill's observation that *achtung* in German can mean both attention and "'respect for persons' to the extent to which they uphold the [Kantian idea of a] moral law" (237). Cull is citing Caygill 357. Partially in keeping with her commitment to avoid positing universal rules, Cull does not elaborate much further.

19 McConachie is quoting linguist George Lakoff and philosopher Mark Johnson's characterization of "embodied realism's" approach to communication (Lakoff and Johnson 93).

20 Rhonda Blair and John Lutterbie, in their introduction to another theatre journal's special section on cognitive science, recommend a list of safeguards for theatre scholars working from scientific disciplines (68).

21 Alva Noë has done admirable work bridging these fields. His *Action in Perception* (2004) and *Varieties of Presence* (2012) have become standard texts within and without philosophy. See as well Gallagher and Gallese et al.

22 See, for example, Merleau-Ponty, *Signs*, especially 39–182/136–295.

23 The term "thick description" was first coined, and endorsed as an anthropological method, by Clifford Geertz.

24 Merleau-Ponty was not immune from just this reproach: despite many examples drawn from his own experiences, Merleau-Ponty's reliance on medical records and psychological case studies in several of his works has led to some criticism of his methodology. For a withering critique, see Sheets-Johnstone 273–318.

25 See, for example, Hill and Paris, eds, *Performance and Place*; Hill and Paris, *Performing Proximity: Curious Intimacies*.

26 As of this writing, the most widely covered case of scholarly malpractice concerns the invention of survey data for a political science paper in the journal *Science*. See McNutt.

27 A highly publicized critique of the concept of "neutral" attention surfaced in a late 2014 viral video depicting a woman walking in New York City neighborhoods and enduring over 100 catcalls in one day (Rob Bliss Creative). The racial politics of the video eventually proved as compelling as the sexual politics to online commentators, but the message attempted was clear: not all attention is "good" and not everyone wants to be noticed.

Chapter 2

Mimicry and the urgency of differences

Behind competing ideas of stage presence rests the conviction that those with (or doing) it make apparent how they are not like what surrounds them. Extraordinary performers are supposed to be in relief from those around them, enacting a powerful sense of being distinct. Phillip Zarrilli, describing himself, notes that only actors possessed of both special training and unique awareness may engender the sensation of stage presence in their audience members ("'... Presence ...'" 145–7). No matter what else stage presence might mean, it expresses a difference.

And so begins its ethical peril: how stage presence defines "the" different dictates its ethical position. Considering stage presence as an expression of how some people are *more* than, for example, means assuming a universal basis from which these performers depart. Stage presence will then figure the experience of difference as a measurant and (counter-)affirmation of self-hood. In this way it will establish a single basis of assessment that both erases the possibility of difference and asserts that it is an essential element of being.

By far the most common mode of assigning difference locates it *in* the person distinguished from his or her surroundings. Difference is then *theirs* or *of* them, which not only accounts for their separation from others but also locates them in a foreground, either of a scene or of society at large.

> If you have it, you don't need it.
> If you need it, you don't have it.
> If you have it, you need more of it.
> If you have more of it, you don't need less of it.
> You need it to get it, and you certainly need it to get more of it.
> But if you don't already have any of it to begin with, you can't get any of it to get started, which means you really have no idea how to get it in the first place, do you?
> You can share it, sure, you can even stockpile it if you'd like, but you can't fake it.
> Wanting it, needing it, wishing for it.
> The point is, if you've never had any of it, ever, people just seem to know.
> (Old Spice)

In this ad, horror movie icon Bruce Campbell ambles from one leather chair to another in a dim den with an endless painting of a ship on its wall, satirizing mid-century United States masculinity while expounding on the nature of "it." The *real* point, of course, is that if you've got "it," you're a man and you wear Old Spice. Although a text reveal at the end of the ad identifies "experience" as the referent of "it," the circular logic of the ad also pertains to the relationship most people have to It as a marker of difference: a precious commodity that you have or don't and by which others will judge you. This is a most unusual commodity, however: like all others, its value is not intrinsic, and yet unlike others, it cannot be bought. But if you would like to make sure people know you have It, might we suggest this deodorant.

Joseph Roach's book on the subject, *It* (2007), traces a lineage of "abnormally interesting people" (1). "It" is not strictly speaking the quality of stage presence; Roach associates it with widespread cultural phenomena and his study concerns the materials of and techniques for constructing public figures of towering interest. Nonetheless, Roach explicitly connects "It" with Eugenio Barba's theories of stage presence and he joins a long line of authors who figure this kind of fascination as a means of separating those "with" it from those without it. He includes in this tradition the Restoration's intoxication by public performance(s) of actresses and the assertions of Charles II's court, as well as Madonna, assorted British royalty, and of course the "It Girl," Clara Bow. In accounting for how these people achieved their fame, Roach proposes "It" as the result of difference understood as identity, something that "resides in the gifted but stems from mutual need" (Roach, "It" 567). Some people possess it and other people want it: "'It' is the power of apparently effortless embodiment of contradictory qualities simultaneously" (Roach, *It* 8).

Jane Goodall, whose book *Stage Presence* (2008) concerns the changing discourses on the power of performers, similarly stresses how different those "with" stage presence are from those without it. Goodall looks less at the *phenomenon* in question and more at how writers have figured it across several hundred years of largely European performance, examining "the rhetorics and imagistic language in which [stage] presence[1] is evoked in different cultural and historical contexts" (7). In particular, Goodall establishes connections between stage presence and "the new order of scientific understanding" (60). Thus, as Sir Isaac Newton achieves fame, so successful actors find themselves described as centers of gravity; as magnetism occupies scientific minds and popular imaginations, so acclaimed performers become magnetic and are portrayed as drawing audiences to them; and as the theories of Anton Mesmer captivate the reading public while earning the disdain of scientists, performers with the power to hold attention are labeled mesmerizing.

And yet Goodall also notes how writers have often referred to forces impossible to understand in order to illustrate that, no matter how much faith an age might have in science, special performers are often figured as embodying a link to unsolvable mystery. When witnesses to performers such as Élisa Rachel Félix and Sarah Bernhardt compare them to ancient celebrants of chthonic rites, they invest stage presence with otherworldliness and an unnatural connection between the dead and living. As scientific certainty waxes, the perception of magic does not necessarily wane, but instead finds expression through extraordinary performers who are connected to what was never understood or, like David Bowie's alter ego Ziggy Stardust, to other planets.

As this last example makes clear, performers with stage presence have often been figured as literally alien. Goodall's project was in part inspired by her uneasiness with the "curious orientalist tendency" that pervades the Western discourse on stage presence (3). In Goodall's case, however, her answer at times requires her to skip over what underpins this tendency. For several pages she attempts to dismiss the exoticism and pervasive fear of female sexuality underlying the attraction assigned to Félix and Josephine Baker. And yet virtually every text she cites relentlessly removes these performers from civilized society and connects them to the demonic and the "natural" (84–5, 95–101, 132–6). In addition, she does not investigate why the performers prominently associated with the dangers and occultism of mesmerism were Jewish. Goodall's avoidance of racism's and sexism's specters in stage presence presents a missed opportunity, especially given her awareness of how twentieth-century European acting theories have tended to obsess over practices from "the East."

In this chapter I take Goodall's lead and position two actor-training programs as sites for reflecting on how performance habituates both attendants and performers to ways of perceiving. In part, this stems from the way that trying to be like someone or something else—a key aspect of most actor training—requires formulating difference. Mimicry informs both how I think of myself and how I imagine others through performance. My encounter with others does not arise simply from their appearance or from my own consciousness—the empiricist and intellectualist positions. It can arise as well from a performed mimicry, and any practice that establishes habits of attending to others through mimicry will provide a literal training ground for figuring how perception copes with and defines difference. Actor training of course proposes different ways of transforming the performer, but it also proposes different ways of attending to others. These are the practices that establish particular ethical conditions both in the classroom and in performance. The training I consider here explicitly interrogates and forms habits of perception and provides insight into how they can both articulate and limit possible responsibilities to others.

In his analysis of habit, Merleau-Ponty claims: "As a system of motor powers or perceptual powers, our body is not an object for an 'I think': it is a totality of lived significations that moves towards its equilibrium"

(Merleau-Ponty, *Phenomenology* 155). What I see, hear, taste, touch and smell—whatever I perceive—arrives not simply through senses that "belong" to me, but across bodies formed by history, biology, and training. Merleau-Ponty here figures habits, the "grouping of lived-through experiences," as accumulations of an active body involved with the world. The body "'catches' (*kapiert*) and 'understands' the movement. The acquisition of the habit is surely the grasping of a signification, but it is specifically the motor grasping of a motor signification" (Merleau-Ponty, *Phenomenology* 144).

As he claims, and as training makes explicit, I do not single-handedly determine these significances on my own—they are as much given to me as found in my actions. In his contemplation on *sens*—the French word for meaning, direction, and feeling—David Morris notes that

> *sens* belongs to a moving body that needs to learn how to move, that learns from others, and that can learn to move differently, that can teach itself to move differently, that itself stumbles upon and encounters differences in ways of moving.
>
> (100)

"Lived-through experiences" are not mine, they are *learned*, even when from myself, and even from a fiction. In one of the only passages that directly considers theatre, Merleau-Ponty reflects on how actors create movement for their characters. Writing from the point of view of the actor, he notes, "What I learn to view as the body of another person is the possibility of movement for me. The actor's art is therefore only an extension of the art which we all possess" ("The Experience of Others" 53). Pedagogy becomes an important site for thinking about how habits and *sens*—meaning, direction, and feeling—are established and encountered as "given." They draw me towards a manufactured balance while convincing me of its immanence, its inherence to my very being.

Habit, a "knowledge in our hands," accrues to bodily awareness and action, and it "relieves us of this very task" of actively interpreting each moment's contact with the world (Merleau-Ponty, *Phenomenology* 145, 154). Habits perform a kind of shorthand, allowing me to more efficiently navigate the world that appears through them. Jack Reynolds writes that Merleau-Ponty thought that habits "inevitably seek to minimize aporias, confrontations, and anything that might disrupt" acquired ways of managing movement through the world (91). However, for Merleau-Ponty habit might be an accretion of behavior, but it does not keep out experiences of the unfamiliar. Morris writes that habit "renders us insensitive to actual situations," but by providing the basis of experience "as determinate insensitivity, habit is the basis of further sensitivity" (91). Habit is the means by which I come into contact with disruptions to the familiar: meaning "is always implied in habits, and becomes express when habits crack"

(Morris 3). The pedagogies of Eugenio Barba and Jacques Lecoq both seek to produce and work from these kinds of cracks.

"Orient-ed" practices

Eugenio Barba left his home in Italy while a teenager, moved to Norway, and from there worked in the merchant marine traveling to Asia in the late 1950s. He found his way to Poland in 1961 and worked closely with Jerzy Grotowski before eventually settling in Denmark to run a theatre company and training institute. His International School of Theatre Anthropology (ISTA) has convened experts in Asian and European theatre for seminars and demonstrations every few years since 1979 and forms the basis for Barba's pedagogical theory.[2] His many articles and books detailing his research are largely revisions of his continuing examination of transcultural principles of stage presence.

Barba's project is driven by his concern with what draws his attention to particular performers and his conviction that this involves practices shared across, but taking place separate from, different cultures. For this reason, Barba explicitly avoids consideration of cultural factors shaping and giving meaning to different performance techniques. Instead, he is interested in a level beyond culture, a level he calls the "pre-expressive" (Barba and Savarese 5, 216–34). Barba describes this as the "basic level of organization common to all performers," and claims that it "deals with how to render the actor's energy scenically alive, that is, with how the actor can become a presence that immediately attracts the spectator's attention, and is theatre anthropology's field of study" (Barba and Savarese 218).[3] What Barba means by "energy" is never explicitly stated, and instead Barba uses phrases such as "personal temperature-intensity" and cites Ferdinando Taviani's description of "muscular and nervous power" (Barba and Savarese 78, 72). Similarly, "presence" remains an elusive concept, the equivalent of energy, something a performer "has" but also something that is always in process, always becoming (Barba and Savarese 52). Barba's collaborator Franco Ruffini referred to the "pre-expressive" level as that at "which the audience finds the performer credible as opposed to legible; not *what* is being expressed but how" (qtd in Chamberlain, "Theatre Anthropology" 178).[4] Ian Watson, Barba's foremost commentator in English, claims outright that "the pre-expressive is synonymous with stage presence" ("Introduction" 7).

Watson's claim reflects Barba's continual assertion that, while each performer is unique, manifesting this uniqueness in a compelling manner is the result of practices that take place at the "pre-expressive" level. All performance includes this level and "the expression level," but training as if the pre-expressive could be separated from expression allows performers to work on their presence, their scenic *bios*, or life (Barba, *The Paper Canoe* 5, 9, 15).[5] In his Introduction to *A Dictionary of Theatre Anthropology: The*

Secret Art of the Performer (1991), Barba states explicitly that he does not "seek to discover laws" and that he only wishes to offer "bits of advice" meant to provoke their own surpassing. Nonetheless, what follows is a tireless determination of "recurrent principles" (Barba and Savarese 6) that consistently positions Indian, Chinese, Balinese, Korean, and Japanese forms as the repositories of admirable techniques in stark opposition to Western theatre, albeit illustrated by select Western practices.[6] Although Barba does not recommend that all actors learn the regimen of eye movements drilled into *Kathakali* dancers or the particular amendments to balance of Peking Opera actors, he unequivocally positions these techniques as a positive good, examples of how to successfully work at the "pre-expressive level."

From these different forms Barba determined five principles that, when wielded by trained performers, achieve the expression of performers' "scenic presence" that makes them compelling: altered balance, dynamic opposition, equivalence, compression, and "coherent incoherence" (Stewart 48–9; Barba, *The Paper Canoe* 25–30).[7] As the first two principles indicate, Barba posits that the "pre-expressive" derives from bodily anatomy or the "'biological' level" (Barba and Savarese 5); for Barba, both bodies and biology lie outside of culture. Accordingly, Barba was comfortable claiming their universal application—if everyone has bodies and they all operate the same, techniques based in "the" body and divorced from their specific cultural contexts will be able to address audience members across all times and places *through* the specifics of cultural performance.

Needless to say, this kind of claim has made Barba into the object of regular criticism on the grounds that his work appropriates and exoticizes "Eastern" practices, denies gender difference, and in general homogenizes both theatre and human behavior.[8] For while Barba readily acknowledges that the precedence of the "pre-expressive" is a "logical and not a chronological" one, he ignores the fact that bodies are not even logically prior to culture or context (Barba, *The Paper Canoe* 9; Barba and Savarese 5). As his critics have argued and as post-structuralist and post-feminist theory insists, even before birth bodies are shaped by cultural and individual constraints that thoroughly implant them in situations well beyond biology. Although the preponderance of adult humans are bipeds structured to locomote from an upright posture, there is no separating the manner in which they do so from the context of their upbringings. The "biological level" upon which Barba relies is a myth, and his principles apply to what Rustom Bharucha has called "ahistorical" bodies (*Theatre and the World* 72).

Watson, who agrees that the "pre-expressive" is "transcultural" and involves a "denial of culture" ("Introduction" 4), nonetheless attempts to refute the charge that Barba appropriates and exoticizes the East by noting that Barba is "ideologically committed to the erasure of otherness" ("Staging Theatre Anthropology" 28). Watson thus reveals exactly how Barba's research practice figures difference by assuming a disembodied subject traditionally (and in this case, explicitly) associated with an independent, straight, Western male. There must be a position from which to enact the erasure of otherness—the privileged transcendental subject. And it is also the very presumption of this transcendental subject that produces the exoticization of Asian practices: the disembodied Westerner supposedly learns how to make himself "present" through techniques of people unaware of the plane of existence on which the Westerner lives. The East is explicitly connected with the body and the West with consciousness, in particular that of the teacher who informs master practitioners from other cultures how their techniques participate in the "pre-expressive" level.[9]

Watson's dismissal of the charge of appropriation similarly turns in on itself. On the one hand, he argues that there is a cultural exchange, with Asian artists both altering Western performers' practice and having their own work changed by their contact with Barba. The exchange occurs during an unequal operation of power in the particular meeting and following the recent history of European conquest that frames it and makes it possible. On the other hand, Watson draws on Fred Turner's argument that the concept of cultural appropriation "is based on a false analogy between cultural and industrial goods," and that the former can be taken from one place "while also remaining intact at their origin" (Turner 260–2). Although Turner is correct to note that for one culture to adapt another's techniques is not to "take" the practice, Watson has already pointed out that the contact between cultural practices cannot help but modify both ("Staging Theatre Anthropology" 29–30).[10] And although nothing may be taken from what Watson calls "the source culture," that culture not only does not remain unchanged, but it is now (mis)represented outside of itself. Appropriation does not involve the theft of property but the transformation of practices according to principles foreign to the practices' context. What the appropriated culture loses may not be its "own" techniques, but rather the ability to claim those techniques *as* its own because they now exist in someone else's terms and discourse. Barba's students learn Indian dance within his system, not the social and religious systems from which it comes. In other words, its otherness is obliterated while its immutable difference is cemented by identification.

Chamberlain suggests that, given Barba's "bracketing" of culture and context, his work might better be understood as a phenomenology of "the actor's scenic presence" ("Foreword" xiv). This repurposing of Barba's work has great merit insofar as it draws on Husserl's foundational phenomenological principle of isolating phenomena in order to stage an encounter between their essence and the transcendental ego. And yet this also explains why such a reframing falls short of rescuing Barba from his critics and his own often unhelpful generalizations: it relies on the early phenomenological belief in complete bracketing. In any event, Barba's consistent turn towards "the East" for inspiration resists the possibility of bracketing culture from an analysis of stage presence.[11]

It may very well be that his principles of movement are widely compelling. And even if this aspect of his teaching deserves criticism, Barba's work involves more than his research of the "pre-expressive," as Watson, Chamberlain, and Nigel Stewart take pains to note. It includes not only intercultural exchanges of training and a particular tension between the "pre-expressive" and the "expression level," but also a system of barter for performance that seeks to circumvent Western systems of value and exchange.[12] Consequently, they argue, Barba's work on the "pre-expressive" cannot fairly be used to characterize the man or the entirety of his work. This seems reasonable enough. Yet it does not prevent Barba from serving as a powerful example of how actor training shapes more than an understanding of acting. As long as it involves mimicry—taking on and in my body the movements of others—actor training shapes an understanding of difference. Barba's research may reveal "the secret art of the performer," but by affirming the "pre-expressive" it demands the abolition of difference while firmly separating non-Western cultures (and people and practices) from their counterparts.

Barba's shortcomings are hardly his own alone: he extends a long tradition of Western actor training and thinking about stage presence that transparently fetishizes non-Western performance in a process that totalizes and dominates the identity of others. Although their projects had divergent aims, celebrated male touchstones of twentieth-century Western acting discourse—Antonin Artaud, Bertolt Brecht, and Jerzy Grotowski—shared a belief in the possibility of accessing and wielding an actor's singular authority. Each of these teachers in their own way staked this authority on their separate experiences and conceptions of non-Western performance: Artaud with his fantasies inspired by witnessing Balinese dance in Paris, Brecht with his admiration for the Peking Opera, and Grotowski's dalliance with Indian *mudras* as part of his training regimen. These writers divorced from contexts of reception and production the ability of different forms to compel the attention of Western European attendants in the early twentieth century, resulting not only in dire misinterpretations but also in a simultaneous appropriation of form and erasure of source.[13] The "foreign" forms of performance activated latent (and not-so-latent) colonialist and Orientalist paradigms of exotic otherness that located an interest of "the" unfamiliar in its opposition to the perceived construction (and inauthenticity) of the writers' accustomed milieux.

More recently celebrated theatre pedagogues have also turned to "the East" for inspiration—Phillip Zarrilli, for one, has acclaimed the movement and meditation practices of India and Southeast Asia in his teaching and performance practice. Although Zarrilli is also a critic of Barba's appropriations ("For Whom Is the 'Invisible' Not Visible?"), his work comes close to "validating" Indian practices with Western theory and science, complicating his role as a conduit for these practices to European students.[14] Anne

Bogart, in contrast, has not only integrated Tadashi Suzuki's teaching into her expansion on Mary Overlie's Viewpoints, but the two systems exist side by side in the SITI company's training. Nonetheless, these two teachers, like Barba, propose access to systems that will help actors achieve what Zarrilli calls (reluctantly, and fully aware of the problematic endorsement of "narcissistic subjectivity") "presence" ("'... Presence ...'" 123). For her part, Bogart cites Barba's concept of *sats*—the quality of energy in the moment *before* an action," something "all actors around the world share" and which, when "intensified and accelerated [...] can be riveting to watch" (73, 74). Whether or not these approaches have been successful (and both Bogart and Zarrilli enjoy considerable endorsement within academic literature and among governmental and private funding bodies), so long as they adhere to the possibility of the "pre-expressive" they will encounter the same problems that ensnared Barba's work.

As indicated earlier, the concept of universality clogs the wheels of actor training or any focused attempt to undo systems of habit. Stuck between the effort to learn, undo, and understand habit lies an assumption of a common basis from which all practitioners can operate. The nature of that commonality will determine the kinds of erasures and endorsements that result from efforts to prescribe actions across times and cultures for a universal aim. "Starting" from bodies as discrete and whole objects erases, among other things, their imbrication with culture.

Addressing habit without further reifying its hidden armature requires an indirect approach, perhaps one disguised as something else.

An introduction to the neutral mask

Jacques Lecoq began his formal theatre training following World War II and quickly found himself working with Jean Dasté, son-in-law of the great French theatre teacher and theorist Jacques Copeau. Wishing to learn more about masked performance, Lecoq left France in 1948 for a three-month stay in Italy that turned into an eight-year sojourn. There, he worked with the likes of Dario Fo and Giorgio Strehler while coming to know the commedia dell'arte traditions and developing his work with masks. When Lecoq returned to Paris in 1956, he opened his own school and taught there until four days before his death in 1999. During that time he trained hundreds of performers, devisers, actors, directors, writers, and dancers.

Lecoq used the neutral mask as a pedagogical tool to help students provide themselves with a "state of discovery, of openness, an availability to receive" (Lecoq et al., *The Moving Body* 38/49).[15] It is not meant for performance. Through work with the mask students may gain a sense of movement without conflict, conflict inherent to drama and the performance of character. After wearing the mask students are expected to have experienced an engaged, physical curiosity for the world uninflected by personal opinion. Lecoq meant for the mask to allow students contact with common experiences by proposing the students address themselves to a sustained equilibrium that perpetually moves forward. He designed the mask to open students to an essential resemblance between themselves and all others.

Given the nature of Lecoq's teaching, it is important to state at the outset that no attempt has been made here to provide a résumé of his work. One of the central challenges with any project that puts Lecoq's pedagogy into writing is honoring the principle of surprise in Lecoq's classrooms. Although Lecoq did describe some of his exercises in writing, he very purposefully did not go into great detail, and as a former student explained, "Lecoq habitually uses rich metaphorical language in an attempt to keep the work at the level of a passionate search" (Wright 72). Indeed, as students we were regularly told, "It's good to be in the fog." To read a thorough description of his work without having had the opportunity to practice it risks spoiling the surprises it holds. One of the saddest things I ever heard at l'École came from the mouth of a first-year student when I was in my second year. One Friday afternoon I was explaining a terrific *auto-cours* (the weekly student-led devising projects) in which a gang of *bouffons* had dragged on stage the corpses of 10 women, who then slowly proceeded to rise from their pile and deliver a stirring choral speech. I had never heard of such a thing, and as I spouted enthusiastically about this discovery, the student smiled at me and said, "Ah yes, I read about that in his book."

What a shame! Nothing I have subsequently read of or by Lecoq has marked me with anything remotely approaching the vividness of lessons learned "on my feet." Nonetheless, Lecoq's work, particularly as it treats the concept of space and difference, can provide an extremely rich ground of analysis. Lecoq claimed that, for his pedagogy, "[t]wo fundamental principles have always been present: the recognition of life around us, and the imagination of the theatre" (Lecoq, *Theatre of Movement and Gesture* 112/13). While this chapter will go into depth thinking about the neutral mask and assemble in one place some of the most trenchant insights others have had about it, I hope that I have left something to the imagination.

It may perhaps be useful to point out at the start what the neutral mask is *not*, especially given some common misperceptions that have attached to its use in teaching. The neutral mask does not hide its wearer. The neutral mask is not a "barrier," it is not "expressionless," it is not "primitive," and it does not "eras[e] the Self" (Felner 157–8). It is not mystical or magical, nor is it blank or empty.

The masks used at l'École are made from leather after a design conceived by Lecoq and Amleto Sartori (1915–1962), made by the latter, and inspired by Jacques Copeau's "noble" mask (Lecoq et al., *The Moving Body* 36/49).[16] The neutral mask offers a face that is "balanced, which proposes a physical sensation of calm," and there are two versions, a "male" and "female" (Lecoq et al., *The Moving Body* 36/47).[17]

Immediately two concerns should arise: are these masks too invested in sexual binaries, and do they falsely impose a sense of cultural or ethnic specificity for this idea of "the" neutral? Mask teacher and Lecoq alum Sears A. Eldredge believes so, which is why he teaches neutral mask using sheets of paper, claiming that they are "more abstract" and less likely to impose their "European heritage" (49). Simon Murray indicates he shares these reservations when he writes of the masks' "questionable universalism," and shares teacher John Keefe's concerns that the neutral masks posit a binary of "'experience versus innocence'" (77). Anthony Frost and Ralph Yarrow seek an exit from cultural or sexual identity by claiming that the neutral mask is an abstraction and note that no face, European or otherwise, has eyes or nose or forehead or skin shade quite like the neutral mask's (233 n.5). (The masks used by Lecoq apparently began their lives a rich brown, but constant use has given them an almost cordovan complexion.) No matter what one makes of this claim, replacing the brown leather of Sartori's mask with a sheet of white paper hardly resolves the problems of the mask's racial specificity. It seems unavoidable that, even if the mask cannot be seen to represent an existing race, it represents *a* racial identity and requires that all students—and at l'École there were usually at least 30 countries represented—adopt it.

Similarly, the sexual binary proposed by the mask appears impenetrable and openly problematic for trans people or anyone who does not believe in identifying entirely as one sex or another. To begin with, Lecoq seems to suggest that the "male" mask is *the* neutral mask and the "female" mask a variant—such at least is the impression when he captions the "male" mask as "the" neutral mask in *The Moving Body* (37/48). Frost and Yarrow attempt to move beyond the sexual poles of the masks by suggesting that students, instead of choosing a "male" or "female" mask, may simply note the different sizes of the two masks and choose whichever one fits their face and physique best (233 n.5). I do the same when I teach using Sartori's masks, and whether or not male students wearing "female" masks or female students wearing "male" masks seems appropriate depends on the body of each student.

And yet, in truth, the masks *are* somewhat different, as Figure 2.1 demonstrates. Master Lecoq teacher Dody DiSanto has observed that the narrowed eyes of the female mask carry an almost antagonistic expression when compared to the "male" mask (personal communication). These differences are not inconsequential and they unavoidably suppose that sexual difference is the basis for all bodily differences. They *can*, if the teacher so desires, also point to a phenomenon treated in greater depth below, namely the occurrence of difference in what is shared. Even with the problems I have identified, having two different masks introduces the notion of plurality into the neutral. As such it might, depending on the teacher's interest,

Figure 2.1 The "female" and "male" neutral masks by D. Sartori[18]

Source: photo by the author.

serve as a way to void the phallocentric model of the "normal" body and open the way to multiple neutral bodies.[19] Henceforward when I refer to "the mask," I do not mean to privilege the male or the female mask, but refer instead to the performer wearing it in accordance with Lecoq's conception of it.

Students wearing the masks are meant to work within its two primary modes—economy of movement and discovery. These refer not only to a lack of psychology (without a past, every encounter is a discovery) but also to bodies moving with "a minimum amount of energy for a maximum return," with all extraneous movement removed (Lecoq et al., *The Moving Body* 90/103). Lecoq referred to this state as one his Seven Levels of Tension, a movement analysis model that corresponds to how bodies function with their surroundings. Lecoq observed how different physical comportments might be aligned with different amounts of resistance offered by the element of movement—for example, a body walking in air operates differently than one chest-deep in water. The amount of resistance offered by a situation significantly affects how I move and thereby changes my relationships with others. When there is only enough tension to prevent gravity's triumph, the body cannot maintain the straight lines that arrive with greater resistance.

Different styles will require different levels of tension, and as one moves up the scale, from less to more tension, different dynamics of physical distance, bodily comportment, and vocal engagement arrive.[20] Many of the movement technique exercises employed at the school rely on the third level of tension, particularly the transpositions of labor or athletic movement.[21] This kind of movement model proposes that one removes all opinion from the movements undertaken. "What's said is said," Lecoq would note, emphasizing that nothing further was required than a "simple" execution.[22] Lecoq here places the neutral mask in the same position Merleau-Ponty imagined for the painter, who "draws on brute meaning [...] in full innocence." In contrast to the writer or philosopher, from whom "we want opinions and advice [...] Only the painter is entitled to look at everything without being obliged to appraise what he sees" (Merleau-Ponty, "Eye and Mind" 161/14). To incorporate the world bodily, their thinking goes, one should do so without any opinion about it—otherwise a kind of rejection takes place and the mover or painter withholds something from the experience of the world in order to keep room for him or herself.

According to this proposition, students can, or may at least attempt to, remove all judgment of a movement; they may perform an action with the force and energy required by their bodies and without conflict. Lecoq suggested that economy of movement allowed students to shed personal or psychological investments that might specify action beyond its universality. The "essence" of a movement could only be achieved through the removal of those opinions, translated into movement, that specify *who* does it. The goal is to perform a movement in such a manner that the performer fades away and only the movement remains. With pantomime, this would result in performing the opening of a door in such a manner that the door becomes more important than who is entering it or what lies on either side.

Along with an economy meant to produce the "essence" of any particular movement, the mask helps situate the student in a state of discovery. The very first thing students do is discover the mask by taking time to regard it, handle it, and spend a few moments wearing it to feel their bodies under it. From there, students proceed through a series of solo improvisations based on the premise that the mask has no past—everything is done for the first time. With the exception of one exercise, students never have to negotiate the hazards of encountering another mask—all improvisations are either done alone or with a "chorus" of other masks operating as one idea, with all of the masks moving separately but in response to a collectively imagined place.

Students begin with "waking," literally starting from a supine position and arising to discover the rehearsal room in which the masked students find themselves. From here, students increasingly engage their imaginations, discovering an imagined environment, and from there the "elemental voyage" of the mask.[23] In this latter series of improvisations, students perform a journey that takes the mask from standing in a sea, across a beach, through a forest, up and down a mountain, across a stream, and onto a plain. The variety of terrain provides a constant spur to and support for the student's imagination. Crossing the different terrains also affects bodies differently, and there are lessons that focus on bodies' connections to the ground in order to identify and perform the different angles and locations of force as bodies navigate water, sand, rock, and grass.

Lecoq spoke of but has not written about a crucial element of the neutral mask work: the mask inclines forward. Lecoq and many commentators have noted that the mask produces a state of "equilibrium," but this should not be taken to mean an absence of movement or tension. After all, the neutral mask operates at the *fourth* level of tension: there is tension between the mask and its surroundings, but a tension without conflict. Rather than standing completely erect, the mask leans forward towards the next encounter, pulled in all of its movements by the world around it. To be pulled suggests both what lies ahead and that the body is brought into movement by where it is rather than who it is. The mask tips forward so that it need never decide to advance—it simply does so.

Removing the possibility of psychological motivation, coupled with the economy of movement, suppresses conflict internal to movement as well as conflict between the mover and the environment. With no opinion about where it is, the mask cannot be against where it is. With the absence of individual opinion, the actions undertaken wearing the neutral mask no longer "belong" to the person performing them, but to everyone observing, who must provide meaning with their own imaginations (and recognition of emblematic movement). In this way the neutral mask provides a means to "recognize what belongs to everybody" (Lecoq et al., *Les Deux Voyages*). To walk across yielding sand, to pick a way over and around thick underbrush, to scamper up a rocky pass, none of these are meant to produce feelings about themselves for the mask, but are simply what the mask does. The mask has no "why," it has only a *where*, places that pull it forward. As such, the neutral mask proposes that its wearers can become "lost" "in" mimed settings. Instead of repurposing an "other" for themselves, students wearing the mask invite their own transformation into something different. The mask displaces movement's motor outside of the body, and students must then negotiate an environment that is both different from them and a function of their imaginations. Students thus stage the way that mimicry can break open a closed system of identity.

Mime, empathy, and locating subjectivity

Lecoq separated pantomime from mime, at least partly to recuperate "mime" from the clutches of the pandemic of buskers inspired by Marcel Marceau's "Bip." More important to him was the attempt to take seriously the dynamics suggested by corporeal mimicry. For Lecoq, pantomime's gestures took the place of words and denoted the influence of an absent object separate from the body. The pantomime indicates a glass of water by cupping a hand. In contrast, mime's gestures are those *of* an object: the mime performs the glass of water with the entire body. The pantomime says, "There is a glass of water," while the mime suggests, "*Here* is a glass of water." Whereas mime concerns itself with porous bodies taking on their environments, pantomime addresses itself to the forms of things, and involves the depiction of objects' limits as they meet with a body's. In Jean-Louis Barrault's words, the "imagined existence of an object will become real only when the muscular disturbance imposed by this object is suitably conveyed by the body" (27–8). Although Lecoq believed that when pantomime was taken to extremes of virtuosity it could become a "theatrical malady" forestalling the development of gesture in theatre, he established it firmly in l'École's pedagogy as a means to an end (*Theatre of Movement and Gesture* 68/96).[24]

Using pantomime under the neutral mask, the student indicates barriers to movement that are not materially there; the student does so in such a manner as to give importance to the obstacle rather than the person crossing it. Through pantomime the body performs imagined barriers to its progress and these serve to propose an imagined location, all while keeping that location separate from—though dependent upon—the body traversing it. With *mime* the performer transposes place itself instead of suggesting a body in a place; the students seek to play place instead of a body in place. Indeed, the body recedes as place advances through mime.

Lecoq considered mime to be more than a theatrical tool and understood it as the primary means by which people learn about the world: "the act of mime is a fundamental human act, a childhood act: children mime the world in order to get to know it and to prepare themselves to live in it" (Lecoq, *Le corps poétique* 33).[25] Lecoq believed that humans constantly mimed their social and physical surroundings as a means of learning about them; all expression and relations with the world were based in the acquisition of worldly traces and images by the moving body. According to this understanding, shared by thinkers from Aristotle onward, human beings appropriate gestures from their caregivers and their environment through mime, literally incorporating themselves into the worlds described and made for them by those with greater power or authority.[26] As athletes, quilters, painters, and scholars know well, much instruction involves drilling in repetition: throw the ball *like this*; tack the quilt *like this*; paint *like this* before you can paint as you like; repetition is pronounced *like this*. And of course, children regularly role-play their parents, their peers, and their teachers, not merely for amusement but also as a means of learning how to be in the world.

Just as he distinguished between pantomime and mime, Lecoq also contrasted the act of miming a sense of place with miming its form, a distinction he borrowed, and altered, from anthropologist Marcel Jousse.[27] Though not as invested as Jousse in whether mimicry was voluntary or not, Lecoq

investigated whether the mime involved exterior form or an interior movement revealed as a shared investment between the body and the world. Lecoq
described this investment as *le geste sous le geste*, the gesture behind the gesture: "this is made by bodily impressions that inspire the body's movement"
(Lecoq, "Le corps et son espace" 279).[28] Morgane Bourhis further explains
that, "Even if the attendants aren't aware of the mimed object itself, they
can still experience actions that have a 'motor of play' that is perceivable in
and as the actor" (27).[29]

It was in search of these gestures that Lecoq used mime in his pedagogy—to push students to move as elements, materials, and place, to move
at the call of something other than themselves. Through mime, performers corporealize what they encounter: "I am facing the sea, watching it,
breathing it. My breath moulds itself to the movement of the waves and
gradually the picture shifts as I myself become the sea" (Lecoq et al., *The
Moving Body* 43/53).[30] Although Lecoq positions the perception of the sea
as a visual act ("the picture shifts"), note that this results from the shared
sensation of breath, linking vision with touch and proprioception as the
body becomes aware of its similarities to the acoustic and visual rhythm
of the waves. Elsewhere, Lecoq uses Jousse's neologism *mimage* to refer to
this process, calling it the expression of "hidden gestures, emotions, underlying state of a character," as well as the expression through movement
of "that which does not have an image" (Lecoq et al., *The Moving Body*
102–3/113–14).

Lecoq followed Jousse and Gaston Bachelard in reversing a dynamic
suggested by German empathy theory.[31] This enormously influential strain
of thought arose from eighteenth- and nineteenth-century art and architecture theory that sought to explain how people perceive, and then how they
take pleasure from, form (Mallgrave and Ikonomou). The term "empathy,"
though drawn from a Greek root, was the English translation of Robert
Vischer's neologism *Einfühlung*, literally translated as "in-feeling" or "feel-
ing-into."[32] Vischer described this as the experience of viewers in the grip
of the human "pantheistic urge for union with the world" projecting their
souls "into" phenomena and tracing them from the inside out (Vischer 109,
106, 108).[33]

According to Vischer, *Einfühlung* enacts a curious fusion of subject and
object: through an identification with the *form* of the object, the viewing
subject occupies it from within, thus transforming the subject–object relation into a subject–subject relation (103). Of course, the two "subjects"
here are the same, namely the initial viewer. Thus viewers are drawn to
phenomena both by the latter's presumed resemblance to a human situation and by a presumed human desire to understand one's surroundings.
Viewers simultaneously achieve and enact this desire by feeling *themselves*
from "inside" the phenomenon encountered. Therefore, phenomena are in
a sense occupied and appropriated by their viewers.

By keeping the viewer's identity intact, the empathy theorists allowed for the suppression of difference even as they sought to analyze how viewers responded to what they perceived. These thinkers essentially anthropomorphized phenomena, installing imagined universal human qualities in them that could then be recognized and claimed by viewing subjects who essentially recognized themselves. Thus, as David Krasner and Dermot Moran note, thinking on empathy required primarily knowledge of *self* (Krasner 267; Moran, "The Problem of Empathy" 271–4, 283ff). Art historian Juliet Koss goes further and emphasizes that, for German empathy theorists, the subject of *Einfühlung* "was implicitly a man of property" viewing art "within the confines of a relatively private realm," namely in the museum or private gallery (144). In other words, empathy was not for everyone.

Lecoq, working from Jousse, Bachelard, and Roger Caillois, broke from this tradition and proposed that when students mimed an object, far from the object being overtaken by the students, the object altered the student. Observing closely the way a particular tree accommodates and resists the wind and attempting to imitate this movement, or observing the way other people walk and attempting to imitate their gait, opens students to new relations with their surroundings without claiming ownership of these ways of being. Mime stages an encounter and a transformation, not an appropriation. The environment alters the neutral mask. Merleau-Ponty, writing about the role of mimicry in child development, notes: "Mimesis is the ensnaring of me by the other, the invasion of me by the other; it is that attitude whereby I assume the gestures, the conducts, the favored way of doing things of those whom I confront" (Merleau-Ponty, "The Child's Relation with Others" 145–6/67–9).[34] This does not mean that I *become* another, but instead that other habits displace my own. These habits are not another's, they are *of* the other, a derivative.

In terms of the neutral mask, to mime or mimic place means to play at taking on the sense of something beyond oneself. As Frost and Yarrow put it, "for Lecoq, 'play' was very much a question of developing the physical articulation of mimetic possibility" (88). With the neutral mask, mime is not a way of knowing that presupposes a stable identity comprehending an object; it is a way of *learning*. Students under the mask do not know or dominate what is mimed but instead open up *mimetic possibilities* in which they are altered by something different from themselves without claiming it. Mimesis with the neutral mask does not repeat or represent or replace another but allows the students to find themselves displaced.

Susan Leigh Foster describes the dangers of assuming that replicating form can produce knowledge. Responding to an entry in Yvonne Rainer's journal about observing and mimicking a dancer in India, Foster cautions that to conceive of literally re-performing another's movement as a form of knowledge suggests replicating a colonial project by stripping movement of "psychological or social frames of reference" ("Choreographing

Empathy" 89).[35] Foster argues that imitating the *exterior* form of movement risks obscuring the labor and values borne within it ("Choreographing Empathy" 86, 88). Imitation in this sense involves a subject whose pure reception of information obscures its (the subject's) interest in particular interpretations of that information. Foster convincingly analyzes how the operation of abstraction and disembodiment played a role in the European colonial enterprise, and yet she leaves open the possibility that alteration by others does not *need* to imply mastery of another. Instead, moving as another can involve learning a manner of being different from one's own. When students mime a tree or the sea, they do not "know" these objects, but they are available to relationships other than their own; these may not be precisely of the tree or of the other person, but they are not entirely those of the student either. Mimicry does not solve the problem of encountering another, but it suggests that the answer will involve transformative contact through movement.

Touch and the flesh

In order to work on the problem of encountering others, Merleau-Ponty first looked to a problem central to perceiving oneself: how do I, how *can* I, perceive myself perceiving? He returned time and again to a foundational phenomenological exercise: placing one hand on top of the other one. As he describes it, when one hand lies on top of the other he is able to feel himself touching *or* feel himself touched, but he cannot do them both at the same moment. Instead, he constantly shifts from one to the other, despite what appears to be the fact of his continuously doing both. This *shift* characterizes both the sensations and his being someone capable of experiencing the sensations. The experience of touching one hand with another and my inability to completely occupy one role (toucher) or another (touched) express the movement that secures the sense of having sense. Touching and being touched cross each other, producing between them the possibility of contact while keeping it at bay. I oscillate between actions, describing an orbit around a sense of self.

Merleau-Ponty characterized this crossing using a term that refers both to the "X" shape made by the optic nerves that cross from the eyes to the opposite side of the brain, and to a rhetorical device in which a sentence's meaning is conveyed by the inversion of parallel phrases: *chiasm*. The *chiasm* serves as a powerful example for Merleau-Ponty because it involves the intertwining of separate components that co-institute a single function. Not only does each component achieve its sense through its operation with others (as opposed to singly), but this operation requires a distinction between components, a gap (*écart*) that makes their intertwining possible. The neutral mask clambering over imaginary objects stages this intertwining—students "remain" bodies and persons and yet appear as such only through an involvement with an environment. In this case, the environment is performed, it is not "really" there, and yet it defines the person moving through it.

The trope of the *chiasm* suggests that object and subject are not so much oppositional categories as they are *kinds of relations* with the world and others. The subject as a "hierarchized system of structures" indicates the possibility of degrees of subjecthood and objecthood (Merleau-Ponty, *The Visible and the Invisible* 239/288) that depend on the ways in which I experience my involvement with others. Relations instead of states, "subject" and "object," describe *how* I am with the world and with others, not *what* I am in the world. Given their layered and shifting movements, they need not suggest a binarized structure of power or meaning. They might instead signal a departure from a unified perspective, "a fragmentation of being, [the] possibility for separation [...] the advent of difference" (Merleau-Ponty, *The Visible and the Invisible* 217/266). This conception of difference does not express power, suppression, or identity, but difference as the arrival of the plural beyond the binary; it signals an ontology and an ethics released from demanding similarity through identity or equality through sameness.

Instead, the difference denoted by "object" and "subject" relations refers to situation and its meaning. A subject relation would be one in which sense *matters*: the subject relations *concern* their orientation with the world and attend to the sense made of it. As my embodied situation continually assembles, I perform subject relations to the extent that it matters to me what may be done with those situations and I depend on others recognizing this performance; my very sense of depth "is a matter of care for being" (Morris 154) that assumes a place among others.[36]

The object relation would be one in which sense, as in both direction and meaning, is given but not known—I perceive something as an object insofar as I remove from it the capacity to be concerned with my engagement, which is to say insofar as I remove from it the ability to meaningfully *respond* to me.

Thus, an image online might appear to be an object, while the same image incorporated into an altar as a totem might no longer appear through an object relation. John Russon goes so far as to note that an "utterly unreflective" plant might still be encountered in a subject relation insofar as it does matter very much to it of what its situation is comprised. The "simple" plant is engaged in a "process of asserting [its] self-maintenance," and it is only by forgetting or obscuring this that I encounter the plant as an object (Russon 297). A plant may not "want" to live, but it *matters* to the organism whether or not it has the resources required to live.

Merleau-Ponty stressed that bodies incorporate the possibility of multiple relations, from indifference to caring deeply about one's situation. He also reinforced the shift from object to subject and the impossibility of being either alone. I require a world and others with whom I take up these relations, and it is these relations that determine my experience of being. This means it is possible to fail to meet each other's needs as subjects:

> the other's gaze does not transform me into an object, and my gaze does not transform him into an object, unless both gazes draw us back into the background of our thinking nature, unless we both establish an inhuman gaze, and unless each senses his actions, not as taken up and understood but rather as observed like the actions of an insect.
>
> (Merleau-Ponty, *Phenomenology* 378)

When I ignore others' capacity to have concern for their care in movement, for their *sense*, I limit the scope of my relation with them; someone may be physically "there" but not perceived through a subject relation as someone to whom I am responsible. Despite their ubiquity, domestic workers and many members of the "service economy" escape notice through just this sort of abridged acknowledgment of their care for their own sense. Many people routinely labor in conditions that actively suppress the experience of concern for their situation.

The chiasmic relationship I have with others gains further definition in light of one hand touching the other: the person involved shifts between toucher and touched and experiences a fundamental reversibility between them. The roles become reversible because a hand, "while it is felt from within, is also accessible from without, itself tangible, for my other hand" (Merleau-Ponty, *The Visible and the Invisible* 133/174). Transposed to *someone else's* hand touching *my* hand, I become reversible with another.

This transposition does not require that I *become* another. I do not understand or *comprehend*—as in to grasp and encircle—another. Yet an exchange of touch can teach me something.

Without proposing the appropriation of the other through a claimed identity with myself, Merleau-Ponty's reversibility describes the experience of movement between relations. The touch of others does not grant me access to their perspectives; rather, it affirms my reversibility as toucher and touched. As someone who touches, I am in the realm of the tangible and am tangible myself; as someone who smells, I am in the realm of the olfactory and may be smelled by others; and so on with all the senses (Merleau-Ponty, *The Visible and the Invisible* 134/175). And to the extent I accept that what I perceive belongs to the realm of the perceptible just as I do, I accept that what I perceive may have a concern for its situation. I am "caught up" in what I perceive and participate in a world experienced through the shifts between sentient and sensible (Merleau-Ponty, *The Visible and the Invisible* 139/181).

Merleau-Ponty risks here a phenomenology of "able-bodied-ness" and "the normal" body possessed of all of its senses. However, his methodology not only accommodates but also anticipates the multiplicities instituted by differently abled bodies. For example, the "visible world" for someone born

blind at birth will be quite different for the person who becomes blind—
both may feel "seen" but this will mean something quite different for each.
Both will "appear" differently to the sighted insofar as they are taken to be
blind. The perceived world is *composed by* rather than simply inhabited by.
Further, senses cannot be isolated from each other; each one engages a world
not singly accessible by that sense alone and so "[w]e must habituate ourselves to think that every visible is cut out in the tangible, every tactile being
in some manner promised to visibility, and there is encroachment, infringe-
ment" between them, as between all the senses (Merleau-Ponty, *The Visible
and the Invisible* 134/175). Diminished sight does not mean an engagement
that is "less than" a supposedly "standard" one founded on an abstraction
of perfect vision; it occupies a position amongst every other as a kind of
engagement with the world. Senses intertwine, and in so doing allow that
each particular intertwining—reflecting how each person perceives according to particular senses—guarantees a place in the perceptible world.

If to touch is to be tangible and to see is to be visible, then my situation
with the world becomes reversible and I can experience the intertwining of
subjectivity and objectification. As Elizabeth Grosz puts it: "The subject and
object are inherently open to each other [...] They are interlaced with one
another not externally but through their reversibility and exchangeability"
("Merleau-Ponty and Irigaray in the Flesh" 46). These shifts describe the
neutral mask and its surroundings, all of which appear through a movement
between them.

Indeed, Merleau-Ponty's reflections on painting describe quite closely the
work of the neutral mask, particularly when he approvingly quotes André
Marchand, himself following Paul Klee. Marchand claims:

> In a forest, I have felt many times over that it was not I who looked
> at the forest. Some days I felt that the trees were looking at me, were
> speaking to me ... I was there, listening ... I think that the painter must
> be penetrated by the universe and not want to penetrate it
> (Qtd in Merleau-Ponty, "Eye and Mind" 167/31)[37]

By performing place through mime and pantomime without conflict, the
neutral mask suggests a movement between a body traversing place and
the place traversed; neither one is perceptible or sensible without the other.

The toucher and touched are distinguishable, but not independent, inter-
twined in a *chiasm* of mutual implication Merleau-Ponty describes as the
"flesh" ("*la chair*") of the world (*The Visible and the Invisible* 133/173).
This "flesh" is neither material nor its lack. Rather, it is an "element" across
which I move as perceiver and perceived (Merleau-Ponty, *The Visible and
the Invisible* 139/182). It accounts for the incorporation of beings and the
world, my fundamental "possession" by the world I perceive and of which
I am a part (Merleau-Ponty, *The Visible and the Invisible* 134/175). The

"flesh" of the world grants the ability of the seer to find the seen while also guaranteeing that the seer may also be seen. It is a third term that further breaks apart a possible binary between subject and object.

As an element by which I come to being, the "flesh" suggests an "anonymity innate" to each person (Merleau-Ponty, *The Visible and the Invisible* 139/181). Insofar as I see, I participate in the visible world with all that is seen. Far from removing me from the material and historical conditions of action, the "flesh" proposes that I "adhere to the domain of history and of geography" (Merleau-Ponty, *The Visible and the Invisible* 115/152). Throughout these domains I am pervaded by the generality of being, a belonging to perception and perceptibility shared by all living things. I am not coincident with what I touch, but what I touch and I both belong to the tangible. This mutual belonging constitutes both an anonymity for each thing in the perceptible world—I share the possibility of perceptibility with all things—and the narcissism of perception—everything perceptible involves the "flesh" of which I am also a part.

However, the "flesh" is not a soup that renders all beings the same; the anonymity of being in general is the very means of differentiation. It bears no relation to Barba's "pre-expressive" because it does not subtend culture but is thoroughly implicated in it: the "pre-expressive" is concerned with "the" body, while the "flesh" is concerned with *embodiment*. The structure and manifestation of the "flesh" arrives through the gap (*écart*) that arranges the possibilities of object and subject relations. The "flesh" is not something *in* which I operate, but that *by which* I am. It is a manner of being achieved through movement rather than coinciding. Nancy J. Holland argues that if the "flesh" is "non-sexualized," then Merleau-Ponty "ultimately fails to create a world in which true difference, sexual difference, can exist" (333). But the "flesh" exists as a means of relation between different terms. Merleau-Ponty does not exclude difference; instead he argues against the possibility of any absolutes, of complete closure as the sign of difference. The terrain of difference requires movement, uncertainty, ambiguity. It requires the failure to identify with another or oneself.

The neutral mask is not neutral

Lecoq claims of neutral mask work that "before sensing the differences we have to sense what is common" (*Les Deux Voyages*). Lecoq attempted through his neutral mask pedagogy to draw students towards an anonymity suggested by the "flesh" but recognizable only by the specificity of the individual. I exist with a world of obstacles, with the material of my embodiment, and the movement across, over, and under these obstacles comprises the work of the neutral mask. The anonymity of belonging arrives through the evocation of a world I recognize, not because everyone has a common experience of specific terrain, but because all perceiving things take part in a perceptible world.

Lecoq spoke of the neutral mask encountering "the tree of all trees," but he addressed a world where multiple perspectives themselves institute the tree of trees. Recall Merleau-Ponty's statement about the table: no one else perceives it as he does, but this in turn is only knowable if others see it at all, and if both he and the other viewers (touchers, smellers, tasters, listeners) all belong to a visible (tangible, etc.) world. The "tree of all trees" is not a *thing* as object, it *is* simply because many may experience it differently. What one person only can perceive will be an object of pure imagination rather than a thing perceptible through imagination *and* the perspectives of other people.

The neutral mask work encourages students to discover a world around them as discovery itself, rather than as a person doing so. Students are to divest themselves entirely of their own mannerisms and move as a principle, not a body. This is not possible.

Lecoq himself was forthright about this: "Of course there is no such thing as absolute and universal neutrality, it is merely a temptation" (*The Moving Body* 20/32). In perhaps his most direct admission that the work of the neutral mask training consists of establishing a principle rather than a skill, in finding the fruits of "failure" rather than codifying success, here is Lecoq in a 1998 interview:

> You could say that I "clowned" my students already with the neutral mask. So they all resemble each other, or they tend to. But the urgency of differences appears precisely in the research of being like the other. In the end, we're never like each other. And these urgencies appear, which the students don't realize, which will, little by little, reveal themselves in their creation, starting with the recognition of life as it is. A tree is a tree, to begin with. And then, how will they sense this tree, which may seem different to each one?
>
> (*Les Deux Voyages*)[38]

As much as students strive to evoke "the tree of all trees" and the "discovery of all discoveries," they are bound to fail. Lecoq often worked with the process of failure, noting:

> I am fascinated by the difference between the geographic pole and the magnetic pole. [...] It is lucky that this angle exists. Error is not just acceptable, it is necessary for the continuation of life, provided it is not too great. A large error is a catastrophe, a small error is essential for enhancing existence. Without error, there is no movement. Death follows.
>
> (*The Moving Body* 20–1/32)

Similar to the magnetic pole that is not the northernmost point, Lecoq charged students with finding a neutral that was not neutral. The neutral, like the *chiasm* that describes the "flesh," is a *principle* more than a *thing*; it is a way of learning about movement.

Likewise, students working with the neutral mask forge a way of learning about how they engage the world. Each pantomimed log brings with it part of the person scrambling over it. And this is the point. Eldredge claims that, instead of "the" neutral, the neutral mask reveals "more of what is distinctly 'you' [...] [W]hat is elicited is actually your *individual* neutral" (50). To this I would add the caveat that "your individual neutral" is as contingent as any other phenomenon: historically, culturally, and physically located as part of a corporeal schema that constantly adjusts. The "you" elicited by the mask on one day will not be the same as the "you" elicited the following day; changes in habit, feeling, and, simply, time all conspire to keep "your individual neutral" a moving target. With the neutral mask, Lecoq proposed a way of moving that would "tempt" students towards a completely uninflected movement. However, as students work to become aware of and deliver themselves from habits of moving, they arrive at movements that specifically and potently characterize how they navigate the world. The movement towards "the" neutral *and back towards an appearance of self* provides a sense of the neutral mask and the student at the same time.

This principle thoroughly undermines Merleau-Ponty's contention that the painter may look at things without the obligation to appraise them. The appraisal will happen whether obliged or not. At the absolute minimum, artists choose what to paint and so must appraise and select a position from which to paint. Consider how, between Monday October 29 and Saturday November 3, 1888, Gauguin and Van Gogh began two and three, respectively, canvasses depicting sites along the same stretch of the southern embankment of the Craponne Canal in Arles (Druick et al. 170–5). Their styles intriguingly similar at this point, the greatest difference between the paintings can perhaps be found in what each artist found worthy of painting. Whether Van Gogh or Gauguin chose best, they chose differently, and this difference arises at least in part from the assessments each painter made of their location.

Lecoq asked students to make themselves a "blank page," but this was "not to diminish their knowledge" or to "reduce" the performer's consciousness (*The Moving Body* 27/39). Rather, he sought to re-introduce students to the inevitable cultural, bodily, and intellectual habits of body, consciousness, and imagination that form their "natural" movements and decisions in play. Aware of these, performers are better suited to enter the state of play so central to engaged performance. By aiming for the common, students distill their movement into a potent performance of themselves. It arrives through a relationship to shared acts of imagination. At the least, it is impossible for the mask to be performed without a body, and a "body reflects its environment, its milieu and its period" (Lecoq et al., *The Moving Body* 27/39). "The neutral" proliferates with each body's difference from others: "The idea that everyone is alike is both true and totally false. Universality is not the same as uniformity" (Lecoq et al., *The Moving Body* 40/51). Far from erasing difference, the neutral mask assists its institution.

Through its lure, its perpetual escape, and its organizing work, the neutral as a principle operates in the same way as the reversibility of the *chiasm*. Merleau-Ponty opens his chapter, "The Intertwining—The *Chiasm*," with his account of touching his own hands and with his claim about the movement between toucher and touched establishing a basis for the reversibility of being. More than halfway through the chapter, he makes this significant qualification:

> It is time to emphasize that it is a reversibility always imminent and never realized in fact. My left hand is always on the verge of touching my right hand touching the things, but I never reach coincidence; the coincidence eclipses at the moment of realization, and one of two things always occurs: either my right hand really passes over to the rank of touched, but then its hold on the world is interrupted, or it retains its hold on the world, but then I do not really touch *it*.
>
> (Merleau-Ponty, *The Visible and the Invisible* 147–8/191)

The principle of reversibility is impossible to achieve in fact because to do so would imply the ability to firmly occupy, simultaneously, a role as object or subject, a possibility Merleau-Ponty has already removed. This applies even more markedly to the experience of touching or hearing another: "I am always on the same side of my body," he writes, referring not only to the *écart* between himself and another, but alluding to the impossibility of being on *all* sides of his own body (Merleau-Ponty, *The Visible and the Invisible* 148/192). When people touch each other, they are not reversible in the sense that they may occupy the other's situation. To begin with, neither one exists completely as a role at any time. Secondly, they are only reversible with each other in the sense that they may touch and be touched. Which is also to say, they are not so much touch*er* and touch*ed*, but touch*ing*. The "flesh" of the world arranges touch, diminishes the binary between subject and object, and discards two roles for a multi-faceted, reversible act.

John Wright notes that Lecoq

> uses the neutral mask to enable his students to work with such openness and availability that the world can make an *impression* on the body [...] [T]he actor is able to let a clear image of the sea make a corporeal impression on him or her.
>
> (76)

The sea appears for attendants through its reflection on the body of the student wearing the neutral mask. This does not suggest, however, that any given part of an environment has the same effect on every body—"the sea" for anyone else will never be "the sea" for me. The neutral mask proposes that students might be able to perform "the sea," and through the attempt to do so discover their "own" sea, the sea that arrives through their particular bodies during the time of the exercise (Lecoq, *Theatre of Movement and Gesture* 69/96). The fact that the observing students recognize the sea in a particular body (or that any attendant recognizes a mimed phenomenon via a performer's body) speaks to the "anonymity innate" to perception as much as to a shared performance language. Different perspectives are part of the "flesh" of the world, and their crossings are what inaugurate a sense of presence (Merleau-Ponty, *The Visible and the Invisible* 84/114). What begins as an assertion of commonality resolves as an engine of difference—an encounter with what is not myself, an encounter that depends on movement and imagination.

And yet the encounter does not in itself secure this possibility. One of the neutral mask exercises conducted at l'École resulted in a kind of failure that models how encountering another can produce stasis and closure instead of movement. In *The Moving Body*, Lecoq claimed that he wanted to avoid the masks having to discover each other because "What could a neutral mask say to another mask? Nothing" (39/51). And yet this was precisely what he asked us to do in an improvisation called The Encounter of the Masks, in which the "male" and the "female" masks were to find each other in the forest. This improvisation engaged the tropes of Eden, lost innocence, and homogenized human experience that some of Lecoq's students have found troublesome. But far from exemplifying the neutral mask work, the exercise stands out precisely because it was so *unlike* the other work we did with the mask.

The most significant element of the mask's encounter with the world is its transformation by and transposition of that world. The neutral mask expresses its wearer and its environment by taking on aspects of their contours and rhythms. The dodging, bobbing water of a brook and the solidity of mountains become apparent insofar as they change the bearing of the student wearing the mask. However, when a "male" mask meets a "female" mask, it becomes almost impossible to transpose the movement of the other. To begin with, both masks are already involved in mapping the same terrain onto their bodies—to change from miming the environment to miming someone *else* miming the same environment quickly reaches a standstill. Students often trapped themselves in a mirror exercise. The next problem was that once students stopped moving through an environment, they would drop their engagement with their surroundings in order to direct all of their attention onto the other mask. And in doing so, the hoariest of gender clichés crept into the work as students assumed what they felt were "basic" behavioral tropes.

Masks encountering another mask figured as Other halt each other.[39] The mask cannot move *through* the other mask as it moves through environments. The other mask arrives simultaneously as completely out-side—resistant to the neutral mask's central work of taking elements of the world "into," and thereby changing, itself—and as completely similar—in the context of the exercise, there is nothing one mask can do that another cannot mimic. The closeness of the mimicry is what poses the problem here: in the other neutral mask exercises, the neutral mask mimicked its environ-ment *and failed*, but here the masks mirror each other *successfully*. The imaginative perception central to encountering difference disappears in the clarity of successfully mimicked action. When working with the neutral masks, students become alienated from their habitual ways of moving in the world through miming the world. At the same time, the neutral mask's mimicry expresses each student's particular ways of moving. The perfor-mance of one's "own" movement follows alienation from it, an alienation denied the mirrored mask. This exercise made apparent that students wear-ing the neutral mask *do* have histories of bodily formation that constrain their movements and their perception; it was upon the grossest exaggera-tions of these constraints that students fell most often. Precisely because students were able to mimic each other in the context of the neutral mask work, the mutability of the neutral mask hardened into the apparent destiny of biology, performed in clichés of male action and female passivity.

Cormac Power writes that "one might argue that Lecoq actor training militates against a metaphysics of self-presence" (78). Taken in detail, the neutral mask can demonstrate how that argument works. Instead of repeat-ing suspect binaries, the neutral mask proposes how the perception and experience of difference are achieved with others through acts of mimesis. Others appear as such because of their ability to render *me* other than I know myself to be, just as the neutral mask stages how environments ren-der the mask into something else. However, when one mask encounters another, its trajectory of alteration meets an *identical* trajectory and the two cancel each other out. The neutral mask encountering another neutral mask cannot be alienated from its own actions and so cannot come to grips with the difference of the other mask. It is not simply that the *failure* of mimesis, rather than its success, opens me up to the difference of other peo-ple. As Homi Bhabha writes in "Of Mimicry and Man: The Ambivalence of Colonial Discourse" (1994), failed mimicry might actually serve a racist policy of obedience and exclusion. Colonial subjects are encouraged to be *almost* like colonizers, to almost mimic their manners, in order to affirm a politically expedient claim of difference.[40] Rather, it is that the failed mim-icry of the neutral mask does not return me to myself or to "the other," but instead transforms my way of being into something else.[41]

Lecoq's work with the neutral mask not only destabilizes "the" sub-ject, it explicitly valorizes and stages the transformation of a subject by an imaginative encounter with another *in front of others*. The mask's encounter with imagined environments takes place through others' perceptions of the mask's actions. The neutral mask is not a tool for a student to use alone—it provides the cornerstone for a pedagogy that not only depends on observation but also prepares students for public performance. The mask puts students in movement, the movement between an appearance of oneself and of others. It does so by staging the processes by which failed mimicry and imaginative perception participate in altering a student's way of moving and of being.

Lecoq and Merleau-Ponty both offer conceptions of commonality that lead, in practice, to assertions of difference. Lecoq used the neutral mask to tempt students with an idea of universality through which students transformed themselves by moving according to imagined environments. When students wear the mask well they are open to an environment, not as the opening of all openings or as discovery itself but as each student's particular failure to erase his or her own history of bodily formation in the attempt to enact "pure" movement. Through the use of pantomime (push back an imagined branch) and mime (breathe with the rhythm of a brook), students enact the transformations other phenomena work on them. With the neutral mask, students are repeatedly drawn to their involvement with place. Thus the mask's mouth is slightly open—to have a closed orifice on the face would act as a marker of separation and would suggest something the mask keeps apart from its environment. Instead, the mask-work can open students to perception powered by imagination and to environments encountered through failed acts of mimicry.

A shared mask leads its wearers on a journey that does not end in failure but truly begins there. The *urgency* of differences only arrives after students try to divest themselves of difference and fail. As with other failures to be considered in this book, this failure generates rather than negates. The neutral mask stages the movement possible during *any* encounter with another, a movement that fails to define "the" other or myself. This movement delivers students not to others or themselves, but to something in between, something new. Both the performing students and the attending students assume responsibility for establishing this in between together (Lecoq, "Le corps et son espace" 279). In *The Moving Body* Lecoq exclaimed of the neutral mask's effect on students, "An extraordinary dimension is being offered to them: *space!*" (38/50).

Notes

1 Many authors shift between "presence" and "stage presence" when referring to the unusual focus given or demanded by a performer. For reasons never made clear, Goodall in particular refrains from distinguishing between these two terms. In order to avoid further confusion, from here forward when an

author uses "presence" to mean something exceptional about a performer or a performance, I will use "[stage] presence."

2 ISTA has met in 1980, 1981, 1985, 1986, 1987, 1990, 1992, 1994, 1995, 1996, 1998, 2000, 2004, and 2005.

3 See also 16, 33, 52, as well as Watson, "Eastern and Western Influences on Performer Training at Eugenio Barba's Odin Teatret"; Watson, "Training with Eugenio Barba."

4 See also Pradier and Taylor.

5 See also Barba and Savarese 218, 7. The possibility of revealing or putting into play an irreducible expression of the actor's self is perhaps the strongest point of connection between Barba and Grotowski, under whom the former studied and served as an assistant, editing the papers that became the seminal *Towards a Poor Theatre.* See also Watson, "Training with Eugenio Barba."

6 See, for example, Barba, *Beyond the Floating Islands* 6.

7 Barba has also reduced this list to three elements: alternation of balance, opposition, and "an operation of compression and reduction" (Barba and Savarese 18).

8 See, for example, Bharucha, *Theatre and the World*; Bassnett; Pavis; Shevtsova, *Theatre and Cultural Interaction*; Zarrilli, "For Whom Is the 'Invisible' Not Visible?" I am not aware of any queer readings of Barba's teaching.

9 This element of Barba's teaching practice, in which he critiques demonstrations of Asian theatre forms, strongly resembles disciplinary regimes of observation and regulation enacted by colonial powers over their subjects. To dispute this conclusion, Franc Chamberlain points out that some of these artists, I Nyoman Catra, Sanjukta Panigrahi, and Kanichi Hanayagi, report positively on these sessions. Indeed, they claim that Barba's re-framing of their movement according to his principles has not only helped them develop their work but has helped them maintain their performance traditions (Chamberlain, "Foreword" xiv). As with Watson's defense above, far from mitigating the sense that Barba positions himself as a master of the exotic, this description of his perceived ability to assist the experts of foreign styles in deepening their own practice explains quite neatly how a Westerner is positioned as a universal master of bodily techniques.

10 Indeed, Watson notes that in personal interviews Sanjukta Panigrahi and Katsuko Azuma "credit their ISTA experiences with giving them greater insight into their own forms [...] and assisted them in the teaching of students." One page later, Watson writes: "Despite their ISTA experiences and insights it has afforded them, Panigrahi and Azuma, for example, maintain that it has had no effect on their traditional performances." It may be, however unlikely, that Panigrahi and Azuma have a repertory of performances that they have managed to somehow preserve from the insights gained from Barba, but it remains to be explained how changing what one teaches one's students of a traditional style is not an alteration of a cultural practice. Whether for the better or for the worse, it seems clear that Panigrahi and Azuma are bringing "back" their experiences with Barba and using them to change the practices in their "home" contexts (Watson, "Staging Theatre Anthropology" 29–30).

11 For example, Barba cites *kabuki* and *noh* training principles when describing exercises meant to help actors achieve [stage] presence (Barba and Savarese 10, 16; Barba, *Beyond the Floating Islands* 17–18, 33–4, 69–71). Barba associates this exercise alternately with the concept of *koshi*, or energy borne of dynamic tension, and *jo-ha-kyu*, a system of movement that emphasizes three stages: retention, breaking, and speed. See also Barba, *Beyond the Floating Islands* 118.

Barba also locates the practice of oppositional movement, one of his core tenets of the "pre-expressive," in "the East," and he credits it with drawing spectators to actions on stage (Barba and Savarese 196; Barba, *Beyond the Floating Islands* 15). Barba does offer examples of the principle in Western forms, including cartoon manuals (how to indicate movement through opposition), Hellenic and Renaissance sculpture, and exercises from Dalcroze, Meyerhold, and Decroux. These latter, however, are figured as "a simplification of the complex architecture of Indian *tribhangi*," a model of spinal posture (Barba and Savarese 200–1, 205).

12 See Stewart, "Actor as *Refusenik*"; Watson, "Introduction"; Chamberlain, "Theatre Anthropology: Definitions and Doubts."

13 For examples of the scholarship on the appropriation of "Eastern" techniques by Artaud, Brecht, and Grotowski see Bharucha, *Theatre and the World*; Bharucha, "A Collision of Cultures"; Shevtsova, "Interculturalism, Aestheticism, Orientalism"; Blau, "Universals of Performance"; Brandon; Chin; Lo and Gilbert; Tian; Tillis. Intriguingly, Nicola Savarese, Barba's long-time collaborator and co-author of the *Dictionary of Theatre Anthropology*, was willing to criticize Artaud while withholding judgment from Barba; see Savarese.

14 See in particular Zarrilli, "Towards a Phenomenological Model of the Actor's Embodied Modes of Experience"; Zarrilli, "An Enactive Approach to Understanding Acting"; Zarrilli, *Psychophysical Acting*.

15 My translation. Given the frequent departures from David Bradby's translations of Lecoq's work, citations from Lecoq's *Theatre of Movement and Gesture* and *The Moving Body* will contain page numbers for the English and French versions.

16 Lecoq encountered this mask working with Copeau's son-in-law Jean Dasté and collaborated with Sartori to make a version suited to Lecoq's needs. Following Amleto's death, his son Donato has continued making neutral masks. Lecoq never worked directly with Copeau, and yet the latter's values pervade Lecoq's work. Simon Murray's description of the strong influence Copeau exerted over Lecoq centers on their commitment to physical training as a preparation for and primary element of theatrical play as well as their interest in "mask work, *commedia d'ell arte*, and Greek tragedy" (30). As Murray notes, however, Copeau's training was expressly designed to illuminate classic texts, while Lecoq's was structured to create new theatre. For more on Lecoq's connection to Copeau, see Murray and Becker 15–43.

17 My translation.

18 These are the masks I use, made by Donato; I trained with masks made by Amleto. Dody DiSanto believes that Donato's masks are not of the same quality as his father's, noting, among other things, that the "male" mask is too small for many men's faces (personal communication). Although I agree with all her observations, I find these masks incomparably preferable to every other version I have encountered, particularly those made of paper or cloth.

19 Lecoq was not interested.

20 The different levels are: 1. Sub-relaxation, 2. Relaxation, 3. The Economic (Efficient) Body, 4. The Supported Body, 5. Decision, 6. Passion, and 7. The Maximum. In class, Lecoq used a slightly different vocabulary: 1 was described as the "Victory of Gravity"; 4 was called "Alertness," and 7, "The Asphyxiation of Movement." For a brief description of each level, see Lecoq et al., *The Moving Body* 88–91/103–4.

21 These genres of movement, it must be noted, are habitually coded as "masculine" in Western culture. Therefore, attempting to perform them "free" from opinion

suggests that they may be de-masculinized. The possibility of this operation is considered below.

22 Jos Houben notes the concordances between the neutral mask and Moshe Feldenkrais's work on "Awareness Through Movement," and Anthony Shrubsall has documented a workshop given by Houben in which these were highlighted. Although Houben claims that Lecoq was more interested in "theatre and space" and Feldenkrais more interested in "educating the sense of the human being," he claims that both continued investigations of "functional, organic movement" (qtd in Shrubsall 105-6). Houben is a Lecoq graduate, a co-founder of Complicite, and currently teaches at l'École in addition to performing and giving workshops worldwide. I participated in a workshop Houben led in Chicago in 2008 and interviewed him later that year in Paris.

23 Bradby translates "voyage élémentaire" as "fundamental voyage." While this captures the centrality of this series of improvisations to the neutral mask work, it loses the connection of the voyage to the different elements (earth, water, fire, air) whose encounter forms an important part of the voyage itself. Lecoq et al., *The Moving Body* 41/52.

24 My translation.

25 My translation; English passage appears at *The Moving Body* 22.

26 For more on the role of authority in instructional mimesis, see Mauss.

27 Lecoq's concepts of *le jeu* and *rejeu* were also at least partly inspired by Jousse. See Jousse 43-84, and compare with *Theatre of Movement and Gesture* 4-5, 68-70/17, 96-7, and *The Moving Body* 22/33. (Bradby, confusingly, takes the end of one of Lecoq's paragraphs crediting Jousse for his explication of *mimisme* and puts it in a footnote that reads as if Bradby wrote it (46-7/56-8). I have written about Jousse's—and Roger Caillois'—influence on Lecoq in "Space and Mimesis," a chapter in the forthcoming *Routledge Companion to Jacques Lecoq*, from which material in this chapter has been adapted.

28 My translation. See also Lecoq and Perret, "Le geste sous le geste."

29 My translation.

30 See also Lecoq, *Theatre of Movement and Gesture* 69/96.

31 Bachelard's influence on Lecoq is the subject of a chapter in *The Routledge Companion to Jacques Lecoq*.

32 Harry Francis Mallgrave and Eleftherios Ikonomou note the first translation of *Einfühlung*, but choose themselves to translate it as "in-feeling"; I follow Dermot Moran and David Krasner's lead in continuing to use "empathy" to refer to this concept of Vischer's and its subsequent development. Krasner, in his excellent analysis of empathy, notes that, long before Vischer wrote, there existed the Greek word "*empatheia*, which signifies the ability to project one's emotions into an object of thought" (71 n.64).

33 The term "viewer" is used advisedly: Vischer and his immediate successors were concerned with aesthetic encounters and heavily emphasized the visual sense. Even August Schmarsow, who emphasized the body in movement, figured this mainly as a roving eye.

34 In Michael Taussig's seminal work on the processes of mimesis between colonized and colonizing peoples, he notes: "The ability to mime, to mime well, in other words, is the capacity to Other" (19).

35 Foster's recent book, *Choreographing Empathy* (2011), is based on this and a series of other articles situating the perception of dance in the context of historical approaches to perception. See also Foster, "Kinesthetic Empathies and the Politics of Compassion"; Foster, "The Earth Shaken Twice Wonderfully"; Foster, "Movement's Contagion."

36 Another way of expressing this would recall J.J. Gibson's notion of "affordances," the environmental features perceived as affording bodies a range of possible actions.

37 For the original Marchand quote in context, see Charbonnier 34.

38 My translation. With Lecoq's version of clown—a vast topic well beyond the scope of this book—the clown sets a clear goal, strives for it, and fails. But in failing, the clown not only awakens laughter, but she or he also achieves something equally, if not more, exciting than the original goal. Lecoq's pedagogy begins in earnest with the neutral mask and ends with clown; the former involves a search for the common that resolves in difference, while the latter involves an acute expression of difference that resolves in what can be shared.

39 I never witnessed same-sex neutral mask encounters.

40 Judith Butler, who has been clear about her debt to Bhabha, famously wrote of how failed mimicry could be used to parody oppressive discourses of identity (*Gender Trouble* 185–7).

41 Writing about "environmental presence," Gabriella Giannachi claims that subjects understand themselves as such *via* environments, through relationships with the circumstances of their location. For Giannachi, "presence is the operation through which the subject witnesses itself as other and then recycles this 'other' so that it may become part of itself" (60).

Chapter 3

A unique phenomenon of distance

I entered the gallery at noon. Attired in capri-length khakis, t-shirt, and vest, with only a few thin lines of yellow paint on my face to signal bird-hood, simply walking in the front door would not necessarily have drawn anyone's notice. Some of the attendants were wandering in the back rooms and others had gathered around the empty area in the main room of the gallery, presumably having figured that the largest bare area would be used for performance. The expectation for a performance had already reoriented attendants to each other and to the gallery; even before my arrival they were transforming the gallery into a performance venue (and the noon hour into a time of performance). All that remained was for the performance to begin.

The gallery sits along the second floor ring of shops and offices circum-scribing the ten-storey atrium of the Thompson Center, a one-square block government building in downtown Chicago. Glass walls fronted all the offices and shops, affording them a view of the atrium and four elevators, each also faced with glass. The entrance to the gallery directed entrants to an information desk that faced the front room. Two galleries opened up behind the information desk, and behind these a long third gallery faced the angled glass façade of the building.[1]

Moving into the gallery I inspected its suitability for a nest. Beginning a task markedly different from any already pursued by the attendants, I felt both a sense of separation and connection: I was up to something else and this signaled the beginning of a shared purpose.[2] The quality and orientation of attention changed, and so changed the relationships between the people in the room. It would be hard to say that these relationships could change *without* an alteration in attention, either in quantity, direction, or quality. Although the attendants and I might have been paying attention to differ-ent objects, we were now all attending to the room and all of its occupants within the shared project of making a performance. In these close quarters, shifts of bodily tension can alter how we perceive our projects and ourselves. How we breathe changes the sound of a room, changes its temperature, changes how people appear. From within the assembled attendants and among the performers, there is almost no movement too small to impact

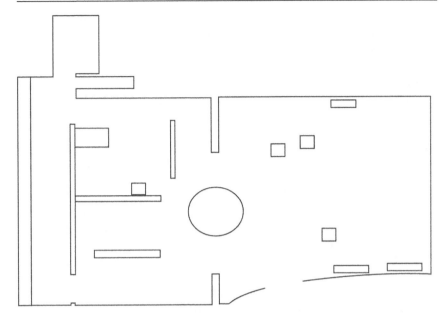

Figure 3.1 Approximate layout of the Illinois State Museum Chicago Gallery
Source: drawing by the author.

the making of a performance. We experience the many relationships at play physically, emotionally, and intellectually—though the extent to which they are felt varies widely. I may offer myself in a direction, or draw closer to an object of inspection, or radiate heat, or shift awkwardly, or talk loudly, or laugh too much, or brush a neighbor's leg with my own. All of these actions communicate a sense of my relationship to where I am and with whom I am. At least, they do if I am paying attention.

I took a radio from under a bench by the windows, brought it to the far wall, plugged it in, and turned on a pre-set AM station full of talk interrupted by static. A new, and unusual for the place, aural element. Gathering an assortment of hidden items from the front room, I made a nest at the far end. Leaving the nest to get some distance to look at it, I entered the assembled attendants and wordlessly sought their opinion and approval for my work. I remained "the performer," and yet our relationship shifted to the extent that attendants offered supportive or critical responses to my handiwork. Many smiles. A few pats on the back. Some embarrassed withdrawals from my inquisitive gaze. By prompting the habitual appraising regard of the gallery-goer, I was attempting to draw the attendants to me emotionally— "See, I'm aware you're here and I'm vulnerable to your assessment"—while also establishing a distance between us—"I'm the artist/art, you are here for me." Whether or not my proximity and displayed interest in the reactions of the attendants suggested accountability for their opinions, a proposal had been made to accept or reject: here is a fiction in which attendant and performance can communicate.

I left the attendants and returned to the nest for further arranging and the declamation of some text. Inevitably, I caught sight in the atrium of ascending elevator riders gathering to stare at me—at us—through the gallery's glass front. When this happened I would stare back, drawing the attention of the attendants to the elevator occupants. Each time, the elevator voyeurs had forgotten their own visibility and physically withdrew in alarm when confronted with our attention. As the direction of attention shifted unexpectedly, so did our relationship to the gallery and to each other. At the very least, the elevators—and their riders—briefly joined the performance, and those of us in the gallery shared a knowing chuckle at the bewildered inclusion of the riders.

I left the nest again and moved through the attendants, taking one gently by the arm and speaking directly to this person as I guided her or him into the next gallery. The others followed without explicit prompt from me, used as they likely were to the performance being where the performer was. A "bird" moving among dead and stuffed as well as painted birds, I offered reflections on the nature of flight, nesting, and loneliness. As I moved around the installation walls, I often abandoned visual and aural contact with the attendants, leaving them free to engage the other birds on display. A portion of the attendants always accepted the invitation to more closely examine the exhibition, turning away from me and the group to investigate one of the displays or paintings.

In the room of contemporary art behind and to the right of the information desk, I passed out cards listing a personal attribute I was proud of. Attendants at this moment regularly surprised me with their responses, such as the performance when the attendants, unprompted, began to read them out loud to me, or the performance where they each, again unprompted, began to perform pantomimes of the qualities on the card. My increasingly manic recitation of failures and hopes brought me back in front of the information desk, and then on top of it, and then leaping off of it, and then spinning, and then running into the glass door to the gallery, and then retreating to a corner. I sank low. Shivered. Attempted long breaths. Lowered my head. The attendants unfailingly recognized that my standing up from this final resting place signaled the end of the performance.

Anne Ubersfeld writes: "Theatrical space can seem like a field of forces whose origins and points of departure are the actors; the scenic space is drawn by them like iron shavings are drawn to a magnet" (71).[3] As I have described about the many moments in *Song*, a performer may "draw" this space by choosing a different relationship to a shared location. And as the leader of the flock, I was able to draw them behind and arrange them around

Figure 3.2 In the back gallery for *Song*
Source: photo by Illinois State Museum.

me. Throughout the performance I regularly and self-consciously sought to participate in altering spaces between the attendants and myself and between the gallery and us.[4] Indeed, *Song* can be described as ticking off each of the five different levels of theatrical interaction suggested by Wilfried Passow and R. Strauss: 1) between fictional characters and their world, 2) between the audience and the fictional characters and their world, 3) between performers, 4) between performers and audience, and 5) between audience members (240). These each address different kinds and objects of attention, different kinds of spaces, between and among attendants and performers. The shifts of space and attention in *Song* belong to a long history of preventing attendants from becoming comfortable with how they relate to performers, a history that includes religious processional performances, court masques, Dadaist soirées, and the happenings of the 1950s and 1960s.[5]

But the spaces of performance can appear to radiate from attendants as much as from performers. In its straightforward propositions for performer/attendant relationships, *Song* demonstrates almost to a formulaic fault how attendants are never outside spaces of performance for the simple reason that the act of attending gives sense and meaning to performance. As Gay McAuley has described in detail, before performers even begin, the process of arriving at and entering the performance venue contributes to the attendants' role in forming the spaces of performance (42–4). Even further, acts of attention can transform virtually any phenomenon into a "theatrical space." Josette Féral writes of how "the simple exercise of watching [...] reassigns gestures to theatrical space" ("Theatricality" 97). More than the actions of the performers, it is attending to the action of others in a particular way that constitutes the manifestation of a space for theatrical performance or, in Féral's word, "theatricality." Féral, touching base with the grandfathers of spatiality in the social sciences—"transitional space discussed by Winnicott, the threshold (*limen*) discussed by Turner, or Goffman's 'framing'"—expands the reach of "theatrical space" well beyond the theatre ("Theatricality" 98).[6] Attendants and performers alike share the work of making the performance area(s) playful; action supposedly tucked into "theatrical space" interacts with attendants and their real laughter, tears, or silence. Attendants and performers share space and place during performance, and the nature of that sharing matters a great deal in organizing meaning and experience—whether attendants feel like external observers or engaged interpreters or mobile participants.

Over the past 25 years theatre scholarship has occupied itself with questions of space and can even be said to have taken a "spatial" or a "placial" turn. As far back as 1981 Ubersfeld wrote, "Theatre is space" (49).[7] Both the increasingly sanctioned popularity of site-specific theatre and the arrival of English translations of French texts on space and place have buoyed theatre scholars and practitioners engaging these concepts in the past decades.[8] A good amount of the scholarly work done has relied heavily on Marxist critic Henri Lefebvre's foundational text, *The Production of Space* (1974). One consequence of his prominence has been that much of the sharpest writing on space has assumed Lefebvre's emphasis on the constraints of material production in the formulation of value and meaning.[9] Cultural geographers Doreen Massey, Edward W. Soja, and David Harvey have also provided important guidance to the cultural materialist approach to place and space.

Without critiquing this approach, John Agnew notes that, when writing of place and space, the *scale* of analysis determines to a large extent how and about what scholars write; this is particularly important to recall when writing about performance as acts undertaken by bodies (81). The cultural materialist scale of analysis has little use for performers—they, like the attendants, are caught in the web of larger forces, perpetually recuperated by the logic of capitalism (or, rather, capitalism understood with Marxist logic); whatever attention can be spared for individual experience assumes it to be the product of social, material culture.[10] The conditions of production are important elements of performance analysis, performance reconstruction, and historical narrative. And as Ric Knowles and David Wiles, among others, convincingly argue, obscuring these conditions in practice or scholarship tends to reinforce existing arrangements of power. And yet, as valuable as Lefebvre-inspired analyses are, they do not address the performer's or attendant's role in making space. In other words, they have little to say to phenomenology.[11]

Three writers in the phenomenological tradition have filled this gap and exercised great influence on theatre scholarship analyzing space: Yi-fu Tuan, Gaston Bachelard, and Edward S. Casey.[12] In particular, this triad offers honey-hued phenomenological approaches to place. For example, Bachelard directed his study explicitly at "images [...] of felicitous space" (17). For his part, Tuan claimed that place was "security" and space "freedom," composing a dialectic along which human beings travel as they seek different sensations and goals (3). In his romanticization of place, Tuan figures it not only as essential to being but also as an unconditionally positive phenomenon; place accrues values, and he insists that these values are never unwanted (154). His emphasis on the desirability of place yokes it to the beneficial security of enclosure, ignoring the fact that enclosures keep out those who want to come in as well as imprison those that would leave.

This approach to place—as essentially welcoming—pervades the resurgence of site-specific performance in the late twentieth and early twenty-first centuries. Site-specific performance rests on the very premise that place is the place to be. The performances discussed by field-leading scholars Nick Kaye, Joanne Tompkins, Mike Pearson, and Michael Shanks use place as a means of providing sensations of belonging—to the place and to the work of excavating its historical and contemporary meanings. Pulled against or submitted to, places in site-specific performance are uniformly addressed as opportunities and almost never as locations to be escaped. Although site-specific performance concerns a very wide variety of practices, almost all of them exist within the theoretical and performance confines of the need to keep attendants in place. These places are there for the attendants—if not as dwellings, then as interpretive sites.

Michel de Certeau, whose *The Practice of Everyday Life* (1980) is another touchstone for theatre and performance scholarship, takes a more skeptical approach to place. He has proposed helpful specificity for performance analyses of place *and* space—two terms often used indiscriminately. He describes place as the "instantaneous configuration of positions" and space as "*practiced* place" (de Certeau 117). To emphasize the relationship of place to power, de Certeau separates it from movement and casts place, in Nick Kaye's words, as an "ordering system, while spatial practices [...] operate as ordering activities" (*Site-Specific Art* 5).[13] Places arrange the material and the social; space not only enacts them, but it has the potential to subvert them by taking unforeseen paths. De Certeau, along with Agnew and Ubersfeld, argues that distinguishing between place and space proves useful in understanding *where* I am and *how* I am.

McAuley noted the "terminological minefield" awaiting scholars writing about space and place (17), and any definitions offered here, no matter how provisional, can and should meet with interrogation. There are a good many histories of the terms, and this book is not one of them.[14] Neither, for that matter, is it an account of the different semiotic varieties of theatrical space.[15]

It *is* an examination of the nature of our involvement with other people, and as such is very deeply concerned with the medium of that involvement. Just what are these spaces? How does attention alter them? What can it mean to cross them or to try to? *Should* I (try to) cross the space between myself and other people? How?

Coming to grips with varieties of space does more than define the medium through which I reach and by which I am separated from others. Describing those spaces proposes a model of what it means to move and be moved by another or to fail to. The juxtaposition of these possibilities and these failures can in turn clarify how I *should* be with others by suggesting the lures and barriers between us. De Certeau's association of movement with space echoes a phenomenological tradition continued here that describes the bond between movement, bodies, and space as the keystone of perception. In this case, continuing that tradition means departing from other studies of theatrical space by pursuing the possible formation of ethics within the structures of performance spaces.

To begin this pursuit I take up the question of space between attendants and performers. I start with a seminal description of experiencing the singularity of something or someone else at a distance. Cultural critic Walter Benjamin published his polemic "The Work of Art in the Age of Its Mechanical Reproducibility" in 1936. In it he posits and analyzes the political implications accompanying changes in perception wrought by the reproducibility of images. In formulating these consequences, Benjamin provides an analysis of how distance modulates experiences of art and other people. Written at a time when the dissemination of images was undergoing radical change, "The Work of Art" resonates just as powerfully in an early twenty-first-century world making a transition from the analog to the digital. In this age, however, artists and attendants seek authenticity not in distance but in proximity.

As I argue, coinciding with others can only be dreamed, and it is a dream that radically diminishes the experience of encountering another. *Sleep No More* (2003/2011), a performance that foregrounds attendant involvement even more than *Song*, provides the grounds from which to consider the ethical consequences of attempts to completely close the distance between others and myself. This "immersive" performance integrates attendants in ways that affirm and challenge assumptions about closeness and authenticity, performance and intimacy, and the experience of ethically compromised attention. I address the techniques of distance from three perspectives: Jacques Rancière's anarchist critique of participatory art, Renaud Barbaras's phenomenology of perception, and Merleau-Ponty's phenomenology of space. Each of these assessments places movement and space at the center of analysis. The first links physical and political encroachment, the second describes the fording of all distances as the work of desire, and the third describes space as the experience of possibility derived from "the flesh" of the world. I argue that proximity, desire, and possibility meet in the foundational perceptual experience of astonishment.

Presence at a distance

In "The Work of Art," Benjamin addressed the dawning political implications of mass audiences for art in early twentieth-century Europe. Benjamin's critique developed a concept that has since taken a central place in the discourse on stage presence: aura.[16] Although most strongly associated with "The Work of Art," aura was first addressed by Benjamin in another essay on reproducible images, "Little History of Photography" (1931). In both essays Benjamin wrote of the "denigration of the experience of aura" through the proliferation of machine-driven reproduction. This in turn signaled how the reign of the cult value of objects would end through the formation of mass audiences for art (Hertz 101).

Benjamin defines aura as "a strange tissue of space and time: the unique apparition of a distance, no matter how close it may be" ("The Work of Art" [1935] 23).[17] The aura is first of all *unique*—it pertains to one object only and separates that object from all others. Hence the association of aura with stage presence in its classic sense—both refer to something special about an actor, namely the appearance of his or her uniqueness. That appearance, however, cannot be separated from the material existence of the actor or object and then exist wholly apart from it. Once an object can be reproduced and those reproductions distributed, the object's aura deteriorates insofar as the image proliferates. Benjamin specifically addresses the case of that stage and film acting and claims that "aura is bound to his [the actor's] presence in the here and now. There is no facsimile of the aura" ("The Work of Art" [1935] 31). Whatever appeal might be found in actors' images onscreen will contribute to the weakening of the actors' auras; as soon as the camera replaces the audience for the actor's performance, "the aura surrounding the actors is dispelled" (Benjamin, "The Work of Art" [1935] 31).

For Benjamin, aura was an effect of singularity and authenticity—any reproduction of the object or its image distorted the object by suggesting its existence in more than one place at a time:

> In even the most perfect reproduction, *one* thing is lacking: the here and now of the work of art—its unique existence in a particular place [...] The here and now of the original underlies the concept of its authenticity [...] The authenticity of a thing is the quintessence of all that is transmissible in it from its origin on, ranging from its physical duration to the historical testimony relating to it [...] what is really jeopardized when the historical testimony is affected is the authority of the object.
> ("The Work of Art" [1935] 22)

With terms like "origin," "authenticity," and "unique existence," Benjamin forcefully links the uniqueness of an object's material existence to its *authority*. This provides yet another association between aura and the classic sense of stage presence—so long as stage presence refers to a kind of command over attendants it will involve authority, the most potent kind of which derives from an actor's singularity. Cormac Power explicitly identifies aura with the classic sense of stage presence in his chapter on "The Auratic Mode of Presence" (47–85).

Mechanical reproducibility precisely threatens an actor's or an object's authority because it threatens the concept of the singular. A reproduction has intrinsically less authority than the "original" because it is neither unique nor first in sequence. In fact, the reproduction loses so much authority that it no longer makes sense to speak of its authenticity; in analog photography every one of the prints made from a film negative could be considered "authentic" (Benjamin, "The Work of Art" [1935] 25). An original appears in only one tense, but reproductions can happen over time.[18] The digital age compounds this effect: not only are there prints made from data, but there are digital manifestations of the same data on screens all across the world.[19]

As Benjamin himself understood very clearly, imagining an enveloping present (or "present-ness") denies the historical specificity that plays no small part in determining how and what one perceives. Utter absorption into the present removes the cultural, political, and economic formation of the perceiver and the perceived and serves, at the limit, as a means of suppressing the labor of those that made possible the place, subjects, and objects involved in perception. It also denies me the exquisite lingering sensations of performances: sore legs from cramped seats, arms suddenly moving upward in recollection of a dancer's gesture, a light-headed stumble at the memory of a thrilling exchange, a sob stifled in the throat recollecting how the dancers plummeted, the sounds that arrive when I recognize the smell of *that* theatre. These may not be performance itself, yet neither are they its remains: they have not been left behind by a performance but are its continuation.[20] It is as hopeless to draw a curtain between moments of performance and the altered bodies that continue on afterward as it is to stop a story from being retold; bodies will always tell where they have been.

By changing my relationship to "original" objects, mechanical reproducibility reveals both the historically contingent character of aura and the ritual use of locating the authority of objects in their singularity. Objects and images no longer have the authority they once had and that was accorded to their (supposedly) unique appearance, whether "natural," "historic," or "aesthetic." The decay of aura signals that, "for the first time in world history, mechanical reproducibility emancipates the work of art from its parasitic subservience to ritual" (Benjamin, "The Work of Art" [1935] 24). Although his discomfort with the relationship between art and ritual is clear, he is no more sanguine about how art was changing in his day and what this meant about authenticity. As Gerhard Richter argues, Benjamin's essay does not document the decay of aura *per se*, but rather argues the consequences entailed by eroding the faith in the "original" that aura was previously thought to convey (240–1). On the one hand there is freedom from an oppressive mysticism; on the other hand there is the experience of media ultimately wielded as a tool to mobilize masses for war (Benjamin, "The Work of Art" [1935] 41).

However, to stay focused on the concept of uniqueness, even as an historical concept, misses the phenomenon that Benjamin associates most strongly with aura: *distance*. The object must exist in a "particular place," and its authenticity is "the quintessence of all that is *transmissible* in it *from* its origin." Although related to the singularity of time as well as place, aura is that which travels from an object to the perceiver; the object has its "here and now," but this cannot be the same here and now as that of the person experiencing the object's aura.

For his first example of aura in "The Work of Art," Benjamin describes an idyllic (middle-class) scene of repose on a warm day, casually observing one's surroundings: "To follow with the eye—while resting on a summer afternoon—a mountain range on the horizon or a branch that casts its shadow on the beholder is to breathe the aura of those mountains, of that branch" ("The Work of Art" [1935] 23). Benjamin describes a cooperation between senses and a productive tension between the near and the far. By connecting breath to sight—to see these things at a distance is to "breathe" their aura—Benjamin assumes the position that vision allows objects to invest bodies. To see is to touch, or, more precisely, to see is to be touched. *But only from a distance.* After all, he writes of the *branch's* aura, not the aura of its shadow that lies on the beholder. The shadow is a medium of the aura's source, not the aura itself. And a shadow requires three things: light, an object, and distance between that object and another surface.

The perception of an effect signals the experience of distance—the thing itself exists at a remove, as far away as the horizon or as nearby as an overhanging branch, but not precisely where the perceiver is. Benjamin describes here not only a distance, but the *movement* that attempts to close it. The eye follows what it sees but does not coincide with it. In the originally published version of his essay he included a footnote that renders the importance of this distance in stark terms:

> The definition of the aura as a "unique phenomenon of distance however close it may be," represents nothing but the formulation of the cult value of the work of art in categories of space and time perception. Distance is the opposite of closeness. The essentially distant object is the unapproachable one. Unapproachability is indeed a major quality of the cult image.
>
> (Benjamin, "The Work of Art" [1936] 243 fn.5)

Cult images *belong* at a distance and they are *meant* to be unapproach-able. Whether mourned or welcomed, the collapse of the distance between object and perceiver characterizes the age of mechanical reproducibility for Benjamin. He recognizes technology as both an engine of this col-lapse and its means. It enables what he identifies as the "emergence of the masses" through the ability to disseminate identical images far from their source. Technological reproduction can "place the copy of the origi-nal in situations the original cannot attain" and allows it to "reach the recipient in his or her own situation" (Benjamin, "The Work of Art" [1935] 21–2). Equalizing access transforms both the perceivers and the work perceived, bringing the former into a collective identity previously impossible while also destroying the cult power of the latter. But the technology also responds to the masses, and Benjamin identifies the dete-rioration of aura as a result of *"the desire of the present-day masses to 'get closer' to things, and their equally passionate concern for overcoming each thing's uniqueness by assimilating it as a reproduction"* ("The Work of Art" [1935] 23).[21] The passion for approachability is a function of and a response to technological reproducibility; the reproducible object offers art to everyone by allowing everyone to approach the artwork. This kind of proximity reduced difference in a radical fashion:

> the stripping of the veil from the object, the destruction of the aura, is the signature of a perception whose "sense for all that is the same in the world" has so increased that, by means of reproduction, it extracts sameness even from what is unique.
> (Benjamin, "The Work of Art" [1935] 23–4)[22]

Benjamin observed the mania for closeness as an assault on the authenticity of objects (and people) in an era when political regimes sought to consoli-date "the masses" in shared missions of revolution, reaction, and conquest. Today bears witness yet again to a heightened interest in closeness, in collapsing the distance between attendants and works of art. This time, however, in the environment of a digitized neo-liberalism, moving closer to a work of art is meant to have the opposite effect it had for Benjamin: instead of destroying authenticity, the approach is meant to secure it. This inversion of Benjamin's formulation surely points to another technological transformation, namely the hegemony of the digital in industrialized econo-mies. The ability to pursue hyperparticular interests online brings with it a change in perception. It also posits once again the importance of *distance* for understanding the role of art (and technology) in composing relationships with others. Reproducibility and access have formed a class of attendant seeking affect in closeness. They now look for authenticity and singularity in proximity where previously, according to Benjamin, proximity denigrated singularity, singularity that could only be achieved at a distance. Before, an object's existence separate from myself established its status as exceptional; today the exceptional requires me next to, if not in, it.

His smell on my neck

Twice I am led into a phone booth where a stranger enters and presses into me. Twice I have lips against my ear, breath on my cheek. Twice I feel lucky, I feel guilty, I feel fake. I've been chosen to have one of the signature private encounters in *Sleep No More*. Not everyone gets to be this close to the actor dancers. As a performer myself the proximity does not throw me the way it seems intended to. I am not disturbed being this close to a performer I don't know. I am comfortable accepting the charge of being touched carefully in a small compartment. I can accept this proximity without hesitation, but it is hard for me to accept it without skepticism. The actors with me are so sincere, so committed. The first, a woman, has joined me "unexpectedly" after I was brought to the phone booth and told to answer a call. My companion and I had been eating at The Heath, the pre-performance restaurant linked to 100,000 square feet of Chelsea warehouse space transformed into the playground of *Sleep No More*. The restaurant and servers are decked out in mid-twentieth-century costumes, explicitly meant to link the setting to the one next door, where *Macbeth* has been transposed to an idea of the films of Alfred Hitchcock. As soon as our server speaks we realize that this is not a pre-performance meal at all, but a warm-up for the main event, an *amuse-bouche* of performance. The servers adopt an air of withholding superiority calculated to inspire mystery. They also bring food and drink to us. Instead of Sartre's waiter, it's the customer here acting in bad faith. I find myself trying to accede to the pressure to play along as someone other than myself in an obvious fiction. At least it feels like bad faith to the extent that I botch my role in whatever scene I am meant to be a part of; the server knows I'm not in the fiction he's offering, but he doesn't stop offering it and we play along with both the pretense and my exclusion from it. I'm embarrassed, eager for the masks that await us next door. Until then, my companion and I find ourselves in a kind of backstage during our server's absence. When I am approached and told there is a phone call for me, I have a split second when I wonder why I haven't been rung on my mobile phone. Ooh. Good. I hold on to that feeling of engagement as I follow the maître d' out of the main room and into a phone booth. He closes the curtain behind me. Now my heart rate increases—I know someone is coming. I hold the thick receiver to my ear and I scan the booth, recognizing that the wall opposite the curtained entrance is not attached to the rest of the booth. A false wall. A door. I'm not supposed to know that it will slide open. I'm not supposed to know that someone will surprise me by—ah, she enters through the curtain. The performer takes the phone and hangs it up. She starts telling me a story and I am working so hard to listen in character. I want to play along, I want to "get the most" out of this chance to be alone with the performer, but I'm not sure what "the most" means here. I don't want to miss out on "the experience," whatever it's supposed to be—and I'm beginning to feel like it most definitely is meant to be *something*. But the rules are not clear—I'm being talked to again as if I am a character in a play, but really the only thing being asked is total credulity. I try to give myself over to the conceit; it's generic noir, so I try imagining high stakes and hidden motives. But the set-up is both too clearly designed and non-specific. Or, if there are specific allusions being made, I'm missing them. It's not occurred to me to look for anything to do with *Macbeth*—which *Sleep No More* reimagines—and I try to find something particular in the allusive, alluring woman in red lipstick and lacquered hair. I'm trying and failing to get it. The mechanics and citations definitely ring bells—the mysterious guest, the seductive guide, the commanding stranger. I'm supposed to feel special, singled out—"one to one!"—but I feel excluded and ridiculous. She asks if I would prefer to take a risk or to remain in safety. I agree to the latter and she says, "A wise choice." I can't tell if she says this regardless of the answer or if it's a specific soothing of what now feels like cowardice. I quietly promise to put myself at risk for the rest of the night, to do the uncomfortable thing. She slides that back wall open, we pass through it, and she returns me to the restaurant where other diners take note. The summons and encounter have worked well: they have aroused a curiosity founded on a fear of exclusion. They have also established proximity as the lingua franca of the production. At five points between the restaurant and the entry to the main playing areas attendants are squeezed together in groups: in two elevators, in a stairwell, a cabaret, and an antechamber. We are regularly being pushed into other people, put into touch. In this last room we are given our masks. Plastic but sturdy, they cover our whole faces with the bottom half sloping out like a beak. With the masks' raised cheekbones and prominent supraorbital ridges, the crowd looks alternately like medieval plague doctors and birds of prey. It's an impressive effect, all the more so when I realize the beaks give not only a look, but also plenty of breathing room under the mask. I begin to feel anonymous. Not to others—they can recognize my clothes easily enough. But to myself. I can be someone else, and that instills me with what feels like an appropriate apprehension. Who will I be in there? The mask is a license, and I can see some of the other attendants adjusting themselves to their own responses to it. There are several groups who have come together. It's a bit rowdy, a bit liquored up, a bit like tailgating. I recall that the other performance venue on this block is the "gentlemen's club" Scores. I wonder what the crowd felt like when Punchdrunk first staged *Sleep No More* in London in 2003 or in Boston in 2009. The mask has certainly caused an internal commotion for me, and my experience of the production so far has consisted mostly of an awareness that my responses aren't the ones I'm meant to have. We're crammed into an elevator and the operator's laissez-faire imperiousness generates some titters and some tense hand-holding. The door opens. An attendant moves out, but before anyone else can follow, the operator's arm obstructs the way. Some attendants visibly recoil in shock as the elevator door shuts suddenly, holding tightly to each other despite the directive to head out on our own. Eventually we are all discharged and I find myself wandering in a maze of branches. I can't find any performers. I can't find a clear way out. It's frustrating. I want to exit, to find something happening. I've barely started, and already impatience. I slow down and listen. I find my way out and into a hallway at the door of a padded cell. There is no way I am going in there alone. I go in, shoulders tensed, knees soft, ready for flight. The fear of being locked in overcomes me and I spin and exit, slowing down as I see another attendant, for some reason determined to hide my small panic. Each movement in this environment tells, not a story, but *my* story. I feel as strongly as ever before that my own emotions and responses are the theme of a production, but so far these emotions relate almost entirely to the structure of the event and not to its content. I realize that not once have I thought about *Macbeth*. Anyone can see me responding to the performance and allow this to be the scene they attend for a moment. Down the hall I see a crowd through a doorway and I follow them as they move into a room of bathtubs. People are pushing me aside, a feeling I come to expect whenever an actor is about to be or has just disrobed. The masked packs of attendants move with the most alacrity and insensibility to others when chasing down an actor dancer who has revealed or seems bound to reveal more flesh. I am finding desire everywhere. I find it in the hurtling crowds hoping for an exposed breast. I find it in the packed second cabaret area, site of a witches' meeting with Macbeth that takes the form of parties I attended in the 1990s—strobe lights, nakedness, horse masks, fake blood, loud music, and a crowd jostling for a better view. I find it in the banquet scene, one of a few recognizable from the source material, where, no doubt, there is less necking. I find it in virtually every duet to be seen in the performance. No matter who the characters are, no matter what the circumstance, if there are two people moving together, the theme is desire, of the heavy-breathing, noses-touching, searching-eyed sort that threatens to spiral into violence. And sometimes does. Burst of movement, glare and pause, burst of movement, rejection/murder and exit. I find it in the second phone booth in which the breath of a performer warms my neck. He has chosen me, taken my hand and pulled me with him in front of other assembled attendants. I don't know what character he is—is he some kind of servant? Now I *do* feel special. I am not simply singled out, I am singled out in front of, for the benefit of, others. He draws the curtain behind us. He talks to me. He touches me. He's going through something, he's playing at going through something. I am eager to please him, to be the attendant he wants me to be. Desire should fill the small compartment and, okay, it can if I want it to, but I waver. Because he's not talking to me. He's not touching me. He's touching a character, and he will repeat these gestures the same way in the next loop of the performance. I am rendered entirely insignificant at a moment I am meant to feel most special. This confusion of status leaves more of an impression even than his dampened costume against my chest. He chokes out "thank you" and leaves. I wait a moment. I want to follow him but I also want to give the attendants waiting outside the phone booth something to wonder about. As the actor dancer has just made so clear, I am not only my own story, I can be someone else's. My nostrils flare at the taste of narcissism. The entire performance is not simply built around each attendant's experience—it is *about* these experiences. All of those desk drawers with notes to pore over, those cabinets to rifle through, those notebook pages to turn—Punchdrunk has left them for *me*, for all of the "me"s in this building, for each of us to feel alone with. If I'm expert enough I might enlarge my understanding of *Macbeth*, but I'm not expert enough, and I find little in these scattered typewritten pages other than my own patience to read them. I do not find any reason to put *Macbeth* next to Hitchcock. I do not find a logic behind the pervasive coupling. But I do find looped opportunities to feel a part of something, to feel apart from something, to feel like what I'm going through is the whole point. The performance is as small as I am and as large. Inside the phone booth wondering about the attendants outside it, I'm asking if I can extend their feeling excluded. Exclusion and selection seem to be the dominant sensations cultivated by the performance. Either I'm close to a performer or I'm not. Either I'm seeing/feeling/touching something no one else is or not. Banquo's two virtuosic solos, the murder scenes staged for voyeuristic effect, the quiet labor of the abandoned bartender, these all register but they are not the main attraction. The main attraction is the possibility of being chosen. I am given many choices—to follow, explore, linger, race, join, separate—but no freedom. The binary system of *Sleep No More* demands that I desire the performers and the closest contact I can have with them. The entire apparatus of the production, its endlessly detailed rooms, its astonishingly choreographed support staff, its indirect direction of attendant movement, has to do with enforcing an aesthetic where attendants can experience a simulacrum of license while everything is controlled to the smallest detail. Balking at that control, even in thought, ejects me from the world of the performance, no matter how closely a performer's smell clings to my neck. I am not being asked to play along after all, but to do as I'm told.

Being together

It can certainly feel as if contemporary performance cannot get close enough. It doesn't want you seated, it doesn't want you out there. It wants you up in its face, up in the action, it wants you moving and sweating. It wants to single you out in a one-to-one relationship and it trades explicitly in desire.

Come on baby, I'm here. I'm here right now in this time, in this space just for you. It's just you and me. Come on, come in, come over here. I have something to tell you. Something I want to show you; only you. What is it? Are you scared? Don't be scared. Just come over here [...] Come on. You know you want to. Yes you do. Why else did you come?

(Paris 179)

Proximity now promises contact with or the generation of something privileged, something authentic. Whether through admission into the (not so) private life of a family on "reality" television or through participation in performance events, getting in close is getting in good. Authenticity is no longer *transmitted*, carried across a distance; now authenticity is sought nose to nose with a stranger. Access depends on proximity. Across the range of responses to proximate performance, one belief holds sway: closeness and intimacy are indissolubly bound as access. Indeed, although proximity might suffice, the goal is now "immersion" in an experience, whether an experimental performance or a branded corporate event (often the same thing). The appetite for immersion has become so bankable that the producers of New York's best-known immersive event—*Sleep No More*—can adopt a kitschy misspelling for their company: Emursive.

In her survey of the genre, Josephine Machon offers a table qualifying the characteristics of "'Traditional Theatre' v. Immersive Theatre" (54–5). It quickly becomes clear that the differences are impossible to sustain with any great rigor—"You may have an extended or intriguing journey to get to the location," "You are physically surrounded by another world," "You are waiting for it to begin," and "You are you" all describe virtually *any* experience of attending performance. Nonetheless, the term "immersive theatre" certainly has a contemporary cachet and designates at the least the re-emergence of interest in participatory performance. Whether or not "immersive theatre" is chiefly a marketing term, its roots can be found in everything from religious festivals to street theatre, to the legacies of Richard Wagner and Atonin Artaud, to Happenings, and to performance art and installation art (Machon 28–37).[23]

The contemporary rage for participatory performance and immersive theatre addresses an impatience with staying apart and a desire to cross over, to draw near. For people living in "an increasingly screen-centric world, immersive theatre offers an alternate reality that is dreamlike and escapist but at the same time visceral and challenging" (Slade). The combination of the dream and the visceral signals for many the advent of an authentic experience kept at bay by both digital communication and the arrangements of traditional theatres. The performance that touches me the most *touches* me the most. If it leaves me apart from it, it leaves me cold. Janet Evans of Punchdrunk notes ruefully that "I went to see *Betrayal* by [Harold] Pinter, expensive seats at the front, and I just thought, they're over there and I'm over here" (qtd in Machon 221). How could someone over there possibly mean as much to me as someone over here? Connected virtually to people across the globe, attendants now want, according to pronouncements of artists catering to them and festivals dedicated to one-to-one performance, to feel their skin warmed by the skin of performers (Machon 25; Chatzichristodoulou and Zerihan 5). As if the person sitting in the next seat in the auditorium had no heat and no smell. As if people could sit in those second-row mezzanine seats they can't really afford without noticing who else settles around them. As if they didn't hear any other astonished sighs at the end of the performance. As if they cannot perceive anything about the attendants out there in the dark. As if laughter and still-ness don't change their rhythm. As if the size of the room didn't change the volume of their voices. As if they could stare through the elevator window at a performance in the gallery below without being seen themselves.

It must be, then, as Leslie Hill and Helen Paris write: "intimate perfor-mance is multi-sensory in a way that real life generally is and performing in a theatre generally isn't [...] [I]ntimate performances employ the hap-tic and the olfactory much more than conventional theatres" (*Performing Proximity* 17). To be sure, Hill and Paris have made several works that foreground the olfactory and haptic between performers and attendants. During a single scene in *On the Scent* (2003), attendants share a kitchen with Hill while she snorts a line of chili powder, smokes a cigarette, pan-fries a pork chop, sprays hairspray, and burns hair (Hill and Paris, *Performing Proximity* 29–33). In *Deserter* (2000), Hill and Paris funneled attendants through a literally overheated "confessional" (Paris 188).

It seems fair to say that, generally, these are not the kinds of experi-ences offered by performances in conventional theatres. Nonetheless, Hill and Paris's claim rests on the conviction that the use of the "proximate senses"—smell, taste, touch—keeps attendants closer to "real life."[24] This is yet another version of both the theatre-as-artifice vs. performance-as-real binary that has circulated for decades and the mimesis vs. life binary that has preoccupied thinkers since at least Plato. What happens on stage remains stranded, separate from the "real" lives of the attendants, however strong an effect the performance might have. Whether or not the events on stage appear "real," they are not the same real as that of the auditorium. Darko Suvin's semiotic approach to space characterizes this binary:

> the constitutive and central qualities of the dramaturgic space looked on are due to *the basic split between visual and tactile space* experi-enced by the audience. The well-known fact of this split has (as far as I know) scarcely been valorized as the decisive factor of theatre, from which all other aspects issue or depend.
>
> (324)[25]

Although Suvin was not familiar with the work of performance artists in the preceding decades who challenged this "basic split," the fact of those challenges and the claims made by Hill and Paris point to its continued currency. The split is honored, attacked, assumed, and theorized. And it remains central to the work of immersive performance, which, by its very designation as such, assumes a standard separation between attendants and performance to be overturned.

And yet, as phenomenology insists, attendants are never separate from their own lives or manner of living during performance. The proximate senses do not remain dormant or separate during conventional theatre. Not only can attendants smell each other, they can smell, for example, the bacon frying at the end of David Cromer's production of *Our Town* (2008); they can even smell performers.[26] Attendants never *leave* "real life" in the darkened theatre insofar as everything on stage appears through embodied perception, just like "real life." Whether I attend to the action on stage, the performer in my lap, or the person sitting behind me unwrapping a cough drop, even if I accept a split between tactile and visual space—a split phenomenology strongly suggests is functional rather than inherent—real life stays close at hand. This means that immersive performance, rather than bringing attendants into a life real like their own, are meant to put *performers* in the real lives of attendants. It's not just the attendant immersed in the performance, it's the performers and performance immersed *in my life*.

Taking the concept of immersion to a kind of logical conclusion, London-based Italian performance artist Franko B goes all in:

> I think to do One to One [performance], to me it's most like you are having sex with somebody, although sex doesn't happen, you have an intimacy [...] I want to try a different type of intimacy with someone I don't know. The nearest I could explain was to an encounter where possibly—although [it] never really happened—some kind of sex happens.
>
> (Qtd in Zerihan 11)

Helen Paris teases this same possibility above with her imagined come-on to the attendant—Come on baby, I'm here. Similarly and more explicitly, in the one-to-one *Kiss, Miss, Piss and Other Stories* (2009), Eirini Kartsaki invites her attendants to kiss her (Zerihan 41–3). It's a performance premise equally radical and banal: if closeness equals access, then the ultimate access would be sex.

This seems precisely to describe the very intentionally frustrated proposition of *Sleep No More*: get close, get sex. Or, at least, sexy:

> As Evan Cobb, who visited the show around 50 times, put it, "I liked who I was when I was there. It allowed me to do all these things I am terrified to do. With the actors I can become a more flirtatious, suave, debonair version of myself."
>
> (Slade)[27]

For many attendants, particularly "superfans" like Cobb who return regularly, the production offers something beyond the chance to like oneself more than outside it; it offers the chance to love. Tara Isabella Burton writes of how she and many others have "fallen in love" during the show, "unable to separate" actor from character or to resist the "emotional reality" in which the relationship between actor and performer rests on "acts of love" ("Immersive Theatre"; "What Fourth Wall?"). She has certainly fulfilled the aspiration of the unnamed artistic associate who tells Agnès Silvestre, "A good one-on-one should perhaps make you fall in love" (qtd in Silvestre). The approach to and of performers, the chance that they and their selected attendants are close—to each other, to something "real," because distance supposedly increases the chance for falsehood—can create a sense of license; the fourth wall breaks, inhibitions break, who knows what will follow.

Co-director and choreographer Maxine Doyle acknowledges that the production plays very purposefully with the thrill of breaking taboos.

> It kind of goes back to the ethos of trying to rediscover the child within [...] We all remember the things that we shouldn't touch but do and then the excitement when we have. I think this work is about that— inviting the sort of forbidden touch.
>
> (Qtd in Kennedy)

Doyle proposes an unnerving conflation of childhood curiosity with the very adult themes and experiences of *Sleep No More*. There is virtually nothing innocent about what takes place during the show, but the impulse to be naughty can certainly be found resting on a childlike assertion of independence. The masks no doubt play a role here. If I feel different from myself unmasked, if the mask affords a measure of disguise, then I have a different experience of possibility; that alone changes the spaces between others and myself. The mask can be a screen that hides me from myself, that hides me from others, a screen on which I can project another image of myself like Cobb did. It can also simply prompt uneasiness about one's own background in masked performance, as it did for Silvia Mercuriali, who describes an experience that resonates with my own: "I get so self-conscious and so scared of fucking it up for them that I cannot enjoy it" (qtd in Machon 192). And yet, while behind every mask roils who knows what desire or embarrassment or curiosity, from the other side the mask-wearers all look the same: they all look like attendants.

As it turns out, *Sleep No More* invites that forbidden touch but still forbids it. Silvestre describes a performance in which Lady Macbeth rises from her bath with arms outstretched. An attendant reads the gesture as an invitation for comfort and approaches, only to be met with a scream from the performer and a crew of black-clad stagehands who stop the intervention and escort the attendant from the premises (Silvestre). *Sleep No More* works through a confused invitation and denial—come here baby, but don't cross this line we did not tell you about. The denial speaks to a potentially productive distance kept by the production, while the invitation aligns with the presumptions of immersive theatre.

These presumptions, as Josephine Machon argues, include the claim that everyday lives pale in comparison to the lives lived in immersion. For her, immersion removes attendants from where they've come, situating the "real" in the performance event: "the audience is thrown (sometimes literally) into a totally new environment and context from the everyday world from which it has come [...] [T]his ludically subverts aesthetic and critical distance, placing the perceiver of the art *within* the art" (Machon 27, 34). In an almost complete reversal of Benjamin, Machon posits an experience of authenticity found within the work of art.[28] She figures the experience as simultaneously outside an "everyday world" and closer to an authentic experience that vanquishes "critical distance." Singularity here resides in "immediate and intimate interaction within the performance" or "*being in the moment*" (Machon 83).

Being apart

For Machon, as for many artists practicing immersive and one-to-one performance, distance presents a problem. It keeps me from what I know and love and what touches me most deeply. Machon approvingly cites Doreen Massey's observation that "we so often and so tightly associate care with proximity" (186, qtd in Machon 133) and prompts readers to seek more responsibility in proximate performances. If I care about what is close by, then the performances about which I care the most, and which will mean the most to me, will take place around me.

Coinciding with the performance grants more than an intense personal experience, however; it also produces a "democratic landscape" and "egalitarian artistic experiences" (Machon 85, 38). Machon turns to French political theorist Jacques Rancière to support her claim that participatory performance equalizes attendants through engagement. Machon compares her desire to get attendants on their feet with Rancière's "society where everybody should be active" (Rancière, "Aesthetic Separation, Aesthetic Community" 63). Attendants here embody the "emancipated spectator" who is not subject to the whims or lessons of the theatre and who instead evades the experts of practice and criticism by "blurring the boundary between those who act and those who look" (Rancière, "The Emancipated Spectator" 19, qtd in Machon 117). And so immersive theatre dismantles the boundary between the act-ers and the lookers: "Rancière's call for an emancipated spectator who becomes an active participant in the work of art is modeled in genuinely immersive theatre practice" (Machon 118).

But Machon gets Massey and Rancière almost entirely backwards. Massey *critiqued* the association of care with proximity, pointing out that it bred "enclosed and excluding spaces" (186). Massey sought, on the contrary, ways to extend care to those that were not familiar or nearby, to break a cycle of localism that she argues contributes to reactionary and xenophobic policies.[29] And far from endorsing immersive theatre, Rancière has offered such a full-throated rejection of its methods and aims that Gareth White notes of the oft-quoted *The Emancipated Spectator* (2008) that it "might already represent a cornerstone of a sceptical approach to experiments with actor–audience relationships" (21).

To be sure, Rancière's radical critique can seem to offer solace to practitioners and attendants seeking to level the playing field, to restore a perceived imbalance between audience member and performer: "spectators see, feel and understand something in as much as they compose their own poem, as, in their way, do actors or playwrights, directors, dancers or performers" ("The Emancipated Spectator" 13).[30] For Rancière, theatre showcases the enunciation of equality in the face of unequal allocations of political position and sensory possibility ("The Paradoxes of Political Art" 139). For example, he pins Plato's abiding hostility to theatre on its capacity to "disturb the clear partition of identities, activities, and spaces" (Rancière, *The Politics of Aesthetics* 8). More than the "immoral content of fables," theatre's tendency to align itself with democracy spurred Plato's exile of this art and all the arts from his ideal city. As Rancière claims, "Politics plays itself out in the theatrical paradigm as the relationship between the stage and the audience, as meaning produced by the actor's body, as games of proximity or distance" (*The Politics of Aesthetics* 12). If an artist seeks radical equality, then it makes sense to dethrone the performers "over there" and place them over here with "us," the attendants. It's our story, too. Such, at least, is the assumption of Hill and Paris and the artists Machon and Zerihan interview for their projects on immersive theatre and one-to-one performance. Proximity equals access, and access both disorders and remedies the distances of exclusion.

In his imaginative interpretation of *Sleep No More*, W.B. Worthen touches upon the queasy easiness of finding Rancière both cheering and deploring the tendency to collapse distance between attendant and performer. Worthen at the outset of his article nods to the familiar line about "individuals plotting their own paths in the forest of things, acts and signs that confront or surround them" (Rancière, "The Emancipated Spectator" 16, qtd in Worthen 82). This seems a particularly apt way of thinking about *Sleep No More*, in which attendants can actually plot their own paths through recreations of Burnham Wood. These spectators are emancipated from their seats as well as from authorial authority. If art invites its publics to make their own meanings and pay attention to their own responses, what could be better than rendering these actions in movement, than setting up actual mazes for attendants to wander and wonder in?

And yet Worthen, a Shakespeare scholar far more engaged with the semiotic richness of *Sleep No More* than I, also recognizes the limits this particular production places on attendants. Having considered the one to ones—of which there are several—in which performers remove the attendants' masks, he first notes that "the scenes of private, unmasked intimacy, however, momentarily suspend our spectatorial distance, anonymity, and apparent lack of responsibility in the event" (Worthen 95). Face to face with a performer, almost always in a small room or compartment (or telephone booth), attendants as Worthen describes them recognize their responsibility for the event as a result of proximity and particularity. As Massey noted with discomfort, often care does not extend beyond the close by. But Worthen concludes shortly after that, "despite its *eventness*, *Sleep No More* immerses its audience in a paradoxical practice: we write our individualized plotlines in our own movements, but are constructed within the spectacle as realist voyeurs, watchers, and *readers*, not agents" (96).[31] Worthen posits that interpretive freedom remains in one realm—a realm of watching, reading, distance—while agency and responsibility lie elsewhere.

Worthen was hunting other game than the political or ethical implications of the production and so does not further elaborate a key element of both Rancière's critique and the assumptions of intimate performance—the experience of "ethical immediacy." In "The Paradoxes of Political Art," Rancière identifies two major varieties of the *"pedagogical* model of the efficacy of art" (136). The first is an "ethics of representation" in which the depiction of a societal problem or injustice is meant to provoke either an aversion to it or a commitment to changing it. In this model, attendants see Tartuffe and, supposedly, learn the ways of hypocrites, "leading, in turn, to the feeling of a certain proximity or distance, and ultimately to the spectator's intervening into the situation staged by the author (Rancière, "The Paradoxes of Political Art" 136). The second, "ethical immediacy," proposes instead that the power of art to effect social change results "first and foremost in partitions of space and time that it produces to define ways of being together or separate, being in front of or in the middle of" (Rancière, "The Paradoxes of Political Art" 136, 137). This paradigm, celebrated by noted theatre-phobes Plato and Jean-Jacques Rousseau, seeks "not to improve behavior through representation, but to have all living bodies directly embody the sense of the common" (Rancière, "The Paradoxes of Political Art" 137). Contemporary artists may no longer seek the expression of this community in the dancing at civic festivals as did Rousseau and Plato, but the dynamic remains the same insofar as "we continue to believe that art has to leave the art world in order to be effective in 'real life'; we continue to try to overturn the logic of the theatre by making the spectator active" (Rancière, "The Paradoxes of Political Art" 137). The model of ethical immediacy demands imagining the theatre as "the place where the passive audience of spectators must be transformed into its opposite: the active body of a community enacting its living principle" (Rancière, "The Emancipated Spectator" 5).

Immersive theatre can be found making a similar claim by placing attendants and performers so close to each other that the interactions between them approach or become like those "in real life." The immediate—temporal and spatial—is meant to deliver spectators directly into an experience that can transform their political position.[32] Representation offers a model of how to behave, and ethical immediacy offers an experience of it.

These positions are not mutually exclusive, as Emma Willis suggests in her analysis of Erik Ehn's *Soulographie* (2012), a presentation of 17 plays about genocide. Although Willis hopes that the plays evade the pitfalls of pedagogical theatre, they appear in her account to almost perfectly embody the two poles of Rancière's schema. In terms of the ethics of representation, Willis claims that the relentless week-long representation of genocide from multiple perspectives is designed to produce an "anti-genocidal ethic" (390). Indeed, she claims that "the political and ethical force of *Soulographie* [is] perhaps best understood as its mandate for social change" (Willis 393). It seems doubtful that there exists an audience for experimental theatre in New York that has yet to assume a position opposed to genocide. But Willis constructs an instantly recognizable formula: such an audience stands to benefit from engaging with representations of genocide on stage. This audience benefits not only from the production itself, whose language purposefully confuses empathy through "subjective drift," but also from finding itself as a community bonded by "a commitment to defying genocide" (Willis 403). And so the ethical immediacy of the productions stems from the work of spectators staging their comprehensions of and responses to the work in a series of talk-backs held throughout the week (Willis 393).

In both perspectives on the event Willis describes a single model in which "critical art" can be found "defining a straightforward relationship between political aims and artistic means: the aim is to create an awareness of political situations leading to political mobilization" (Rancière, "Aesthetic Separation, Aesthetic Community" 74). It should be noted, however, that Rancière explicitly derides such one-to-one correspondence between artistic intention and spectatorial response: "there is no reason either why understanding the state of the world should prompt a decision to change it" ("Aesthetic Separation, Aesthetic Community" 75).[33] Even further, he notes the fundamentally backward-looking nature of art around the corner of the "ethical turn" and doubts "the ethical couple of a community art dedicated to restoring the social bond and an art bearing witness to the irremediable catastrophe lying at the very origin of that bond" (Rancière, "The Ethical Turn" 200).[34]

Rancière critiques the efficacy of immediacy based on his conviction—shared by phenomenology and argued above—that there is no "real life" people depart when attending the theatre. In Rancière's words, "There is no 'real world' that functions as the outside of art [...] Instead there are definite configurations of what is given as our real, as the object of our perceptions and the field of our interventions" ("The Paradoxes of Political Art" 148). These configurations constitute ordering systems of perception, what Rancière called the "distribution of the sensible" (*The Politics of Aesthetics* 7–12). This serves primarily to put different classes of people in their proper place within a political ecology by determining "who can have a share in what is common to the community based on what they do and on the time and space in which this activity is performed" (*The Politics of Aesthetics* 8). Rancière understands the distribution of the sensible as a means of enforcing political arrangements, but he also explicitly describes how it is equally adept at placing spectators in one place and actors in another (even if only to stage their eventual union). "The mandate for social change" that follows from attending a week of performances about genocide imagines very specific places for producers of art and their attendants, but no less than an immersive performance that strictly orders performer and attendant roles.

The impulse both to animate attendants and to get them closer to real life assumes the distribution of the sensible as the natural order; it proceeds from the erroneous supposition of a separation between art and "real life" and between spectatorship and activity. But, Rancière asks, "is it not precisely the desire to abolish this distance that creates it?" ("The Emancipated Spectator" 12). It certainly does not hurt a theatre company to oversell the daily alienations that the show in question will alleviate for its potential audiences. And yet, far from attendants requiring art to emancipate them, they require their *own* enunciation. After all, attendants to theatre were never passive: "Being a spectator is not some passive condition that we should transform into activity. It is our normal situation. [...] Everywhere there are starting points" (Rancière, "The Emancipated Spectator" 17). Performances do not emancipate attendants. Performances are not even the ethical subject—the people attending them are.

For Rancière, it is *the spectators who emancipate themselves*. More than works of art, the work of interpretation models emancipation. Art may propose a reordering of sense, but "these sorts of ruptures can happen anywhere and at any time [...] they can never be calculated" (Rancière, "The Paradoxes of Political Art" 143). At any moment people might respond to what they perceive in a way that upsets the way in which they are supposed to perceive. Emancipated spectators enunciate themselves as a collective by displacing their supposedly proper place in relationship to art (Rancière, "Aesthetic Separation, Aesthetic Community" 57–8). Instead of serving as material for works of art forging or revealing or mandating a social bond, instead of acquiescing to the imposition of value offered by a performance, emancipated spectators initiate "a conflict between sense and sense [...] a conflict between a sensory presentation and a way of making sense of it"

(Rancière, "The Paradoxes of Political Art" 139). Disordering the configurations of what is given as real depends not so much on activist art as on activist spectators.

In two different essays Rancière demonstrates this redistribution of the sensible by turning to a ninenteenth-century revolutionary journal in which a joiner composed a fictional diary of his brother. Looking out the window of a home in which he has been hired to lay floorboards, he imagines himself sailing out over the landscape to enjoy it more than the neighboring homeowners. The worker occupies "the place of work and exploitation as the site of a free gaze" (Rancière, "Aesthetic Separation, Aesthetic Community" 71). Similar to Féral's passersby who manage to attend to events as if they were theatre, Rancière's worker institutes a different relationship to his surroundings that disorders the "proper" place of art. In another description of this publication, Rancière notes that this displacement precipitates an "overturning [of] the 'proper' relationship between what a body 'can' do and what it cannot" ("The Paradoxes of Political Art" 140). The laborer is not supposed to have the time or ability to appreciate a landscape. By re-placing the category of worker with that of the museum-goer, the laborer redistributes the sensible. Instead of art producing "a collective body," attendants manifest "a multiplication of connections and disconnections that reframe the relation between bodies" (Rancière, "Aesthetic Separation, Aesthetic Community" 72). Rancière here describes not a work of art, but *a work of attention.*

The varied performances of this work establish that the attention of the expert and the novice alike hold the capacity for disturbing the order of perception. It is a "capacity that makes everyone equal to everyone else. This capacity is exercised through irreducible distances; it is exercised by an unpredictable interplay of associations and dissociations" (Rancière, "The Emancipated Spectator" 17). In turn, the community of sense that arises is not draped in consensus. It appears instead as a "dissensual figure," an assembly engaged in perceiving objects designated for other perceptions and other perceivers. By creating a break in the "proper" use of perception—in Nicholas Ridout's example, cooks choosing ingredients at market are not meant to know of, much less compare themselves to, Michelangelo picking marble for his sculpture (Ridout, "Mis-Spectatorship" 180)—a dissensual community undertakes a shared labor that redistributes rather than affirms.[35] It is a "community structured by dissociation," capable of "being together" in labor while "being apart" both from each other's experience of the work and from the artist's intentions (Rancière, "Aesthetic Separation, Aesthetic Community" 58–9).

Through shifting modes of attention, attendants/emancipated spectators achieve an "aesthetic distance" between themselves and the intentions of artists (Rancière, "The Paradoxes of Political Art" 137). Rancière hinges his emancipatory politics on this distance, even while insisting that the distance between art and "real life" is constructed, a distribution of the sensible that deserves scrambling. While the action of attention achieves a "blurring of the boundary between those who act and those who look" (Rancière, "The Emancipated Spectator" 19), it does not result in the coincidence of art*work* and attendant; rather than bring them together, it establishes an emancipatory distance between them. As Peter Hallward describes this dynamic, "It is because the spectators never wholly identify with what they see, because they draw on their own experiences, because they retain a critical distance, that they are able actively and knowingly to engage with the spectacle" (145). In contrast, the community supposedly welded together by immersion in a performance or work of art leaves no room for critique, dissensus, or knowledge.

While distance for Rancière establishes the authority of emancipated spectators by keeping them unapproachable, distance for Benjamin establishes the authority of the artwork by keeping *it* unapproachable. For both, distance remains crucial even as it channels power in opposite directions. And in both cases something happens to those who attempt to cross these distances: they lose agency as political and ethical subjects. Approaching the work of art might dispel its cult value, but it also congeals people into the masses ready for political manipulation by a proliferation of images. Similarly, closing the gap between the spectator and the artwork produces stultifying consensus and adherence to a single experience and meaning of reality. For Rancière, the paradox of political art is that the action required to make a difference in the world of politics depends on the straight line from cause to effect that signals the compression of distance and the arrival of consensus.

In his drive both to identify the engine of enunciation for emancipation and to avoid an oppressive consensus, Rancière leaves unexamined what might prove to be key characteristics of the phenomenon of distance. He insists on different kinds of distance—between artist and attendant, between attendant and artwork, between what anyone knows and does not know—but he does not dwell on how they arise and what they signify in themselves. For Rancière, distance functions as "the normal condition of any communication [...] the path from what she already knows to what she does not know" ("The Emancipated Spectator" 10). Distance sets the scene for knowledge.

A phenomenological approach, however, suggests that distance might instead hold what can never be known. Even further, it suggests that distance does not herald the suppression of responsibility but its generation. A phenomenological approach fleshes out Rancière's political one by describing the process of separation as an experience of the lived *and* the possible, a path of knowledge and the basis of an unresolved strangeness. As such, it can alleviate the condition Rancière believes endemic to contemporary ethics, namely the conflation of "norm and fact" which amounts to little more than the elevation of the is/ought fallacy ("The Ethical Turn" 184). The phenomenological description of distance and depth provides a world as I experience it *and* a world as I might.

In the Introduction to his collection *Signs*, Merleau-Ponty writes of the tension that underwrites the ability to perceive others while allowing them their distance from what is known: "They are definitively absent from me and I from them. But that distance becomes a strange proximity as soon as one comes back home to the perceptible world" (15).

Distant possible orientation

The world of perception exists because of and through distance. Without it, I am coincident, immersed, blinded. I require distance. Within myself, between others and me. Without distance there can be no movement. And without movement there is only death. Without space between others and myself there would no longer be any *relationship* between us. As Renaud Barbaras puts it: "we should say that it is because the perceived thing is intrinsically distant [...] that it makes possible a relation with a perceiving subject" ("Perception and Movement" 82). Coinciding with another annuls the possibility of relationships because none can be made without distance. Barbaras notes that an essential quality of embodiment, the inability to comprehend being entirely, derives from this distance:

> it is not because we are embodied consciousnesses that the perceived world is distant; it is rather because perceived being implies an essential distance that our experience is partly obscure, that is, embodied [...] [T]o appear means to appear at a distance.
>
> ("Perception and Movement" 82, 83)

For Barbaras, distance does not enable clarity so much as it preserves an obscurity indissolubly bound to all appearances.

Each thing of the perceptible world holds this distance within it because everything of the perceptible world exists *both* as an experienced thing *and* as a representation of a total world that can never be perceived. Each thing is an object I can experience. Each thing is an object whose entirety I can never experience, not at once, not ever. Each thing is an object whose entirety escapes me because its appearance affirms the existence of a perceptible world whose totality—a totality that encompasses me—remains forever incomprehensible. Each thing is an instance of the world, is a part of and emblematic of it. Paradoxically, for the instance of the world to be perceived, the world to which it belongs enters into shadow. Distant, obscure, invisible: "the essence of appearance consists in the givenness of an infinite that separates and brings together each manifestation with what appears in it; it relies on *the givenness in person of the impossibility to be given exhaustively*" (Barbaras, *Desire and Distance* 77).[36] No matter how close I get, so long as I can perceive a thing it will present me with the inexhaustible totality of a world. Each manifestation in the world is a manifestation *of* the world, "something invisible that it presents in its invisibility" (Barbaras, *Desire and Distance* 78).

That seems like a tall order for, say, a prop on stage. It might seem less daunting to imagine another person involved in the presentation of the invisible in its invisibility. And yet the principle remains the same: anything perceived exists through a horizon that cannot be crossed. Beyond that horizon might exist the endless paths leading from the prop to the families of the workers who made it and beyond, or the endless paths leading from another person to her past and everyone who took part in it. Understood this way, the one-to-one encounters in *Sleep No More* might operate less as the fulfillment of intimacy denied others and more as the heightened frustration of access. Perhaps this is the lure the superfans cannot resist. Perhaps I am not meant at all to understand the character giving his telephone booth confession with skin next to mine. His motives, their role in a narrative or event, my role in each, our relation to each other and to the attendants left outside the curtain, perhaps these are not meant to bring me closer to him or them or *Macbeth*. Perhaps instead they illuminate the separation that persists not only within all intimacy but also within all perception. Perhaps.

Even so, the scent of lipstick and the damp warmth of a touch in a phone booth linger—remind me that the distance into which the perceived thing withdraws does not foreclose the possibility of approach or touch. These sensations affirm as well the fundamental movement of perception. To perceive is to encounter the perceived thing's manifestation of an untotalizable world. Barbaras argues that only by moving towards another, and so instituting distance, can I perceive the thing or the person through which that distance appears. Left alone, turned away from, others and objects lose their depth for me when I abridge my relationships to them. The institution of each thing's horizon arises from a movement towards, a movement that contains an excess of itself: "Insofar as there is perception only as the limitation of a totality it indicates, all perception calls forth essentially its surpassing and therefore gives rise to a movement" (Barbaras, *Desire and Distance* 124). For Barbaras, perception involves the constant renewal of movement because the distances of the perceived world never finish. Perception's excess belongs to movement, to its surpassing, to its constant departure: "it is because no perception can calm movement's constitutive tension that it gives rise to new perceptions" (Barbaras, *Desire and Distance* 96).

In Barbaras's terms, this means that movement does not concern *need* because needs can be met. A satisfied need suggests the destruction of distance between what I need and myself; it suggests the coincidence of the needing and the needed and the denial of distance. Barbaras thus concludes that *desire* must be the basis of perception. Desire is inflamed when its demands are met because "the object of desire can never be present *as such*" without then ceasing to be desired (Barbaras, *Desire and Distance* 112). The desired is precisely that towards which I move without ever coinciding. To perceive is to move because I am separate from the perceived, and to move is to desire because the excess of movement depends on never reaching its goal. Desire thus "attains something only through that which exceeds it and opens in a way upon the infinite" (Barbaras, *Desire and Distance* 123).[37] If perception were founded in need, Barbaras argues, it would find itself capable of stopping, which would distort the continually evolving movement of the subject. Needs end and enclose; desire continues, instituting and maintaining distance between itself and others. For Barbaras, it is not distance that calls forth desire, but desire which "unfolds the constitutive distance of the sensible." By aspiring to something it cannot ever possess, it brings me into contact with the world that can be experienced (Barbaras, *Desire and Distance* 125).

Placing desire at the heart of perception certainly speaks to the habitual association between closeness and intimacy assumed by much one-to-one and immersive performance. Sometimes this association can be staged with brutal coercion and manipulation. In La Fura dels Baus's *XXX* (2002) some attendants are bullied into physically exposing themselves; in Ontroerend Goed's *Internal* (2007) the actors use "pick up artist" techniques to manipulate attendants in one-on-one interviews to expose themselves psychologically, only to reshape and announce those secrets in the least flattering way in public later on. Sometimes desire can be folded into the gentle admiration for stars such as Patrick Stewart and Ian McKellen. Or it can be guiltily obscured by the critical celebration of young, fit women getting naked for experimental performance. Attendants in performances such as *Sleep No More* can stage it. It can be found in the long history and mythology of performers sexually available to esteemed attendants. Whether as attendants desiring contact with performers or performers representing desire between themselves, desire floats freely at the theatre. And yet its function there also points to the limitations of desire understood as the ground of perception and the root of subjective experience.

On the one hand, *any* state that regenerates through perpetually escaping its termination can function the same way desire does for Barbaras; in a way this very generalization establishes desire's central role in perception. What desire desires is not an object or person *per se*, but the ungraspable totality of the world opened by the object or person. It is into this horizon that desire continually plunges, and its failure to arrive at the end of it signals and prompts its everlasting movement. But the same could be said of curiosity or astonishment. Desire requires distance more than distance requires desire. In this sense Barbaras generalizes desire almost beyond recognition because it recognizes no determined object, only what escapes it, and this is the same for every object of desire. Even further, the movement of the desired away from the desiring becomes a kind of repulsion, like a positive magnet's compulsory reaction to the approach of another one. The desired doesn't evade—it is driven away.

On the other hand, desire addresses not simply a movement towards, but *possession*, the having of someone or something. A subject arising in attempted acts of acquisition cuts a compelling figure. But it does not describe a figure that emerges both as a movement towards and as an expression of the perceived thing. The *chiasm* of touchers and touched presents subjects who arise not simply through their *own* movement but through the movement of the perceived towards them. In an unusually sensual passage from *The Visible and the Invisible*, Merleau-Ponty writes of the multiple directions and dimensions of perception: "Movement, touch, vision, applying themselves to the other and to themselves, return towards their source and, in the patient and silent labor of desire, begin the paradox of expression" (144/187).

Desire, as Barbaras understands it, skips this multiplicity of movement and misses the passing of the perceived and perceiving during perception. His distance of desire is uni-directional and two-dimensional. Although he vividly describes the function of and endless regeneration of desire and distance, ultimately his is a flat description. Merleau-Ponty adds depth and dimension to desire and distance, rendering in their place the phenomenon of space. Space for Merleau-Ponty is not simply a span, a distance to be moved across even if never completed. Space is the experience of possibility.

Merleau-Ponty understood depth to announce "a certain indissoluble link between the things and me" (*Phenomenology* 267). And yet, unlike Barbaras, for Merleau-Ponty this depth did not extend from a subject to the perceived or trace the singular trajectory of desire. Instead, because depth is "not indicated upon the object itself, it quite clearly belongs to the perspective and not to things" (Merleau-Ponty, *Phenomenology* 267). By this he means that depth involves situations between perceived and perceiver rather than qualities proper to one or the other. Instead of a distance the subject travels through desire, depth establishes a relationship that extends in multiple dimensions.

To the uncrossable distance between perceiver and perceived, Merleau-Ponty adds depth. As Anthony Steinbock explains it, depth for Merleau-Ponty "makes something seen or heard to co-exist with other sights or sounds by allowing some to be concealed as background" (340). A world of distance keeps me from things because they are far away. A world of *depth* and *space* keeps things from me because they are far away *and* partially hidden. Or more precisely, partially unknowable. Co-existence here refers to a world in which the embodied relations between each thing maintain an invisible for and of each other thing. This invisible is *of* and makes possible the visible. Depth introduces the experience of horizons. Horizons are not simply openings to what I cannot perceive—they are essential barriers that make possible the invisibility of what lies beyond them. Unlike the repeatable separation of distance, the space between others and myself "ceaselessly changes" (Lecoq, "Le corps et son espace" 273), in part because the specific obstacles—material and imagined—that partially hide me from others are never the same. The result is a world enlarged from juxtaposition into co-existence—I am behind, above, next to, before, and after others.

Far more than a discursive complication of space is at stake. John Wylie writes of how, for Merleau-Ponty, depth suggests a world "composed by differences rather than by identities, as an ongoing *differentiation* rather than an *identification* produced through the categories of subject and object" (526). The term depth—*profondeur* in French—already suggests something beyond, the possibility of the unknown and the unknowable. Barbaras's subject as desire acquires, or seeks to. The subject as space *opens*. The two-dimensionality of distance gives way to antagonism, while the multi-dimensionality of space gives way to what Marjorie Grene calls an "ontological pluralism" that not only acknowledges but depends upon experiences foreign to any given subject (607). The subject becomes distinguishable in the way it opens to the world around it, not simply in the way it moves through it.[38] This kind of space supports a porous subject, "the subject defined as a *field*, as a hierarchized system of structures opened by an inaugural *there is*" (Merleau-Ponty, *The Visible and the Invisible* 239/88).[39]

This description of space proposes a fundamental change to the relationship between the perceived and the perceiver that Barbaras describes. The perceived does not await the always-deferred arrival of the desiring subject. Instead, perceivers always express a relationship with the perceived that arises from both of them *and* from the space between them. Perceivers constantly change so as to become "the body that is required for perceiving a given spectacle" (Merleau-Ponty, *Phenomenology* 262). The "given" does not pre-exist me; it is that which appears to me in my particular actions of perception. When attendants go to a performance they have the opportunity to make themselves available to a manner of appearing. They can reject it, of course, and in that case they will enlarge the inevitable difference between their perceptions and those of other attendants. It would surprise me not at all to learn that an attendant at *Song* retreated from the premise that I "was" a songbirdman or indeed anything other than an awkwardly made-up guy in ill-fitting khakis. And as I have described above, I regularly felt my failure to arrange myself for the spectacle *Sleep No More* offered. "Not getting it" may result from a failure of imagination, will, or timing, but the world given to me in these failures is no less real. At the very least, performance foregrounds the always available opportunity to recognize the arrangements of attention that reveal my actions to myself.

Attending performance also foregrounds how one person alone never does space. Space involves perceivers and perceived—it is the means of their involvement. As such, it cannot be said to be determined by one or another, even in the situation of a performance, where attendants arrive precisely to adopt the spaces of the performance. Merleau-Ponty describes how "between me and events there is a certain leeway (*Spielraum*) that preserves my freedom without the events ceasing to touch me" (*Phenomenology* 299).[40] I am bound to others, but they do not determine me; and between us we can find *play*. *Spielraum* translates literally as "play space," but is usually translated as "elbow room," "room for maneuver," or "leeway."[41] In all cases, freedom exists as a response to constraints, not as their absence.

Arranging myself in the act of perceiving the world, what Merleau-Ponty calls "the gearing of this subject into his world" (*Phenomenology* 262), requires the work of orienting myself in different situations. In order to perceive, I require a grounding orientation that arranges and reveals my relations with others. I am not simply "a thing in objective space," but "a system of possible actions, a virtual body [...] defined by its task and situation" (Merleau-Ponty, *Phenomenology* 260). The perceived world both calls forth and answers my possible actions. My sense of orientation, my ability to exist in relation to things and the world, does not derive from the facticity of my body but from situations—settings for action. Orientation is achieved not *from* my body, but through its shifting capacities for action in relationship to others. The spatiality of bodies concerns not simply depth, but the depth of possibility. Merleau-Ponty writes that "depth cannot be understood as the thought of an acosmic subject, but rather the possibility of an engaged subject" (*Phenomenology* 279).

The term virtual used above reiterates that space and time are intimately connected, that perceiving space always involves an engagement with time. The possible and the virtual concern relations with time, in particular the way in which the past and future are embedded in the present. The past comprises a matrix from which the possible gathers and to which it constantly alludes; the appearance of the present is the manifestation of different possibles. Bodily abilities derive from habit and experience; what seems possible will always be specific to each person. Likewise, the virtual is the future embedded in the present insofar as it refers to something that is not *now* possible. Which is to say, a "virtual body" is a body engaged in a situation not currently possible; its conditions include those of the past and present, but require arrangement in the future.[42] Merleau-Ponty called the sensation of being able to make these arrangements the "intentional arc," and described it as the feeling of being able to direct himself towards projects not yet realized (*Phenomenology* 137–9). Thrown out around me, recalling my past and formulating my futures, the intentional arc confirms my situatedness while proposing changes to those situations. Elsewhere, he describes how "one's self-expression is an exchange between that which is given and that which is about to be accomplished" (Merleau-Ponty, "The Experience of Others" 55). Merleau-Ponty leaves unsaid that the intentional arc requires more than the formation of bodies, of learned ways of acting and perceiving. In order to change my situation, in order to leave the confines of the possible and the actual, I need *imagination*. Imagination, the creative redistribution of the actual into the virtual, hosts the institution of space between me and others; it grounds relationships in what is and in what can be.

Performance—of any kind, from the conventionally fictional to the supposedly real—pushes past Merleau-Ponty to suggest that instituting space requires imagining it. There is almost never only one thing for bodies to do, almost never only one possibility. Situations resist taxonomies because they are instituted by imagining bodies possessed of the capacity to surprise. This is among the reasons why space can never be reduced to the categorization of bodies and places, and why the same arrangement of bodies and material can be different spaces for different people.

Space is always a matter of potential as well as actuality, of what may be as well as what appears to be. The perception of the (im)balance between the possible, actual, and virtual might describe a sense of space's different qualities. A "dead" space may feel like one drained of the virtual and the possible, while a "charged" one might feel like one where the virtual seems more prominent than the actual.[43] Imagination does not contrast with the actual or the real but is inseparably involved with it. Spaces are the always embodied, always imaginative relations with the world and with others. Space understood this way holds the descriptive *and* the virtual, the way things are and the way they might be. The tension between them holds something beyond desire: astonishment.

Notes

1 Chicago dancer and choreographer Ginger Farley had originally written the text of *Song* for her installation *Fertile Muck* in 2003. Alerted by the assistant curator Doug Stapleton that the Illinois State Museum Chicago Gallery was programming an exhibit of John James Audubon's bird studies ("The Birds of America, Prints from the Illinois State Museum Collection") along with contemporary Illinois artists' responses to birds ("While All the Tribes of Birds Sang"), Farley arranged to have the piece presented as a lunch-time performance in the spring of 2007.

2 Reflecting on a similar situation at a performance in which an otherwise non-descript person transformed a gallery, McAuley writes, "it seemed to me that there must have been some special quality of bodily tension or purposefulness that triggered our attention and told us that here was a performer rather than another spectator" (105).

3 My translation. For Ubersfeld, "scenic space" (*espace scénique*) is "the abstract collection of signs onstage," and concerns the spaces of performers exclusively, while "theatrical space" (*espace théâtral*) includes this space as well as the relations between performers and attendants (53).

4 These movements also served the thematic concerns of *Song*, the writing of which was inspired by choreographer Ginger Farley's captive songbird who never stopped singing for a mate that would never materialize. She wrote a monologue exploring the varied and futile ways of attempting to express ourselves and reach others.

5 For semiotic and cultural materialist historical analyses, see Carlson and Wiles.
6 However, for Féral this space, once established, never quite involves the attendant:

> By watching, the spectator creates an "other" space, no longer subject to the laws of the quotidian, and in this space he inscribes what he observes, perceiving it as belonging to a space where he has no place except as external observer.
> ("Theatricality" 105)

The inception of this theatrical space depends on but immediately excludes the attendant, much like Husserl's *epoché*. For more on Féral and Husserl, see Camp.
7 My translation.
8 Overviews of site-specific performance include Kaye, *Site-Specific Art*; Pearson and Shanks, *Theatre/Archaeology*; Hill and Paris, eds, *Performance and Place*; Birch and Tompkins.
9 See, for example, Wiles; Knowles; Rehm; Briginshaw; Boucris; and Wilcox. Lefebvre proposed a "conceptual triad" composed of "the perceived, the conceived, and the lived," namely spatial practice, representations of space, and representational spaces (39). Although consistently noting different varieties of space, he repeatedly resolves them into products of industrialized capital. Lefebvre was primarily concerned with *production*, understood as reproducible, organized group labor, a focus that drives analysis away from individuals and towards larger forces (68–85). While he posited the individual human body as the site of perceiving space, and as capable of "generat[ing]" space, this merely concerned space as a unique "work" (in distinction to a "product"), and did not reflect "social space," *into which* individuals are born (162, 170, 216 and 32, 46, 57, 68–70).
10 I am grateful to Philipa Rothfield for insisting that Marxism and cultural materialism *do* account for individual experience, albeit as a byproduct of social and economic arrangements.
11 Knowles does provide an exceptionally perceptive analysis of actor and director training in Western Europe and the United States, including an account of the possibility for subversion inherent in Lecoq's training. However, any room for maneuver offered in this early chapter disappears by the end of his book's chronicle of the seemingly limitless recuperative powers of the forces of production (Knowles 24–52).
12 See, for example, McAuley; Lutterbie; and any number of articles from *Modern Drama*'s 2003 issue (46.4) on space and theatre.
13 My emphasis. See also Pearson and Shanks.
14 For genealogies of these terms see, for example, Casey; Jammer; Kern; Lefebvre; Low and Lawrence-Zúñiga; Massey; Sack; Ströker.
15 See, for example, Wiles; Suvin.
16 The term is a cognate in German: *aura*.
17 The previous English translation by Harry Zohn, from which the title of this chapter is drawn, translates "*Ersheinung*" as "phenomenon" instead of "apparition" and reads as "a unique phenomenon of distance, no matter how close it [the object] may be" (Benjamin, "The Work of Art" [1936] 222). In his earlier essay, "Little History of Photography," Benjamin had defined aura as, in Edmund Jephcott and Kingsley Shorter's translation, "a strange web of space and time: the unique appearance of a distance, no matter how close it may be" (Benjamin, "Little History of Photography" 285).

18 Many performance scholars have adopted the position that performance—as opposed to broadcast or recorded events—can exist all at once. For example, Josette Féral wrote that performance had "no past and no future" (Féral, "Performance and Theatricality" 177); Peggy Phelan associated presence with a "maniacally charged present" and famously asserted that performance is chiefly characterized by its constant disappearance (149). Phelan in particular is careful to argue that the presence of performance rests on an absence, but her yoking of the two produces performance as an Alpha and Omega: nothing is left over from it. There is no supplement that does not destroy performance (148, 149ff). The phenomenon of performance is secured by the continual slippage of materials into the vortex of the present, which is to say, by their continual *absenting* themselves.

19 Philip Auslander has taken this baton from Benjamin and carried it through several articles and books. His chief point has been that technology that broadcasts performance poses serious challenges to the idea that an original experience of performers must be located in physical proximity with them; see Auslander, "Humanoid Boogie"; Auslander, "Live from Cyberspace"; Auslander, *Liveness*.

20 Rebecca Schneider points out that insisting on performance's ephemerality derives from a habit of archival practice that defends its importance both by asserting that performance disappears and that it can only be known through certified remains. See Schneider, "Archives: Performance Remains"; Schneider, *Performing Remains*.

21 Original emphasis.

22 The political danger was clear to Benjamin: the formation of a "cult of the audience" all too easily placed at the disposal of fascist states (Benjamin, "The Work of Art" [1935] 33).

23 Oliver Grau has traced the long association between the term "immersive" and digital art and "virtual reality." In both digital and performance environments "immersive" means roughly the same thing—the experience comes close to feeling like "real" life.

24 Hill and Paris draw heavily from Edward Hall's work on space and social relations. See also Hill and Paris, *Performing Proximity* 6–14.

25 Original emphasis.

26 Hill and Paris aren't the only performers to forget this. After attending a one-man show at the 200-seat Forum Theatre in Stuttgart, I effusively complimented the performer on how brilliant it was when near the end of the show he took on the character of a drunkard and took off his shirt, which released a powerful body odor into the auditorium. Much to my embarrassment, he had no idea what I was talking about.

27 To be sure, it costs good money to be this debonair—with tickets running between $75 and $126 over the four years of the show's run so far, Mr. Cobb has spent no less than $4,000 there. This is a relative bargain compared to The Box, a burlesque show co-owned by one of *Sleep No More*'s producers at Emursive, Simon Hammerstein. The Box has locations in New York and London and charges $1,000 to reserve a table. Here, Hammerstein says, "That's what I'm selling: mystique and mystery and sexual openness" (French).

28 Michael Fried famously theorized the concept of attendants disappearing into the artwork in his eye-wateringly pungent attack on "theatricality," "Art and Objecthood" (1967). Fried sought to defend the all-encompassing pres*ent* of modern art from the durational pres*ence* of minimal art. On the one hand there

was the "present-ness" of modern art, an *a*temporal experience of an artwork whose objecthood was purportedly irrelevant. Here, the originality of the object can only be experienced in a vanishing temporal encounter. When faced with the modern artwork the viewer is entirely consumed by the present of the art's revelation—the artwork exists all at once "in" the present. On the other hand, and threatening the integrity and isolation of the modern artwork, minimal art produces the effect of presence by foregrounding an experience of time's passing.

29 Joan Tronto also warned against the potential parochialism of care ethics (256–7).

30 Rancière's concluding thoughts on the emancipated spectator makes this claim of interpretive equality:

> it is a new scene of equality where heterogeneous performances are translated into one another. For in all these performances what is involved is linking what one knows with what one does not know; being at once a performer who deploys her skills and a spectator observing what these skills might produce in a new context among other spectators.
>
> (Rancière, "The Emancipated Spectator")

31 Original emphasis.

32 Gareth White elaborates a counterargument that draws on his extensive experience creating, attending, and teaching participatory theatre. For White, once "participants" enter into the actions of performance, they put their own subjectivity on stage as a material of performance. Far from offering to close a gap between the attendant and the performance, "accepting an invitation puts a participant in a position of having to respond, and thence having to view their own response as part of a work of art" (201).

33 See also "The Paradoxes of Political Art" 140–3.

34 Claire Bishop's sustained scholarly critique of participatory art rests squarely on Rancière's doubts. See Bishop, *Artificial Hells*; Bishop, "Antagonism and Relational Aesthetics"; Bishop, "The Social Turn: Collaboration and its Discontents."

35 Nicholas Ridout also demonstrates this point in his account of "mis-spectators" in the same essay cited here and described in Chapter 1. Unlike Machon, whose survey of immersive theatre features interviews with theatre-makers but not theatre-goers, Ridout considers the liberating experiences of art by turning to the people in attendance, or at least as they are represented in fiction.

36 Original emphasis.

37 Although Barbaras nowhere references Luce Irigaray in his book, her earlier observation about the relationship between desire and "interval" bears a striking resemblance to his own: "The *locomotion toward* and *reduction in interval* are the moments of desire (even by expansion–interaction). The greater the desire, the greater the tendency to overcome the interval while at the same time retaining it" (Irigaray, *An Ethics of Sexual Difference* 48).

38 Phelan, who did not cite Merleau-Ponty here, formulated a very similar idea of subjectivity when she wrote, "Subjectivity can only be 'had,' that is to say, experienced and performed (through the performance one has the experience of subjectivity), in the admission and recognition of one's failure to appear to oneself and within the representational field" (91).

39 My emphasis on "field."

40 The German appears in the original French, and Landes has translated "*jeu*," literally "play" in French, as "leeway."

41 I am indebted to Dermot Moran for his kind assistance translating and explaining this term.

42 These observations were inspired in part by Elizabeth Grosz's thoughts on Henri Bergson (*Architecture from the Outside* 3–29, 91–105).

43 The concentrated experience of possibility anchors an account of presence by Jon Erickson, in which presence involves "the possibility of future movement [...] [P]resence is based not only in the present, but in our expectation of the future" ("The Body as the Object of Modern Performance" 239). Erickson has revised his understanding of presence more than once since ("Presence"; "Tension/Release").

Disorienting

In this chapter I posit a kind of stage presence called centrifugal space in order to continue elaborating how failures in the grounding of perception can generate responsible involvement with others. Beginning with a phenomenological account of the theatrical blunder, I explore Bernhard Waldenfels' approach to encounters beyond recognition, when responses to the strange announce an unrecognizable set of possibilities. Locating these possibilities in Merleau-Ponty's phenomenology suggests different kinds of attention associated with the variety of spaces between performers and attendants. I offer an account of centrifugal space as an ethical rapport of disorientation, arguing that when I lose myself as the source of possibility, I am thrust into an experience of intersubjective embodiment held at bay by habits of identity. I describe this as a play of space that enacts and requires the imbalance of social relations, in particular those associated with the allotment of attention.

Gabriella Giannachi and Nick Kaye write that the concept of presence "draws attention to a spatial relationship and hence a re-positioning of being in relation to this other that is somehow in front of them" ("Presence" 104). This suffices for the experience of presence, in which one is re-positioned while always maintaining a frontal relationship with phenomena. The perceiver is altered, but she or he remains the center of perception. I propose that for the centrifugal space of stage presence I am re-situated in relation to a phenomenon that ceases to stay frontal during disorientation. Which is to say, I lose my sense of myself as the center of orientation in exchange for a shared uncertainty.

By design and by accident

During a 2010 performance of *Moon Water* (1998) by Cloud Gate Dance Theatre of Taiwan, their music, pre-recorded and played over a sound system, began repeating the same notes over and over.[1] At first my companions and I were unsure if this was a musical choice or not, but after someone backstage made three very obvious attempts to get the CD to play properly we understood that it was a mistake. The music then cut out completely. But the curtain did not come down and the lights did not dim. Instead, the dancers continued dancing. As my jaw slowly descended, my torso began rising, and my neck began moving forward, the dancers appeared to adjust themselves. It seemed as though the dancers braced themselves for the task of performing the rest of the piece without any musical accompaniment. Their coordinated breath seemed to evolve as its own score, their focus seemed to enlarge, their limbs seemed to become suppler and more defined, and their movements seemed to unfold in a more resistant element than before. For my part, I was doubled over with amazement. I strained forward to attend as closely as possible to any perceived changes from their habitual movement that might signal their improvised accommodations—even though I was unfamiliar with the piece and was hardly capable of actually recognizing changes to their choreography or affect. The stage became an arena of unclear possibility and challenge. It was no small disappointment when the music returned.

How can it be that when things go wrong they can feel better than when they go right? More precisely, how can it be that when *it appears to me* that something has gone wrong I orient myself more closely to the action on stage? What was happening on that stage might still fall within the classic theory of stage presence, in which performers, expanding "circles of concentration" or maintaining awareness through breath, govern the direction and quality of the audience members' attention.[2] It seems most likely that the dancers were reconfiguring their attention to each other and to their movement as the music failed. As mentioned in Chapter 1, these acting theories, while perhaps useful approaches for actors, either flatten the experience of stage presence into a formula or exclude attendants while reiterating their submissive role in relation to the actor. Zarrilli, echoing Jane Goodall, claims that stage presence cannot be accidental and only appears "when performers have confidence in and have clarity about the precise nature of their performance score" ("'... Presence ...'" 145).[3] And yet this describes the Cloud Gate dancers both before *and* after the musical mishap, and it was only after that I felt myself engaged with something special.

The kind of stage presence Zarrilli claims for himself may be a *kind* of stage presence, but ultimately it affirms the tradition that keeps the performer separate from and dominant over the attendants. Because stage presence never exceeds the control or practice of the performer, attendants do not have a choice over how or to whom they attend: performers demand a particular response and are granted it. Alteration, movement, and involvement in this kind of stage presence lie in the will (or training or "being") of the performer to whom the attendant is not responsible but obedient.

More practically, this model cannot account for any interest exercised by the attendant eager to find out how the performers will recover from a loss of grounding. And yet the experience of actors encountering unexpected obstacles can generate incredible excitement during performance: actors fighting desperately to recall their lines in moments of confusion; actors collapsing in helpless laughter at something supposedly outside the realm of their character's imagined world; dancers organizing themselves to contend with a technical glitch. These performers experience a loss of ability (to remember, to "act professionally," etc.) while attendants can still experience such moments with great enthusiasm. There are of course moments when a failure spurs not excitement but pity, embarrassment, or disgust. The *reasons* for this are surely numerous, but the experiences may be described as those in which disorientation seems either conclusive—there is no hope for the performer—or habitual—a function of an actor's or company's established lack of preparation, for example. Which is to say, the performers and attendants experience a failure that does not signal possibility opening onto the unknown but instead confirms the known.

I am using the term "disorientation" to describe the experience of losing one's bearings—subjective, material, imaginative—during which the world perceived becomes strange. When disoriented I don't know where I face, in which direction I project my body, or where "home" may be; my sense—as in meaning and direction—of myself dissolves. Attempts to *re*-orient suggest the extent to which I am habituated or committed to the posture of certainty or security. The nature and costs of the investment in certainty often escape scrutiny in moments of panicked seeking for the limits I feel necessary to function in the world. People are varyingly habituated to orientation—to knowing which way they are and are going. During onstage failures, losing this orientation can be profoundly unnerving—and those of us who have forgotten not only our lines but also, for what seems like ages, *where* we are, can attest to the depth of the sensation. But surely this also extends to attendants who sense something strange about that actor who suddenly looks pleadingly at a scene partner. In each case, performers and attendants attempt to re-find themselves. And each moment can teach them more about themselves than a moment in which they are certain.

No matter how closely I watch otherwise, when something goes wrong for the performers I attend differently than when everything goes according to plan. Reflecting on the experience of attention when actors get lost can suggest a great deal about the stakes of orientation in perception. The shift in attending signifies more than the onset of a voyeuristic thrill at observing a harmless crackup; it encourages thinking more deeply about the relationship and responsibilities shared by those perceiving and perceived. Attending to failures in performance suggests that only when considering the performers' *and* the attendants' sense of possibility will an ethical rapport grow between them.

These kinds of failures, it should be added, are not the planned and conceptualized disruptions of the companies Sara Jane Bailes examines, nor are they like Judith Halberstam's interpretive acrobatics queering popular culture. While it is possible to call resistance failure and failure resistance as they do, the failures Bailes examines are both chosen and fictive, and those Halberstam reads are discursively imposed. Failure can certainly generate possibility, but it's not failure if you're not trying.

No, these are moments of performance when the plan is lost and, if only briefly, performers and attendants try to find their way again. Nick Ridout analyzes some of these moments in *Stage Fright, Animals, and Other Theatrical Problems* (2006), one of the rare studies of why certain kinds of failure on stage not only fascinate but also speak to the nature of performance. In Ridout's virtuoso historicization of how theatre's failures of representation serve to heighten a sense of theatre's danger and power, he argues that the simultaneous fascination with and repulsion by spectators' own frailty serves to direct their attention to events on stage. Ridout's study operates by answering the *whys* of interest in mistakes on stage, and his Freudian readings of culturally specific milieux provide a strong complement to a phenomenological approach. It may very well be that the spectacle of an actor failing to suppress his or her helpless laughter fascinates because attendants understand the actor's plight to be an emblem of a more general bodily failure to regulate the passage and eruption of the interior to the exterior (Ridout, *Stage Fright* 129–50). Or it might not. In either case these events can be productively described as moments of re-orientation as the actors attempt to right the course of the performance. I might take pleasure in this or find it woeful, but the actors can still be understood as attempting to find their way out of a situation. If space arrives through attention to possibility, "corpsing" actors can be understood as scrambling for a possible exit from their failure to constrain their laughter.

Similarly, the particular fascination of animals on stage may be effectively *explained* as the enactment of coming to terms with a failure of the theatrical sign system to hide the animality and exploitation of actors (Ridout, *Stage Fright* 96–128).[4] It might also be *described* as a heightened awareness of the animal's sense of possibility threatening to overturn the system of the performance. If, in attending to these animals, I attempt to comprehend their possible actions, I can assign a variety of responses—nervousness, moral discomfort, or excitement—to my failure to fully grasp of what they are capable. And again with actors who "dry" on stage, forgetting and attempting to recall their lines. In contrast with actors who accept that the lines are "gone" and let their shoulders and their efforts sag, actors who try to claw the lines back engage attendants with the experience of not knowing how they will act next, allowing me to entangle myself in the projection of their possible actions.

The perception of effort seems crucial here—the sensation that actors are *re*-orienting themselves to terrain made unfamiliar by the sudden loss of habit. There can be little doubt that an attendant unaware of the problem would likely attend much differently than I did. And as any performer will admit, they are often pained by mistakes of which the attendants haven't the smallest awareness. It's not simply being lost that matters, but the attempt to un-lose oneself in a new order of experience. This kind of disorientation strips performers—and attentive attendants—of their accustomed sense of possibility. It demands the awareness and acceptance of something else, of possibilities outside of one's own, of an order of experience derived from elsewhere. This kind of disorientation offers something strange.

Before the wanting-to-know

The seeds of this strangeness can be sown with the neutral mask work described in Chapter 2. Through sustained efforts at miming other ways of moving, students expose themselves to other possibilities—neither their own nor those of the mimed objects. Even further, in the effort to move these possibilities, the students express their *own* constraints as forcefully as ever. In an account of expression in Merleau-Ponty's work, Bernhard Waldenfels observes that "the paradox of expression consists in the fact that an expression is really much more an expression the more vigorously it is moved, incited, and claimed by others" ("The Paradox of Expression" 100). What I perceive and what I do are ways of the world coming to experience through me. I am, each of us is, everything is, an expression of the world, of *a* world whose totality forever eludes us. The most profound expression of myself will be motivated and inhabited by specific relations with others and it will be founded on a depth that cannot be dissipated. Jack Reynolds notes Merleau-Ponty's concern with taking the *specificity* of these relations seriously: "the worst of infringements on alterity is to privilege it simply as that which is forever elusive. In the end, this engenders an 'anonymous, faceless obsession, an other in general'" (190).[5]

From these traces found in Merleau-Ponty, Waldenfels hints at his own preoccupation, one that speaks to the experience of stage presence as much as it does to expressions of others: the strange.[6] Unlike the "other" separated from the same—a being locked into a dialectical whole—the strange embodies that which escapes the order of experience. The concept of the strange poses a challenge at the basis of all perception: how can I encounter something not myself in a manner that neither appropriates it into a previous system of understanding nor exiles it entirely from contact? In other words, how can I perceive things that I don't expect to encounter without rendering them part of pre-existing experience? On the one hand, a theory of perception that relies on recognition insists that the strange exists only through its confirmation of the perceiving subject's primacy—I perceive others through various acts of transference, empathy, and projection. On the other hand, a theory of perception (or ethics) that intends to respect an absolute difference between perceiver and perceived renders the latter entirely inaccessible: "a language that is entirely alien to us could not even be understood as a language" (Waldenfels, *Phenomenology of the Alien* 76).

In order for the strange to avoid appropriation by the perceiving subject in an act of recognition, it must remain outside comprehension while within perception. It must be a phenomenon that "shows itself only by eluding us" (Waldenfels, *Phenomenology of the Alien* 35). Patrick Burke writes that for Merleau-Ponty "wonder is the motivating power of perception itself" ("Listening at the Abyss" 93), and Waldenfels develops this idea by positing the encounter with the strange as the defining act of perception. Waldenfels suggests that to *truly* express the existence of something other than myself I must leave it clouded in depth. Just because something is different from another does not mean it is strange to it—"if we distinguish between an apple and a pear or a table and a bed, we are certainly not saying that one is the stranger or strange vis-à-vis the other" (Waldenfels, "Réponse à l'autre" 360).[7] The strange resides not simply outside myself, which would posit the centrality of my location, it establishes all my limits by existing outside them: "the same is distinct (*verschieden*) from the other, but the self is separated (*geschieden*) from the strange. The strange is not simply other, it is elsewhere [...] [I]t is, as Merleau-Ponty said, 'an originary form of elsewhere'" (Waldenfels, "Réponse à l'autre" 362).[8]

Not only does the strange come from elsewhere, it cannot be anticipated. The strange thing *comes to* my attention. Care and direction might still characterize attention without originating from me. The action of attending arrives unexpectedly: "what is strange emerges by befalling us, amazing us, frightening us, or tempting us" (Waldenfels, "Strangeness, Hospitality, and Enmity" 93).[9]

However else I might feel about the strange, I will feel something powerful and it will involve a great deal of care. Waldenfels aligns the strange with pathos, an overcoming by something outside of myself and of any reason I possess. Consequently, he finds the opposite of pathos not in sense or meaning, but in *apathy* (Waldenfels, *Phenomenology of the Alien* 27). I *could* pay attention, but in my apathy I do not. As Waldenfels puts it, "This does not mean that there is an unchanging amount of data from which certain elements are selected, whereas others remain unselected; rather, attention forms an 'affective relief'" (*Phenomenology of the Alien* 64).[10] It's not that I attend to some things and not others, it's that I care to attend to some and don't care to attend to others. I do not always choose this care, however: "Far from the habitual secondary attention which expects something that is not yet present, the originary attention waits for something that will never be fully there" (Waldenfels, *Phenomenology of the Alien* 65). I care for something I do not yet know, much like the songbird singing his heart out for a mate he has never and may never meet.

All of these characteristics speak to the possibility of finding stage presence during theatrical blunders. Either through expert simulation or transparent reaction, performers in the midst of an unexpected problem can invite my participation in straining towards a solution. Here Waldenfels describes encountering the strange in a way that feels eerily familiar to me as a survivor of onstage wipeouts:

> The alien as alien requires a responsive form of phenomenology that begins with what challenges us, calls upon us, or puts our own possibilities in question in an alienating, shocking, or amazing fashion before we enter into our own wanting-to-know and wanting-to-understand situation.
>
> (*Phenomenology of the Alien* 36)

To be sure, the wanting-to-know can follow hard upon the realization of the strange—I doubt that more than a few moments passed between the Cloud Gate dancers hearing the skipping CD and their wondering if what was happening was happening, and if it was happening how they could manage it. This would put them roughly where I found myself soon after, on the verge of an unrecognized possibility, encountering the strange through a response that arose from the uncomprehended. Such, at least, is how Waldenfels attempts to solve the problem of encountering something radically strange: through a response to it. This solution prompts two crises for perception.

The first situates the response in a curious temporal realm because it is not strictly speaking *subsequent* to the strange but constitutes it: "the call [of the strange] only becomes a call *in the response* which it causes and precedes" (Waldenfels, *Phenomenology of the Alien* 42).[11] A response requires a call, but I only experience the call through the action of my response. The causality in question pushes time *back* rather than forward—instead of the call making the response possible, the response makes the call possible *as an experience of something unknown and unknowable*. In the face of this paradox Waldenfels shrugs his shoulders: "the alien experience is strictly speaking impossible" (*Phenomenology of the Alien* 54). And yet, "it is a lived impossibility" (Waldenfels, "Réponse à l'autre" 373). I can experience a surging, creative response to that which I cannot know.

Which leads to the second crisis: the response involves the creation of a new order of experience. Waldenfels writes that "responding in its full sense does not give what it has, but rather what it invents in responding" (*Phenomenology of the Alien* 38). Only invention evades appropriation while permitting perception. Which is to say, the strange lies outside the realm of the known and can only be encountered through an act of creative expression in response to it. Because the response does not reside entirely in the perceiving subject, it allows the subject to encounter the strange outside of the borders of knowledge or comprehension. I experience the strange through my transformation in response to something that only appears to me through this response.

This does not mean that the strange only exists through me—my response incorporates a reordering of experience beyond myself. My responses do not begin when I speak or move; they begin with the unavoidable look, the inevitable touch, the inescapable attention that situates me in the world at all (Waldenfels, "Réponse à l'autre" 368). The experience of responsibility begins to take shape in this response, in its reordering of possible sense. Waldenfels, however, cautions against assuming too great a role in the expression of the strange: "We invent *that which* we respond, but we do not invent *that to which* we respond and which gives a certain weight to all that we say and do" ("Réponse à l'autre" 374). The creative response produces other possibilities that confirm an experience of the strange without claiming it. "Radically alien is exactly that which cannot be anticipated by any subjective expectations or by any trans-subjective conditions for possibilities" (Waldenfels, *Phenomenology of the Alien* 18).

Beyond the conditions set between myself and others *as we are*, Waldenfels finds Merleau-Ponty's concept of space as a *Spielraum*. My embodied situations involve my body as a "system of possible actions," with my sense of space fusing the actual and the imagined (Merleau-Ponty, *Phenomenology* 260). Waldenfels proposes that, *when I pay attention*, embodied situations can involve the strange as well, and so transform my own systems of possible actions. My encounter with the strange, my disorientation, results from a fundamental ambiguity that opens up within myself, between others and myself, and between what makes sense and what cannot be understood. Waldenfels' phenomenology of the strange maintains that ambiguity while also examining it, which forges a path directly towards stage presence. By accepting the challenge of the strange, "the putting into perspective of all that appears gives way to a putting into the abyss which maintains recesses, absences, the 'je ne sais quoi'" (Waldenfels, "Réponse à l'autre" 367). The character of the relationship between myself and the "je ne sais quoi" cannot be taken for granted because of the varied ways of paying attention. So long as I can *come to* attention as well as attend to, "attention cannot decide on the 'that,' 'what,' and 'who' of experience, but it certainly can decide about the '*how*'" (Waldenfels, *Phenomenology of the Alien* 64). The strange brings with it and places at the center of perception the advent of ethical choice—which "how" I follow involves me in specific ways with others. These different kinds of "how" lead towards or away from a "lived distance" between others and myself and characterize different kinds of space between us. Only some will maintain the strangeness of our encounters.

Centripetal and centrifugal space

Movement refers movers to their environments and to adaptations required by one's own and the world's constraints, and Merleau-Ponty marked a difference between "concrete," or goal-oriented, movement and "abstract"

movement. Each one concerned a different kind of context for movement, a background that "is immanent in the movement and animates it"
(*Phenomenology* 113). He characterizes the difference between the two
backgrounds by observing that while "the background of concrete movement is the given world, the background of abstract movement is, on the
contrary, constructed" (Merleau-Ponty, *Phenomenology* 113). In his example, a gesture beckoning his friend arises from the situation of their distance
from each other, just as a repetition of the gesture if the first is met with inac-
tion will arise from a modified situation. The "world as given" here includes
the perceived (emotional, material) relationship between the two men, and
so the gestures arise from this situation rather than being "built up" without
reference to a perceived situation. "If I now execute the 'same' movement,
but without aiming at a present or even an imaginary partner [...] then my
body, which was just previously the vehicle of movement, now becomes the
goal of movement" (Merleau-Ponty, *Phenomenology* 113–14). His use of
scare quotes here confirms that he is arguing precisely that these are *not* the
same movements; the first works towards a goal and from an actual situation, while the second becomes unmoored from the mover of the gesture.

Merleau-Ponty in his later works disavowed such a neat separation
between abstract and concrete modes of movement. The point of introducing them here is the association he made between them and different kinds of
space. Concrete movement he links with centripetal space because it "takes
place within being or within the actual [... and] adheres to a given background." Abstract movement's connection to centrifugal space derives from
how it "takes place within the possible or within non-being [... and] sets
up its own background" (Merleau-Ponty, *Phenomenology* 114). Centripetal
and centrifugal spaces suggest that embodied and imaginative relations with
others can still be perceived as having or lacking a source. Centripetal space
locates the perceiver and the perceived within the limits of their recognizable bodily constraints. It clamps attention to a source. Centrifugal space
recognizes a radiating experience of possibility that does not adhere to any
person's particular situation. The differences between these two spaces do
not concern kinds of movement so much as they concern kinds of attention.

Without insisting that a situation is *strictly* "concrete" or "actual,"
centripetal space classifies encounters with the "classic" version of stage
presence. Spectacular performers make themselves *objects of attention* and
institute a space that adheres closely to their bodies. Their bodies are, in
comparison to the preponderance of attendants, "inaccessible,"[12] and their
possibilities override and subsume those of the awed attendants. Because
centripetal space is still *shared*, the extent to which I perceive a performer's
abilities as radically disconnected from the bodily projects of the attendants
becomes the extent to which I—as an attendant—collude in the isolation
of the performer. In order to recognize or identify the virtuoso, attendants must accept their own sense of falling short of the virtuoso's abilities,

imagined to reside uniquely "in" the virtuoso him or herself. Bettina Brandl-Risi describes this phenomenon when she writes that a virtuoso "surpasses standards and expectations by producing a perplexing and excessive difference [... and] stages himself both as the subject of the performance and as the object of the amazement this performance evokes" (11). The standards and expectations clearly belong to the attendants; they are the ones casting someone at the end of an unbridgeable distance as an object.

To be sure, this kind of isolation earns its own sort of attention. It is a variety of attention, however, that participates in excluding others from myself by defining them exclusively in terms of my own identity. Its pleasures are real, but they bring with them a rigid objectification. They can also bring with them a queasy awareness of my own participation in this objectification when I admit to being part of a centripetal space during performance. And as much as that participation embarrasses me, it also provides an opportunity to closely consider centripetal space.

The touring production of *I Want to Dance Better at Parties* (2004) by the Australian company Chunky Move came to Chicago in the spring of 2007. The piece explored the various relationships Australian men have with dance, whether as a profession, personal expression, social activity, or religious rite.[13] Throughout, the voices of several documentary subjects (all male) combine with literal and abstract transpositions to create a "personal, expressionistic, postmodern reverie" (Smith). During the piece I often found myself focusing on dancer Kristy Ayre, who was formidably adept at clogging, ballet, and modern dance idioms. She also embodied an appeal well rehearsed by Europeanized media: with her long, blonde hair trailing her rapidly articulating and slender form, she was a recognizably athletic, thin, Western European beauty. And if I am honest I will argue that the kind of relationship instituted between us may best be understood as this kind of centripetal space that isolates and defines rather than shares and entangles.

To begin with, there was her costume, whose shorts emphasizing her legs operated within the context of the relentless objectification of (women's) bodies. Costumes are an ancient means of directing attention on stage, both to whole bodies and to parts of bodies in performance, and of indicating everything from a character's rank to the production's budget. They are as semiotically rich as pretty much anything else on stage. In this case, no matter what significance might be argued for her dress in the local context of Australia, Ayre's shorts also, if not primarily, functioned to draw attention to her legs. While the costume designer (Paula Levis), Ayre, and the choreographer all might participate in this act of objectification, the act cannot be completed without a particular quality of attention from the attendant. After all, the appearance of someone's legs does not *require* his or her objectification—that act must be completed by another.

Very few dances do not invite attention to particular parts of dancers' anatomy. Dance intended for attendance tends to work by proposing that the movements of parts of dancers' bodies engage attention. At the limit, moving bodies might be perceived as the essential movement of perception and an opening onto the depth between movers and attendants. And why not? All the same, in most evenings of concert dance, movement does less to express the bottomless depth of being than to express an exquisite line or curve or story or idea. Attendants can agree that the dancers are more than the dance and then move on to the pleasures of attending to the dance (after which even the idea of that "more" evaporates). Nonetheless, within the context of objectification proposed by the activity of attending to movement instead of the movers, attendants still retain the possibility of different kinds of attention.

In Ayre's and my case, a particular kind of attention sundered perceived and perceiver, and this closure marked the ends of the virtuoso's and the non-virtuoso's bodies. Although we shared the space of the performance, I attended to her body's system of possible actions as so far removed from my own that I experienced my relation to her as one of closure, not openness. Bodies are by their nature open to each other, yet my experience of hers was marked by the disquieting sensation of a certainty that our difference lay outside of me and entirely in *her*. I experienced her as both unlike *and* comprehended by me. There is without question pleasure and excitement to be had in experiencing this distortion of how perception expresses a co-institution with others. Nonetheless, it insists on separating the performer and the attendant, and it fills up and hardens the depth between them by foreclosing the constant inhabitation by the strange.

Notably missing from the experience of centripetal performers is the sensation of reversibility essential to perception and embodied being. As discussed in Chapter 2, this reversibility is *imminent*, marked both by the confidence in a shared world of perceptibility and by the failure to reverse identities with any other. While I cannot exchange places with another, and while I do not perceive as they do, I do share belonging to a world *of* perception. The concept of reversibility invites awareness of divergent perspectives and allows for the experience of difference located in the movement between unreachable points. When, as with the virtuosic performer, that mutual movement is excluded, I find another enclosed by unreachability instead of opened through space. Others then appear to me through identities rather than moving multiplicities, as certainties rather than the ambiguous commingling of the known and the unknowable.

Instead of investing in the possible, centripetal space solidifies, insists on what "is" instead of what may be. Jack Reynolds writes of centripetal actions as "habitual" in the sense that they rest in the sedimentation of meaning accrued by the subject (89). These kinds of actions not only reify appearance, but they also demand that attendants remain who they have already imagined themselves to be; alterations that occur in this relationship remain in the domain of the perceived object. In this description, Ayre appeared inaccessible to me only insofar as I staked my attention to an arbitrary difference between us that removed rather than bound us in a mutual implication.

"Concrete" movement and "physical" space refer to the over-determination of task-oriented movement drained of perceiving subjects. In contrast, centrifugal space takes movements and involves them with *potential*. The resulting movements and space carry the "function of 'projection' by which the subject of movement organizes before himself a free space in which things that do not exist naturally can take on a semblance of existence" (Merleau-Ponty, *Phenomenology* 114). This space appears as the realm of the virtual; the movements here have a place and grounding among other people, but they also take on their meaning through the imagined and the strange rather than through the familiar. This space of strangeness describes a kind of stage presence in which excited attendance to performers might express varied causes—skill or mishap—and varied contexts.

In the case of *Moon Water*'s mechanical problem, the adjusting dancers and attendants instituted a space that vibrated with possibility and the strangeness that accompanies attempts to re-find a displaced sense of location. Through this kind of space, attendants can perceive the extension of virtual bodies that do not yet exist but whose imminence may be felt by performers and attendants alike. Unlike centripetal space, which telescopes down to performers and isolates them from attendants, centrifugal space requires both the active attention of others and a lack of concrete expectations for the future. Attendants and performers draw themselves up to find a way through a strange terrain rather than to equip themselves for an habitual task. The disorientation that jettisons "expectation[s] of the future" brings me into a shared uncertainty with particular performers different from what I experience with those performers to whom I attend but who precisely *do* meet my expectations—even when those expectations are that the performers surprise me. The strangeness of centrifugal space concerns a mutual and imaginative re-orientation in which attendants and performers test habits of perception and action.

Centrifugal space carries me away from a center and emphasizes the possibility inherent in the reversible relation. Rather than a quality that draws attention to the body of the performers and that seems to close space around it, centrifugal space involves attendants with other situations, with another experience of space. Whereas "classic" stage presence, or centripetal space, collapses a sense of space and insists on a closure between performers and the attendants, centrifugal space draws them into a vivid openness. It does so by involving them with the virtuality of space, its capacity to harbor creative—which is to say, perceived but unfamiliar—arrangements for all of its participants.

Centrifugal space concerns a kind of attention to what transforms and surprises rather than to what rests, to what surrounds rather than to what inheres in individuals. This description accommodates a central mystery of stage presence: when people seem not simply volatile or unpredictable, but disposed toward the world in a way that indicates they need more room than their bodies take up. Saying "Gosh, you always seemed so much taller" reckons with the discrepancy between how much seemed possible in relation to the other person and how much seemed possible according to an abstract measurement. Of course, this person is not "actually" however many inches or centimeters tall, but *also* that.

With the virtual more pronounced than the actual, centrifugal space speaks less to an action of the performer than to a relation. Excitement comes not *from* a person, nor is it *in* someone who has or is doing something *more* than. Rather, through centrifugal space, attendants engage with a sense of possibility *neither their own nor another's*. The virtuoso expands my sense of *human* possibility ("I didn't know that was possible!") but does not alter my own; my horizons expand, but the point from which I perceive them does not. In the disorientation of centrifugal space, however, when I lose certainty about what separates another's possibilities from my own, I lose my anchor of perception. I may then enter into a more exposed and more responsive relationship with others, one that allows for the creation of an ethical rapport.

Tere, Clare, Donnell, and Drag Ronald Reagan

Unsurprisingly, centrifugal space often arises with actors portraying characters who are disoriented. A Hamlet or a Medea can be expected to lose their footing, and indeed attendants may judge the performance of these characters according to the experience of dissolution. This holds particularly true for characters with whom attendants are not previously familiar, like Paula Gruskiewicz's panicking empress in *Waiting in Tobolsk*, discussed in Chapter 1. I drew myself into Gruskiewicz's foundering empress and her uncertain grasp on her environment without expectation of madness feigned or otherwise. Much the same happened with the EL2 Stage Works Production of Tennessee Williams' *The Two-Character Play*.[14] Clare (Tere Harrison) and Felice (Jason Fleitz) are actors and siblings who find themselves abandoned on the set of the next stop on their tour. Harrison's portrayal of Clare embodied a fierce and jagged oscillation between affectation and sincerity, playing at desperation while shrinking in fear from the possibility that her failures were real rather than those of her characters. A pervasive panic accompanied Harrison for most of the performance as she shifted unexpectedly between Clare and the characters this character played at playing.

Above all, Harrison's shifting relationship to the set of the play (within the play) communicated Clare's vertiginous moves between her characters and her relationship with her brother: one moment the set was a fiction acknowledged by the characters, the next it was a hallucination of their childhood home; one moment the backstage (of the play-within-a-play, but visible on stage in the Williams play) was outside that home, the next it was backstage of the theatre in which Clare and Felice were trapped, the next it was the wreckage of Clare's mind. Which is to say, she was off-balance for much of the evening. And so was I, constantly alert to what Harrison might do next and attending to every possible action she might take. The result was that, rather than having my attention fixed to her entirely, I attended to the relationships unfolding between her and the place around her. I involved myself most with the *space* between her and her surroundings. In these cases the possible became more involving than what was "actually" happening. The *stage* was the area of attention, rather than the person occupying it.

As a kind of relationship between performer and attendant, centrifugal space might come and go: this kind of relationship need not last for the entirety of a performance. This is another way of describing the performer who "has it" and then "loses it" at another moment. Donnell Williams never "lost it" during the performance of *My Fellow Americans*, but I did experience shifts from one kind of space to another.[15] *My Fellow Americans* was a meditation on the presidency of Ronald Reagan and on the people his policies excluded from the "shining city on a hill." Through dance, text, and music, a company of five performed the mixture of anger, bitterness, and compassion evoked by this popular president whose policies did so much damage to the American people, particularly the growing population of people suffering from HIV/AIDS. Laura Molzahn of the *Chicago Reader* wrote, "Carpenter blows apart the clichés of Ronald Reagan's presidency by bringing out their surreality, tying them to unexpected emotions, or both." At times during the piece Williams seemed to draw the stage almost entirely to him, becoming the sole focus of attention; and then almost immediately afterwards the Hamlin Park Fieldhouse seemed to vibrate with potential movement. One series of these moments involved a solo of confident swoops and staggered steps, performed while wearing a full-head Reagan mask. And six-inch stiletto heels. And nothing else save skin-tight black shorts and plastic-wrap around his torso.

Now, there is no way for me to untangle my attention to his movement from his striking appearance. Attending to his control over the jerking steps in those heels and the transfixing sight of Reagan's head atop an African American man's drag persona rendered spaces centripetal *and* centrifugal: through the collapse of space onto his body, our relationship became one characterized by closure and rigidity, while his unexpected rhythm and my unwillingness to firmly assign an identity to an almost-bare-chested drag Reagan opened us to the uncertainty of disorientation. At times the space between him and what surrounded him had shrunk to the surface of his shrink-wrapped body and with it the embodied experience of projected possibility. At other times, during centrifugal space, I was disoriented by my response to his movement and appearance; I attended to how the room was changing and changing me during the solo, and my embodied experience of projected possibility expanded through the windows. The strange did not attach to him—or me—but instead arose between us.

During some fleeting moments of his solo I was involved with a kind of attention that relied on a centralizing and objectifying relationship with the perceived. I have purposely chosen a white woman and a black man as "the perceived" for this straightish white male attendant because doing so fore-grounds the histories also at play here—or *can* if I choose to attend to them. Doing so certainly makes me uncomfortably aware of my own position, which is very much the point in singling out centripetal space. In addition, it is no mistake that in both these cases the performers' costumes revealed their bodies to many different types of attending. And yet, as I argued above with Ayre, no one kind of attention was *necessary*.

In performance the kinds and vectors of attention depend on the attend-ants. Indeed, at other times in this same sequence I found myself disoriented in the strangeness of my response to Williams' movements and appearance. As long as I was not trying to locate Williams or keep his movements and appearance at bay, as long as I was attending to them in a manner that required a creative response to them, a centrifugal space opened between us. During the thrill of that solo *he* was not the strange or its ambassador; strangeness unfolded between us.

This kind of strange does not depend on arresting (or revealing) cos-tumes. Later, dressed in khakis and a light-blue business shirt with the collar open, Williams sat in a folding chair and sang an a cappella version of Queen's "Another One Bites the Dust." While Williams sang, Carpenter danced a solo to his right, struggling to leave his own chair, then engaging in a series of thrusts, grabs, and feints before collapsing back onto the chair. Williams' voice came clear but empty of emotional affect, and he leaned slightly forward, his body focused far ahead of him. My attention to what might happen around him arose not out of curiosity for how *he* would respond or what it would mean to him, but in a way simultaneously more generalized—a sense of possibility for whatever was around—and more specific—these possibilities concerned *me*. The difficulty of clarifying "my" relation to the space of performance from Williams' marks the inauguration of the experience of centrifugal space.

Part of this experience involved Williams turning Queen's song from a boastful promise of violent reprisal into a plaintive but detached account of the devastating march of AIDS through the gay community of the 1980s: "Another one bites the dust / Another one bites the dust / And another one gone, and another one gone / Another one bites the dust. / Hey, I'm gonna get you too." As I'm sure a number of other attendants were as well, I was aware that Queen's lead singer Freddie Mercury himself died of AIDS-related pneumonia in 1991. Just as there was no way for me to separate my attention to Williams' earlier solo from his appearance in relation to mine, there is no way for me to separate my experience of this moment from my prior knowledge of the song. And this is very much the point: that centrifugal space cannot be understood as something pertaining solely to the performer. Part of the sense of possible action that pervaded the playing area *for me* had to do with Williams re-casting the song, one I happened to know from my own 1980s childhood. This change from the recognizable into something else, the experience of alteration, also signals the co-institution of centrifugal space.

I do not mean to claim that Williams or I *knew* this was our experience or that we sought it. I *do* mean to claim that this kind of description provides the framework for situating performers and attendants in a relationship better suited to ethical attention than the classic description of stage presence.

Attendants do not achieve the foundational space between themselves and the performers, but instead co-institute it together with them. The particular kind of stage presence I call centrifugal space stages and magnifies this experience of the strange. It is not simply a matter of an attendant undergoing an alteration of perception. Centrifugal space involves the ability to alter *and* be altered—the movement between toucher and touched—and it requires attendants and perceivers to share it. Performers are more than aware of the heightened availability and awareness that arises in the most charged of encounters with attendants. I am suggesting that this concerns not only their own practice but that of the attendants as well; both are in play.

Accordingly, images of centrifugal space are difficult to achieve because they require both performers and attendants. Williams looks amazing in Figure 4.1, but he is alone—which, by itself, can never reflect the nature of perception as I argue centrifugal space does. Indeed, for this reason the image serves as representation of the centripetal space that does not participate in stage presence. To effectively convey stage presence would entail either engendering the experience of stage presence between the viewer of the image and the image itself (rather than representing it *in* the image), or depicting performers, their environment, and the attendants, and all of them must be perceptibly involved in the movement of imagination.

Three images from Barba and Savarese's *Dictionary of Theatre Anthropology* illustrate this difficulty. In a section on "The performer's presence," Barba offers images of Iben Nagel Rasmussen performing on a street in Sardinia in order to demonstrate the qualities of "extra-daily technique" he believed were fundamental to making a performer compelling (92). Barba's accompanying text explains how Rasmussen effectively marshals the different techniques of his training to demonstrate her presence. And yet the images tell a different story. In one, Rasmussen is pictured marching behind two women who appear completely unaware of the actress. Whatever may be said about her technique matters little to these women. In another image she is passing by an older woman standing in a doorway with her arms folded, studiously

Figure 4.1 Publicity still of Donnell Williams for *My Fellow Americans*

Source: photo courtesy of Cheryl Mann Productions.

performing her desire to not be impressed. No matter how well these images convey Rasmussen's technique of deploying opposition in movement, her failure to register with the two women in front of her and the older woman's defiance make it difficult to associate these situations with any kind of stage presence in which the attendants are necessary participants.

In the third image, Rasmussen stands on her toes beating her drum. Behind her, a boy has his hand on the frame of a door and a foot inching toward it; he appears to be cautiously keeping her in his sights. In the other doorway, in front of Rasmussen, there are two women, one middle-aged and the other older. The former has her arms on the latter's shoulder and leans into her laughing. Both she and the young boy are, in my analysis, attending to Rasmussen without foregoing their own centers of perception—his caution asserts his trepidation, and the younger woman's enjoyment and posture of relaxation assert her status as onlooker. The older woman, however, seemingly unaware of her companion's touch, leans into Rasmussen with brow furrowed and hands held as if they were also wielding drumsticks. Through her mimicry she is taking on another system of possible actions, adapting her body to another set of constraints. Or so it seems. This is of course an interpretive exercise. And yet it can also demonstrate that only an image that depicts a shared involvement between performer and attendant will be able to represent the experience of stage presence enacted through centrifugal space.

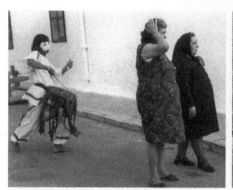

Figures 4.2–4 Iben Nagel Rasmussen in Sardinia

Source: images courtesy of Routledge.[16]

I want to emphasize again that I am not suggesting a complete exchange of orientation between attendant and performer. My attunement to new possibilities does not mean they become my own, nor that I understand or occupy the situation of a performer. The simultaneously mutual and different experiences of disorientation embody the "strange proximity" of a relation to others who cannot be known and yet *whose unknowability fosters a shared experience of the perceptible world*. I perceive the world through an orientation to possible actions that institutes space with others. During centrifugal space I allow myself to lose my own sense of orientation around my habitual system of possible actions. I become *dis*oriented. Elizabeth Grosz, drawing on Roger Caillois, writes of how "direction, centeredness (centricity), location, dimension, and orientation [...] derive from the particular relations the subject has to objects and events" (*Space, Time, and Perversion* 93). When these relations involve a mutual overwhelming between performer and attendant in the experience of centrifugal space, each of them alters direction, centeredness, location, dimension, and orientation. My habits of perception and relation briefly dissolve and I am forced to confront the lengths to which I will go to (re-)assert what I find familiar or recognizable. I am left with a choice to orient myself into a strange world centered between others and myself or in myself.

The reversible relation of perception is incomplete, marked by the inability to occupy the situation of another *or one of my own*. Garner wrote of "rival perceptual centers" (*Bodied Spaces* 46) among performers and attendants, and while I also recognize multiple perceptual centers, I do not believe that they are in competition. I follow Merleau-Ponty's suggestion that the reversibility of the "flesh" does not result in a Hegelian dialectic but in a multiplicity realized through the experience of space. Multiple perceptual centers work in concert and through mutual overlapping to render the performance perceptible to begin with. The perceptual center of an actor with whom I experience centrifugal space does not conquer my own perceptual center; instead, the different centers together assert their instability and intertwining. They alter each other by their mutual opening. What this alteration feels like cannot be generalized because attendants and performers experience disorientation in their own ways: losing certainty of direction does not mean and feel the same even to the same person. Nonetheless, through centrifugal space I am invited to take responsibility for how I institute space with others through the expression of oriented yet distant possibility.

This poses a crucial question about perception and perceptibility: in the case of disorientation it must be asked, *for whom* is it not simply enjoyable but also safe to lose one's bearings? There are places where certain marked bodies lose their way only at their own peril. Whether sought or stumbled into, disorientation changes the sense of my body's possibilities, a privilege often connected to the situations afforded by race, sex, sexuality, and class. Matrices of power underwrite the pleasures of disorientation.

For some people disorientation is dangerous and a privilege held by others. Even further, this privilege might depend on the erasure of those without it. I may only become unlatched and may only accept the responsibility of responding to another in the context of particular lives shaped by forces and phenomena often beyond my capacity to alter. Not everything of which I am capable is experienced as being possible, and this discrepancy accounts not only for the dynamics of inequality but also its possible subversive and creative functions.

Abilities and possibilities

Promoting the idea that I may be involved with another's sense of possible action requires addressing one of the most persistent criticisms of Merleau-Ponty's phenomenology: that he figures a world determined by "the" body in action. This is to say that he stands accused of abstracting and homogenizing the abilities of diverse bodies into those of the ideal, straight, male subject operating without constraints in a world free of history or culture. While one may easily mistake in Merleau-Ponty's early work a generalized model of the body, he consistently insists on the body's location in specific contexts that not only alter but found perception. For example, he writes of "the social world with which we are in contact through the simple fact of our existence, and that we inseparably bear along with us prior to every objectification" (Merleau-Ponty, *Phenomenology* 379), and of the cultural and historical contexts that condition perception of "the" color red (Merleau-Ponty, *The Visible and the Invisible* 132/172–3). And in a 1960 article he writes, "in fact and in principle, it is impossible to establish a cleavage between what will be 'natural' in the individual and what will be acquired from his social upbringing" (Merleau-Ponty, "Child's Relation" 108).

As Grosz has persuasively argued, Merleau-Ponty offers philosophers ample resources for rethinking traditionally binarized theoretical models that habitually erase and/or subjugate the experience of bodies that are neither white, male, or heterosexual, nor without physical or mental disability. In particular, she points to ways Merleau-Ponty's thought not only resists easy claims that it irrevocably privileges certain bodies over others, but also offers feminist thinkers the basis for founding a non-essentialist ontology. By establishing the locus of experience *between* binaries (mind–body, individual–society), he deauthorizes "the" body as a source of truth and draws attention to how bodies form and are formed by the social. Sex and sexuality for Merleau-Ponty constitute elements of orientation rather than aspects of "the" body. For Grosz, Merleau-Ponty's insistence on the partiality and constraints of experience leaves open important questions about *whose* embodied knowledge passes for accepted knowledge ("Merleau-Ponty and Irigaray" 40–2). In addition, the development of

Merleau-Ponty's reversibility thesis explicitly recognizes the advent of the "plural" in existence and provides directly for the arrival of difference at the heart of perception and being rather than as additions to or distortions of a male subject (as Judith Butler and Luce Irigaray have argued).[17]

However, these criticisms offer productive specificity to Merleau-Ponty's account by detailing the ways in which, in particular, socially gendered bodies and senses of possibility are formed differently. Iris Marion Young, in her influential essay "Throwing Like a Girl: A Phenomenology of Feminine Body Comportment, Motility, and Spatiality" (1989), described differences between masculine and feminine movement derived from the impositions of male-dominated discourse and culture. In her analysis, these gendered roles and language produced weakened "feminine" movement that was constrained and discontinuous. Young noted in a later reflection on this essay that even her own initial critique accepts male motility as universal; she thus failed to account not only for the formation of "male" motility but also suggested that women's motility is *only* shaped by its restriction and thereby strips women of their "full humanity" ("'Throwing Like a Girl': Twenty Years Later" 288–9).

Perhaps there is not much use in writing of "masculine" or "feminine" movement, as opposed to "feminine- or masculine-coded" movement. Labeling movement "masculine" or "feminine" risks obscuring that movements are associated with *constructions* of "masculinity" and "femininity" in different discourses, while suggesting that certain kinds of movement are inherent to different sexes. As has been observed before, claiming a movement's gender risks needlessly binarizing movement and turning from its formation by race, sexuality, class, and myriad other factors. Merleau-Ponty was well aware of this:

> We have no grounds to speak of "the" masculine and "the" feminine since each civilization, according to its mode of existence, elaborates a certain type of masculinity in correlation to a certain type of femininity. But within any given society one finds *sexual stereotypes*.
> (*Merleau-Ponty à la Sorbonne* 495)[18]

And yet Young is surely correct to point to significant and recognizable ways in which different classes of people experience their bodies, which is to say, form different systems of possible actions. As Sara Ahmed notes in *Queer Phenomenology* (2006), the "I can" of bodily intention depends on others *allowing* me to perform actions; my abilities are inseparable from conditions of possibility that are not made by me alone. "'Doing things' depends not so much on intrinsic capacity or even on dispositions and habits, but on ways in which the world is available as a space for action" (Ahmed 110). At the same time that I can claim my experience of the world is instituted by the limits to a range of actions, I can recognize that these limits are neither exclusively my own nor those of others. In her account of the phenomenology of political repression, Janice McLane observes, "if human beings exist through shared corporeal schemata, we must ask ourselves just what schemata are being shared" (138). I may learn a range of possibilities circumscribed by multiple forms of institutionalized denial and privilege. In which public square would you not think twice about "the" possibility of kissing your partner? Are you in a state that legalizes discrimination against your sexual being or actively persecutes you for it? How do you, as a mixed race couple, experience "the" possibility of going for a stroll in a neighborhood where one of your races predominates? Possibilities are not intrinsic and are all too often foreclosed for "other" bodies.[19] This is not to suggest that "white" bodies operate freely, as they demonstrably do not. However, in many circumstances they operate within *habits* of freedom applied to bodies (un)marked as white: "what phenomenology describes is not so much white bodies, but the ways in which [...] such bodies are not 'points' of stress" (Ahmed 138–9).

How to embrace a loved one must of course be learned, but Ahmed insists on remembering that it must also be experienced as *possible*. The "successful" body, as Merleau-Ponty's countless examples of bodies modified by history and circumstance make clear, is a fiction; each form of ability carries with it not only individual accomplishment, but also the inheritance of sedimented histories accompanying all learning of bodily movement. In Rosalyn Diprose's words, "my possibilities are borrowed from the bodies of others, always with an incalculable remainder" (54). There is not "a" successful body, there are multiple bodies variously engaged in shared projects. When those projects demand that my possibilities derive from someone else, I am circumscribed. Everyone is, as Iris Marion Young noted, the shape of these enclosures, each one of which documents histories of institutional and personal oppression.

And yet the involvement of these bodies also makes possible the sensation described above: that I am oriented not to my own sense of possible actions but to one arriving from between myself and others. In this experience of the strange, "the place where I begin is not my own" (Waldenfels, "Réponse à l'autre" 372). It is not any other's place, either; it is one that comes into being through my response to the strange. In the "lived impossibility" of a response to another that precedes my understanding that a call has been made at all, I begin in a place imagined between myself and an unfolding relationship with another. The constraints felt by performers and attended to by others can contribute to the sensation that they do, or do not, "have much presence." If I fail to attend to the possibilities of others I'm with, I banish the strange and abbreviate their—and my—intentional arcs. A failure to accept my disordering by the integration of other possibilities for action amounts to a failure of attention, and it denies others and myself the opportunity to change the space between us.

Although not referring here to the theatre, Merleau-Ponty writes perceptively about acting when he observes: "To play is to place oneself momentarily in an imaginary situation, to enjoy changing one's 'setting'" (*Phenomenology* 136).[20] This kind of play produces Waldenfels' "lived impossibility" in which "I am there where I cannot be" ("Réponse à l'autre" 373). Waldenfels, however, associates this impossibility with pathos and suffering as the result of something "tearing us out of the familiar" (*Phenomenology of the Alien* 26, 65). But why can't this displacement and disordering be enjoyable? Perhaps not quite *ecstatic*, but nonetheless an invigorating experience of movement? Perhaps discomforting, but nonetheless a welcome awakening to the tension between knowing and unknowing? Stretching towards these poles will, if I do it right, use muscles metaphorical that need the exercise and will be sore afterwards.

After all, stage presence is a *thrill*, not a comfort; it is exciting, not pleasant. During the centrifugal space of stage presence, during the disorientation of the strange, this thrill does not derive from performers but from creative responses to them. As an attendant, my excitement and sense of possibility do not involve the performers' qualities so much as my changing orientations and theirs. As a performer, the thrill and sense of alertness that I associate with a "good" performance is not a function of "my" work, but of a particular attentive relationship developing between the attendants and me. It makes no sense to describe a performer as having or doing stage presence if there is no one in attendance. And whereas the charismatic or virtuosic performer suggests an unreachable state for attendants whose awe reflects the hardening of difference as identity, centrifugal space requires a heightened involvement with each other. It isn't mine or anyone else's, it is not stable, cannot be located, and is always strange.

The "charged" centrifugal spaces are not those commanded by a performer; they are those in which ambiguous and emerging senses of bodily possibility intertwine. These spaces enable an encounter with the radical strangeness of embodied, intersubjective existence. Following the kick of playful disorientation, attendants and performers begin to come to grips with another sense of space. My sense of situation alters and I shift my systems of possible actions for another—not *the* other's, but one not my own. Without inhabiting another's body or situation, through a mutual encounter people can experience what Merleau-Ponty calls a "mysterious slippage" that destabilizes without making another into something recognizable:

> If another person is really another, at a certain stage I must be surprised, disorientated. If we are to meet not just through what we have in common but in what is different between us, [this] presupposes a transformation of myself and of the other as well.
>
> (*The Prose of the World* 142)

The exhilaration of these moments speaks to the experience of myself as an opening subject. Given the inexhaustible depth of the world, the subject who opens onto the world of perception is the astonished subject. The desiring subject pursues and perpetually closes in; the astonished subject opens up to possibilities other than its own by accepting an encounter with the strange. This is ultimately *any moment of attention*. For Merleau-Ponty, wonder lay at the heart of both the phenomenological enterprise and the act of perception. Echoing Plato and Aristotle, he said, "Philosophy is *thaumazein* [wonder], the consciousness of strangeness" (Merleau-Ponty, "Man and Adversity—Discussion" 236). It is not the deciphering of strangeness or its solving, but an awareness.

Accepting the strangeness of the world is not submission but a committed action. It requires attending—direction and care. And the act of attending to the centrifugal space of stage presence, contrary to Merleau-Ponty's assessment that theatre restricts my responsibilities to others, offers an experience that opens me to my profound involvement with others. Astonishment moves in many directions—the astonishing moves *towards* me, I move not away from it back into myself but towards a new configuration of the possible, and the world extends its depth again into the unknowable. Wonder forms me—it opens me to my inability to comprehend the world that appears through anything and anyone I encounter. It is not simply a question itself, it is the beginning of an answer to a question the world asks of me. This opening heralds the first step of expressing the world through a creative response to it. And far from translating others into a set language, the ensuing expression operates as the founding arrangement of newly possible meaning (Merleau-Ponty, *Signs* 67). In Burke's words, "wonder is the strangest of all experiences because it is openness upon the strange. It is strangeness itself" ("Listening at the Abyss" 93). Wonder is paying attention.

Notes

1 The Dance Center of Columbia College presented *Moon Water* at the Harris Theater in January of 2010. Performers: Chou Chang-ning, Hou Tang-li, Huang Mei-ya, Ko Wan-chun, Lee Tzun-chun, Lin Hsun-fang, Liu Hui-ling, Shen Yi-wen, Su I-ping, Tsai Ming-yuan, Wang Chig-hao, Wen Ching-ching, Wong Lap-cheong, Yang I-chun, Yu Chien-hung. Choreographer: Lin Hwai-min. Set Design: Austin Wang. Lighting Design: Chang Tsan-tao.
2 See, for example, Zarrilli, "Senses and Silence in Actor Training and Performance" 61–3; Frost and Yarrow 130–1); S.A. Barker.
3 See also Goodall 33.
4 See also States, *Great Reckonings in Little Rooms* 32–7.
5 Reynolds here quotes Merleau-Ponty, *The Visible and the Invisible* 72/100.
6 Waldenfels addressed the difficulty of translating *fremd* into English in the preface to a collection of lectures he gave in 2004 (*The Question of the*

Other viii). After offering "the foreigner, the stranger, the strange, the alien, or simply the Other," he seems to settle on "the stranger" before admitting defeat: "It seems to me that the *Fremde* is one of those cultural keywords which, though not untranslatable, are ultimately over-determined through translation" (viii). Mark Gedney translates *fremd* as "the strange" in "Strangeness, Hospitality, and Enmity" (2011), while David J. Parent and Alexander Kozin and Tanja Stahler use "alien" in their translations of *Ordnung im Zwielicht* (1996) (*Order in the Twilight*) and *Grundmotive einer Phänomenologie des Fremden* (2006) (*Phenomenology of the Alien: Basic Concepts*). Among the possible over-determinations to follow any of these translations, I have chosen to foreground the connotations associated with "the strange" for three reasons. To begin with, in early twenty-first-century America the term "alien" broadly serves the discourse of populist anti-immigration politicians fulminating against "illegal aliens." Waldenfels explicitly treats the difficulty of intercultural encounters (*Phenomenology of the Alien* 70–84), but these can remain potent without associating him or myself with the barely concealed bigotry in anti-immigration rhetoric. The second reason is that Waldenfels notes that *fremd* concerns three different kinds of difference, each of which he translates into several languages ("Réponse à l'autre" 359). For the French, he sticks to *étranger* and *étrange*, and in English he equates "foreign," "alien," and "strange." And as noted above, he has himself chosen "the stranger" over "the alien." Lastly, Waldenfels nowhere hides his debt to Merleau-Ponty, and the latter gave a significant weight to *l'étrange*, as I will show below. All citations from Waldenfels will include the translator's choice of word; when the cited text is in French this will be mine.

7 This and all other citations from "Réponse à l'autre" are my translation.

8 Waldenfels places this quotation from Merleau-Ponty at page 101 of *Le visible et l'invisible* but I have not found it there in any of the English or the French editions.

9 See also Waldenfels, *Phenomenology of the Alien* 26.

10 The term "affective relief" is Husserl's (*Analyses Concerning Passive and Active Synthesis* 216).

11 Original emphasis.

12 This is Barba's word to describe the virtuosic body (Barba and Savarese 8).

13 The production I attended was at the Museum of Contemporary Art Chicago in March of 2007. Performers: Kristy Ayre, Antony Hamilton, Martin Hansen, Jo Lloyd, Lee Serle, and Adam Wheeler. Choreographer: Gideon Obarzanek.

14 Presented in Chicago at the Viaduct Theater in 2005. Direction: Ellie Heyman. The 2013 Broadway revival featured Amanda Plummer and Brad Dourif, two actors who have made careers out of playing eccentrics. Indeed, the *New York Times* played up the actors' history of playing "lunatics" and called the play "demented" (Brantley, "Brother, Can You Spare My Sanity?").

15 Presented in 2009 at Chicago's Hamlin Park Fieldhouse. Performers: Peter Carpenter, Lisa Gonzales, Suzy Grant, Atalee Judy, and Donnell Williams. Direction and Choreography: Peter Carpenter.

16 Barba and Savarese 92, figures 59–61.

17 On difference in the reversibility theory, see Chapter 2. Rosalyn Diprose writes in detail about Butler's troubled engagement with Merleau-Ponty, and although she does not explicitly address Irigaray's work, Diprose's entire book can be understood as a rebuttal of Irigaray's claim that Merleau-Ponty's *oeuvre* suffers from ocularcentrism (Diprose 66–70, 202 n.16, 203 n.4).

18 Translation by Talia Walsh ("The Developing Body" 50).

19 In *Black Skin, White Masks*, Frantz Fanon addresses how an ability is conditioned by racial histories that narrow possibilities for bodies read, and felt, as black. Detailing his alienated awkwardness reaching for a cigarette at a table in the company of white bodies, he unveils the ways in which his body, not simply recognized as black but as black in a specific place and era, affects his movements in ways that separate him from other bodies (111; qtd in Ahmed 109).

20 My translation. The original French reads: "Jouer c'est se placer pour un moment dans une situation imaginaire, c'est se plaire à changer de 'milieu'" (*Phénoménologie* 168–9).

Chapter 5

The ground of ethical failure

A refusal

I had walked out at intermissions but I had never actually turned my back on a performance and certainly had never turned my back on student work. Nine students and I had waited in the Bunge Studio at Beloit College while five other students left the room to prepare a performance they had worked on over the past two weeks. The prompt I had given was for each of them to create and administer a questionnaire and to then use that material as the basis for a performance. After several minutes, one of the students reappeared wearing all black and silently summoned us to follow her. We left and proceeded down a long hallway, past a set of doors, and into a carpeted stairwell that provided access to the backstage of the 300-seat Neese Theatre. Another guide appeared above us and we followed him up and up the stairs, past the lobby level, and up to the level housing the lighting and audio booths, as well as overflow costume storage. The lights were mostly low. Doors were slammed behind us. The guides occasionally barked orders at us. The sense of menace was both overplayed and unavoidable, at least to someone with my fear of heights and mild claustrophobia. We arrived at a door. A guide pounded on it and another guide opened it. She instructed us to descend the stairs behind her. The stairwell was concrete, lighted, and the well it circumscribed was bordered in glass. As we made our way down, the "guides" yelled into the atrium and slowly the figure of a man, naked, covered in dirt, rustled at the bottom of the well. We arrived at the bottom landing, a cramped concrete area with two closed doors to the side and behind us and the glass well bottom in front of us. The guide above announced the man's crimes against a government whose agents we were given to understand these guides represented. Another guide materialized behind us shoving the man's wife into the landing with us. She and her husband howled for each other before she was pulled through a door that closed behind them. The remaining guide standing with us commanded us to look at the prisoner as he was executed. That was when I turned my back. I heard what I later gathered was a bag of leaves and dirt emptied from above onto the man, who collapsed under the material.

I had initially started to obey the guide and turn. I had followed her so far, and when you're told to do something in a theatre, you tend to do it. I realized that I was agreeing to play a part in a fiction that I did not want. I was not being spoken to as the member of a theatre audience, invited to watch a performance. This performance operated by slotting us into a fictional world in which a guard was ordering us to be complicit in the death of this prisoner. As an audience member, I was willing to play along with the performance. As an unwilling cast member in a drama, I felt revulsion at the situation. As the teacher, I wanted to see how the students staged the death. I was also paying attention to the other students in the audience. None of them had been to a promenade performance of this kind before, and many of them appeared shaken. And so I turned my back from the prisoner in an attempt to change the role the performance had given me. I tried to perform for the students that they didn't have to watch; that they had a choice; that their attending to the event could be resisted; that, as attendants, they had agency, if only the agency to turn away. I wasn't sure if I was being cowardly or if I was taking too much room in the performance, or if I was simply following a clouded aesthetic impulse driven by the physical arrangement of our bodies in the enclosed area.

The guide standing with us led us through the dressing room area of the theatre, up a flight of stairs, down the original hallway, and, after depositing us in the studio, she shut the door behind her, signaling the end of the performance and the beginning of the post-performance debriefing.[1]

We had much to discuss. Although they all expressed deep appreciation for the work of their classmates, many of the students had indeed felt intense emotional distress. We spoke about the process of making the piece and what the performing group's questionnaire had addressed. We spoke about how some of the students had felt the greatest discomfort when they were compelled to watch the degradation of the prisoner. They had sensed, as I had, that this moment demanded acquiescence with the character's treatment. The performers were pleased to affirm that this had been one of their concerns—how the spectacle of bodies tortured by the violence of the United States military created a fraught connection between those bodies and their witnesses. This led us to consider the possibility that not seeing an event might be the most ethical response to it.

The conversation began to turn on the idea that the ethics of a performance—its adherence to a set of conclusions about what is good and bad—resided not only in the content of the performance but also in the *way* in which its attendants perceived it. We grappled with the idea that the performance demonstrated the horror of state violence in a way that raised questions about the demonstration itself. A divide appeared between the ethics of the performance and the ethics of attending to the performance: a performance might make an ethical claim—confining other people is bad— in a way that was itself unethical, for example by confining the experience of audience members in a space that did not examine so much as demand complicity in violence. Our role as witnesses to represented violence cast doubt on the ethics of making violence perceptible. For one thing, if I am an expression of what I perceive, then attending to violence means that I express it, that I am essential to its continued passage in the world. I imagine this was the source of more than one student's—and my own—concern. Further, and for another thing, by expressing this violence I risk the possibility of amplifying it more than the experience of the person who endured it. It may be that in allowing myself to attend to violence or its representation I do not carry forward a warning or a testimonial but instead legitimate and perpetuate it.

"No response is appropriate"

Problematic dynamics of attending have certainly played out on much larger stages. The furor surrounding Brett Bailey and Third World Bunfight's *Exhibit B* (2010–) offers a familiar thicket of contesting claims and presumptions concerning the nature of attending and of attending to representations of violence.[2] Heightening the stakes considerably, the installation and the reactions to it explicitly linked the act of attending to contemporary racialized violence. Through meticulously researched and reconstructed tableaux, *Exhibit B* recreates—perhaps too closely—the "human zoos" of the nineteenth and twentieth centuries in which Africans were displayed before their colonizers in Europe. In each installation a local black performer or two stood, sat, or lay down in scenes depicting a genealogy between colonial violence and the contemporary treatment of African immigrants by Western European governments. In one of the most commonly repeated images from the performance, a woman sits on a bed naked from the waist up with her back to the attendants and with a manacle and chain around her neck. The caption of the tableau in the installation relates the story of African women kept in sexual slavery by a German colonial officer in 1906 Namibia. The performer stares at attendants through a mirror on the wall she faces. In another, a man sits alone in a row of airplane seats, his mouth covered in duct tape, his wrists bound to the armrests, and his legs and ankles tied together; two pairs of shoes rest before the empty seats next to him. The caption relates the stories of 14 asylum seekers such as Samira Adamu and Aamir Ageeb who were killed resisting their enforced return to the countries from which they had fled to Europe between 1991 and 2010. Each installation bore a similar caption describing the scene depicted and listing the "materials" used in the display. The installation ends with a room in which attendants are invited to record their experiences. These are placed alongside the reflections of the performers, each of whom has provided accounts of their daily confrontations with local institutionalized racism.

I did not attend the installation. No one in London did, either. After acclaimed and protested performances at festivals in Avignon, Berlin,

Grahamstown, Brussels, and Edinburgh, *Exhibit B* was to be presented by the Barbican in London in September of 2014. Following protests and an online petition signed by 23,000 people who had never attended the performance, it was canceled the night of its premiere and never opened in London. When the production reached Paris later in the year, it was met with protests in which blood was shed by police corralling protestors, five of whom smashed the glass doors to the venue before being intercepted by security.

Nonetheless, anyone can still gain access to what fueled the protests. Because it was not the show that offended—almost no one protesting had attended any of its numerous installations across Western Europe—but *images* of the show that riled its opponents. The images are silent, just like the performers.[3] At first glance, the images present passive black bodies enduring oppressive *situations* without anyone visibly enforcing the situation. Nothing can be seen to keep the live bodies in place, and this presumably contributes to the sense that the exhibit reifies the powerlessness of black bodies and the passivity of oppressed black subjects. Whatever moral benefit might be assigned to the installation would presumably have to rest—if the images of it circulating online and in print fairly depicted the event—on the continued objectification of black bodies. As non-attendant Dr. Kehinde Andrews put it in his call to boycott, published in the *Guardian*'s "Comment is Free" blog, "Exhibit B is offensive because it perpetuates the objectification of the black body that is a standard trope of society."

The claim of objectification stems in part from the fact that these images fail to include any representations of the white bodies inflicting the violence. Their absence—and that of the director, who is, as virtually every critic noted, white—as much as the presence of the silent black bodies, spurred outrage and opposition. John Mullen, a professor at l'Université Paris Est and organizer of an unsuccessful petition to block the Paris performances, argued: "It shows a lie, really. It shows the victims without the perpetrators. The black victims are silent, immobile and fetishized, while the colonialists are absent" (qtd in Carvajal). And Sara Myers, who never attended the performance and who spearheaded the online petition that succeeded in canceling the show in London, wrote that it would be "more striking and send a clearer message" to include white bodies. Insisting that Bailey was a racist, Myers did not clarify if she was referring to the publicity images or the performance, nor did she clarify what this message would be or why it would be clearer. The point can still be made that without the representation of the agents of violence these images—and perhaps the installation they picture—freeze their subjects not simply as victims, but as inevitably accepting their role. Not only do the images and the installation fail to depict the scenes of resistance that were part of overthrowing these regimes of colonial violence, the Africans depicted in them remain, in images online, still and accepting.

The publicity images also risk freezing the event in the past. Indeed, Myers explains: "I want my children to grow up in a world where the barbaric things that happened to their ancestors are a thing of the past." It is not clear if Myers is opposed to contemporary representations of historical violence or if she wishes to portray racial violence of this sort as a thing of the past. The petition does suggest, as do most advocates of suppressing art, that *Exhibit B*—or, more precisely in this case, the publicity images of it— has a dangerous power, though it is not clear whether this power is entirely detrimental: "the colonialism this piece purports to expose does nothing more than reinforce how effective it was and remains as a caging instrument of white supremacists" (Myers).

Beyond the absence of the contemporary immigration officers or colonial officials, the images lack an element that was very much present during the performance. Each installation's plaque listed among others the same two materials: the living performers and the attendants. Unlike the image on the cover of this book, none of the publicity photos for the 2014 tour included depictions of the attendants.[4] This fact can certainly be marshaled against the show: what does it say about *Exhibit B* that its publicists felt the best way to advertise it visually would be to use images that, by their removal of the active engagement between attendants and performers, positioned its performers as passively complicit in the violence they were representing?[5] This could be seized upon to indict the production for, in Andrews' words, "arrang[ing] an interchangeable set of black bodies" (Andrews and Odunlami).

Andrews happens to have been addressing one of the performers (Stella Odunlami) and offers uncomfortable evidence that *he* was the one who failed to see the particularity of each performer. As a non-attendant, he might not have known about the presentation of performer experiences in the last room. This element of the production might then frame the engagement of local performers as a mindful practice of attending to the specific histories of the performance location and the particular kinds of institutionalized racism faced in each city. Further, the production was typically sited in historically significant locations. For example, in Brussels *Exhibit B* occupied a church in which undocumented immigrants had once sought shelter.[6] For Bailey's part, he acknowledged how the images were offensive and publicly stated that he wished they had never been used to begin with (qtd in Ebony).

From the accounts of performers and attendants, the interactions between them that were missing from the publicity images constituted the real point and the real power of *Exhibit B*. By confronting the mobile, living gaze of the subjects in the "human zoo," attendants had the opportunity to explicitly place themselves in the schema of continuing racial violence. For Lyn Gardner, "the silent, unmoving figures at the centre of each one of the installations makes us confront how we look, where we look and what we are prepared to see."

Critics such as Andrews, Mullen, and Myers attacking the *images* of the show rather than the performance miss this defining dynamic of the piece. Mullen charged that the installation did not include "the perpetrators," but this ignores the possibility that "the perpetrators" are very much present in *Exhibit B*—as the attendants. Barend Blom describes the shock of receiving the gaze of the performers and then the second shock when he recognizes that he has "start[ed] behaving as in any museum." Faced with the dawning realization that his attention constantly teeters on the edge of a violently objectifying gaze, he fears that "no response is appropriate" (84–5).

French historian Pascal Blanchard observes that the experience of the roughly 35,000 Africans displayed in human zoos before 1.5 million Europeans between 1810 and 1940 is not widely known. Ignorance of these practices and their contemporary manifestations in effect supports the ongoing projects of colonialism and policing black bodies. All the same, and without acknowledging this specific history, critics such as Myers noted that black Africans and their descendants hardly needed to go to an installation to understand their place inside regimes of European racist violence. As the performers' written testimony affirmed, the experience of local black people already carried the weight of colonial history and its contemporary expressions in government brutality. Although the performance need not have been revelatory in order to function as a reflection on contemporary racism, *Exhibit B* had far less "news" for Africans living in Europe than it did for white attendants. This point was made repeatedly against the installation, which was framed as exclusively serving the needs of white audiences.

Exclusively served or not, those needs make a stark appearance in one performer's account of her experience in the production. Berthe Tanwo Njole, also company manager for *Exhibit B*, performed in Poland as Sara Baartman ("the Hottentot Venus," who is perhaps the most recognized example of the practice of human zoos). A group of men had found each other in the exhibit, and when they came across her they laughed and made comments about her body. Afterwards, each of them returned one by one to apologize to her (qtd in O'Mahony). Tiffany Jenkins, the author of *Contesting Human Remains in Museum Collections: The Crisis of Cultural Authority* (2011), writes of *Exhibit B* that

> the work is about our engagement. The black performers look us in the eye as we look up at them on the pedestals and, in one case, in a cage. That the actors look you in the eye is designed to make you feel uncomfortable, and most critics have described this interaction as a devastating experience—which it is.
>
> ("Exhibit B: A Guilty Pleasure")

Blanchard claims in an interview that the actors "fix the spectators with an unpleasant stare which precisely retranslates the horror of these zoos." Unlike the majority of spectators, the actors know about the history of human zoos and about their continued existence in Paris until 1937. The actors are "completely aware, and their contempt in this respect is intolerable. And by the way, they are the ones we ought to listen to on this subject."[7] The actors from the Edinburgh production could indeed be heard from. They released a statement in support of the London performance, ardently defending the work of using their embodied attention to engage the attendants:

> In that moment when our eyes meet, we cease to be objectified and become human. Some people literally jump back. Some break into tears; others immediately look away. Others still gaze deeper as their eyes well up [...] They cry because they didn't know what was done. They cry because they realise how it is still being done. They cry because they realise that the past impacts the present. They cry because they experienced this personally. They cry because they didn't. Reading the pages and pages of comments from the audience left at the end of the exhibit attests to this, but we don't need to read that. We see it in their eyes.
>
> (Nyirenda et al.)

A fully fleshed out debate over *Exhibit B* would include a great deal more than can be offered here. It would require an examination of the instances and the failures of dialogue between cultural institutions and the publics they purport to serve, a consideration of the role police play in securing freedom of expression for protestors and artists, and an analysis of the historical traditions of European anthropology and ethnography and their relationship to human zoos and the theatrical form of tableaux vivants. And it would also have to include the reflections and provocations of the installation's director Brett Bailey. His comments before and after the London and Paris protests depict an anguished artist but do not reveal an overly scrupulous interrogation of his work and his role in it.[8]

The point of delving into *Exhibit B* here is to demonstrate the difficulty of assigning a simple "good" to attention. It might seem at first blush that bearing witness to the continuation of colonial violence in the policing methods of contemporary Europe is commendable. According to Andrews, however, "If you pay to see it you are colluding in the worst kind of racial abuse" ("Exhibit B").

Like most censors, Andrews is convinced of his own capacity to predict precisely both the intention of the artist and the inevitable reaction of the public. His critique runs very close to demands that women cover up in public so as not to "provoke" straight men. The desire of cultural guardians to determine what gets attention and what does not presumes that artworks exist outside of their perception by others and so can impress upon their publics meanings that are relatively stable and identifiable—or at least identifiable by their critics. If such presumptions seem unrealistic, it bears remembering that they spring from the conviction that performance *matters*. Censors are worth thinking about because they take as seriously as anyone that the relationship initiated by attending to a work of art will continue to determine or influence the behavior and responsibilities of the attendants afterwards.

Further, Andrews insists that bearing witness to violence is not the same thing as bearing witness *against* it. After foregoing the idea that an artwork can *only* be attended to in the way its artist (or its critic) intends, there remains an encounter with more than one outcome. Rancière would certainly have some cutting remarks about the moralizing of *Exhibit B* and its assumption of a straight line between representing horror and doing something about it. Attending to a representation of violence does not automatically ensure that I oppose it. Witnessing violence or degradation might in fact require my participation in it, and this was clearly a, if not the chief, concern of many opposed to *Exhibit B*.

A curious split takes place here, however. Can an artwork be said to require the objectification of its performers? Is it the performance that is degrading or the way of attending to it? If *Exhibit B* is as problematic as its critics contend, doesn't their censure belong to the attendants (whose responses they imagine) rather than the performance-makers? The very fact that a rejection of the work was possible suggests that the proper place for concern lies with the attendants, not the performance. *They* are the ones making the objectionable meaning, they are the ones perceiving the untrue thing. The most vociferous critics did not attend the work in part because they insisted there was only one way the work could operate on its attendants. However, their position depended on the possibility of *attending differently* to the work. If I can reject the objectification of *Exhibit B*, then perhaps what I object to is not the performance but a way of attending to it. This pertains as much to provocative twenty-first-century art as to, for example, the "comic" scenes of sexual threat in *Tartuffe*. Under what conditions can someone enjoy these scenes without sharing complicity for the violence in them that the *actress* endures?[9]

It seems certain that a primary condition would be the belief that the performers have taken up their roles with the kind of awareness Blanchard found in conversation with those involved with *Exhibit B* in Paris. It is a commonplace that actors have no ethical agency because they are always speaking someone else's lines or following someone else's direction. But of course even after they decide *if* they will do this—actors can and have rejected roles—*how* they do this matters a great deal. In "Resisting the 'Organic': A Feminist Actor's Approach," Lauren Love describes how actors can make choices—within the confines of the text—that insist on the agency of a character and an actor under any circumstances. In her most detailed example, concerning her portrayal of Gwendolyn in *The Importance of Being Earnest*, Love describes conventional staging choices that diminished the power and subjecthood of her character. She met these with a series of adjustments to the locus of her attention, the posture of her body, the direction and rhythm of her movement, and the kinds of goals sought by her character. All of these she undertook in order to both elaborate on Wilde's text and to prevent the character(ization) of Gwendolyn from existing solely for the benefit of her paramour (Love 283–9). Nonetheless, it remains possible for an attendant to this performance to attribute these choices to the director or the script or any other influence. Whatever meaning Love's tactics might have for the production, how they make meaning depends on how attendants approach her work as an actor. They can place her anywhere along a continuum from puppet of the director and playwright to active and engaged agent of her own expression.

Without explicitly endorsing—yet—the presumption embedded here that agency lies at the heart of ethics, if I consider that performers are operating under physical or ideological compulsion the qualities of attention shift. The scale of coercion might begin with the imagined economic imperative to "make it" in the performance industry by submitting oneself to whatever conditions will achieve fame and fortune. Participation in a rigged system might be used to excuse taking part in a production but it can also be used to condemn it. The charge of complicity was certainly lobbed at the performers in *Exhibit B*, who were—despite their explicit arguments demonstrating the contrary—painted as "selling out" in order to move up.[10] The question of complicity and coercion can certainly proceed further, and when it reaches a limit case the ethics of attending gain even sharper focus.

Writing about captive African Americans posing for daguerreotypes in 1850, Harvey Young notes that the subjects were ordered into poses that would serve the work of the Harvard professor who commissioned them (26–50). Typically pictured in profile and frontal positions, subjects Alfred, Delia, Drana, Fassena, Jack, Jem, and Renty sat and stood in various stages of undress but in near total stillness for over a minute. Young addresses the multiple temporalities of photographs, how they not only serve as an indexical representation of the past, but also as a projection towards a future observer. Young considers in this light the various interpretations of the forward gaze depicted in some of these images. Some critics locate agency and a measure of control in the fixed gaze of the subjects. Alan Trachtenberg suggests that the subjects "perform" for the camera, and that within the role of "specimen" the critic might find a defiant gaze, a look "back" at the daguerreotypist Joseph T. Zealy. After all, as Young adds, "blacks, throughout the era of captivity and into the post-emancipation years, could be punished or killed for looking a white person in the eyes" (47).[11] Young, nodding to Cherise Smith, nonetheless suggests that the conditions of captivity and the actual production of the daguerreotypes make the defiant gaze an unlikely conclusion (35).[12] For this reason, he concludes that "the reproduction and re-presentation of [Delia's] image, continue[s] to objectify her," and that "the hypervisibility of Delia's image promotes her objectification" (H. Young 38). As such, Young chooses not to represent any of the images of her or Drana. However, and owning up to his vulnerability to the charges he has just made, Young does offer two reproductions of Renty (217 n.27).

Writing after Young and taking up his analysis of the temporal shifts of photography, Rebecca Schneider considers another example of "performing" under duress in *Performing Remains* (2011). Reflecting on the photographs of prisoner abuse at the American detention center Abu Ghraib in Iraq, Schneider notes that the images owe their power not only to what they contain but also to their ability to circulate. Schneider writes that, for the prisoners, the taking of the images was meant to produce a "shame that will occur (again and again) as a result of the image's circulation. The shame is meant to take place not only *in* the digital image but *as* the image; that is, as the image in a future circulation" (*Performing Remains* 162).[13] Each time someone looks at them, the abuse of the prisoners continues. The positions into which the prisoners were forced were degrading, but the promise to circulate these images constituted, constitutes, the next act to the torture. The posing and taking of photographs said to the prisoners, "more people will see you this way." In other words, every time I look at a photograph of the torture at Abu Ghraib, there is a sense in which I inevitably enact the degradation of the prisoners through my attention.

This returns to the position of those that closed down *Exhibit B* in London: the work exists outside me to the extent that it determines entirely how I attend to it, if not how I take action afterwards. To face the artwork is to submit to its proposed way of being attended to. The challenge posed in this particular case becomes: how am I to bear witness to the cruelty of those American soldiers in that prison, the American political system that produced it, the history of the site that housed it, and the experiences of the men who endured it? And what of the situations large and small contributing to the experiences of Alfred, Delia, Drana, Fassena, Jack, Jem, and Renty? To what am I attending—an idea, a movement, a shape, a person? Schneider, after Toni Morrison, proposes that "the action we take in response is 'in our hands'" (*Performing Remains* 168). But might it still be impossible for me to face these images without degrading the people pictured in them? What would it mean for me to attend to these people ethically? And might my doing so involve turning my back on the images and enactments of their suffering?

Witness and the loving eye

As these troubling cases can attest, to witness invokes the location of perception—a witness must have been *there*—while also suggesting how an event becomes an event through its having been witnessed. In these senses witnessing aligns with attending. Additionally, witnessing has a juridical coloring—adding "a" in front of "witness" suggests a crime. To witness someone or something is to have been present when something went wrong. For Kelly Oliver the question of witnessing goes yet further, beyond the law, to directly address the emergence of subjects, the coming into being of someone whose expression of the world's meaning matters both to him or her and to others. For this reason, Oliver introduces a formal ethical character to witnessing related to its role in subject formation as well as its juridical and historical uses. She begins with the explicit goal of understanding subjectivity from "the position of those othered in dominant culture" (Oliver, *Witnessing* 6). From here she pursues an understanding of witnessing that links its radical inclusion to its necessity for subjecthood.

Oliver offers the concept of witness as an alternative to the drive for recognition. As she argues in *Subjectivity without Subjects* (1998) and *Witnessing* (2001), this drive does not produce inclusion in an ethical community so much as it characterizes attempts by oppressed groups to gain traction within political systems that produce inequality. So long as survivors of violence seek visibility from a (juridical, political, social, discursive) system that not only allows but also depends on that violence, they remain trapped within that system as objects. For Oliver, the common usage of recognition derives from a subject–object dichotomy inherently characterized by closure and antagonism. To suggest that someone can exist outside of recognition is to posit both a "unified, self-contained" being capable of granting recognition as well as a "pathology of oppression" that accepts a violent break between people (Oliver, *Witnessing* 2, 3).[14] In a dynamic hearkening to the dialectical struggles outlined by Hegel, subjects come into being through contests with each other—I do not "have" a sense of myself to begin with but must wrest it from others.[15] While these schemas can account for my responsibility to other people, they do not merely describe oppression and objectification, they require it (Oliver, *Witnessing* 5–7). In order to designate recognition as the entryway to subjectivity, one has to first establish an other that is objectified and initially excluded. This exclusion also follows the logical position that ethics first requires the recognition that someone belongs within the orbit of ethical behavior. If I either need or demand recognition in order to achieve subjectivity or inclusion in an ethical community, I have found myself, to begin with, in a system of oppression.

As Oliver notes, while traumatic exclusions and antagonistic contests might be "effective in *explaining* the existence of war and oppression, if *normalized* it makes it impossible to imagine peaceful compassionate relations with others" (*Witnessing* 7). Oliver's argument develops from her observation that within the intersubjectivity installed in the pattern of recognition and exclusion can be found the ability to address another as well as respond to another. *This*, rather than neo-Hegelian conflict, constitutes the root of subjectivity. In order to separate address-ability and response-ability from their familiar placement in dynamics of oppression,

Oliver invests them with the work and responsibility and privilege of the witness. I am a witness insofar as I address others with what I have experienced; I am a witness *to*—to others and events. To witness is to bring an experience or event to others. I am also a witness insofar as I receive the experiences of others; I am a witness *of*—I respond to the offer of another's experience. To witness is to respond to and to address another, similar to the way that attending requires a call to attention and an imaginative response to that call.

Subjectivity remains *inter*subjective, and my awareness of myself in the world still requires action from others. To exist in the world is to have an exchange with the world. Echoing Merleau-Ponty—and his critics—Oliver reaffirms the intercorporeality of experience: by existing bodily I need something from others and they from me. But instead of providing recognition, which inserts me into a set of standards and roles that preexist me and may indeed function to actively weaken my social and physical abilities, others offer a response to my address to them. Their act of witnessing affirms my own and I emerge as someone capable of addressing others. At the very same time, these acts of responding embody their own coming into subjecthood. I continue to exist as an appeal to others, but I also exist as the response to them.

Not just any response, however. Only those responses that offer continued responses from oneself and from others can be considered part of witnessing. Responses that limit the response-ability of others are considered "false witness."[16] The kind of response Oliver demands of witnessing, then, goes beyond a simple reaction or answer. A "response" operates as a kind of affirmation of another's process of witness. It acknowledges that others can only come into being as subjects through their ability to address and respond (affirmatively) to others (as witnesses themselves). Not only does Oliver find that "that which precludes a response destroys subjectivity and thereby humanity," so too does the suppression of the ability to address another: "the subject is the result of a response to an address from another and the possibility of addressing itself to another" (*Witnessing* 90, 105). The ethical determination here depends on the advancement of witnessing and coming into subjecthood. Subjecthood can only be had through assisting others coming into subjecthood, and this work—witnessing—constitutes the central responsibility of each subject.

> Subjectivity is responsibility: it is the ability to respond and to be responded to [...] Reformulating Eva Kittay's analysis of relations of dependency, a subject who "refuses to support this bond absolves itself from its most fundamental obligation—its obligation to its founding possibility."
>
> (Oliver, *Witnessing* 91)[17]

Without a commitment to the embodied subjecthood of others through witnessing, my own subjecthood diminishes and I slide towards objectifying myself.

The act of witnessing *of* does not come from knowledge or authority. The one who receives witness is the one who does not know what the witness knows. I do not ask for confirmation of what I know in order to respond to another, and I do not ask for the delivery of facts that I can find otherwise; "not everything that is real is recognizable to us" (Oliver, *Witnessing* 106). Unlike the juridical witness, upon whom depends the establishment of a verifiable narrative, Oliver's witness testifies to something beyond the visible. Namely, "what the process of witnessing testifies to is not a state of facts but a commitment to the truth of subjectivity as address-ability and response-ability" (Oliver, *Witnessing* 143).

Throughout *Witnessing* Oliver turns to a scene described by Shoshana Felman and Dori Laub when a gathering of psychologists and historians watched videos of survivors of the Shoah (*Witnessing* 1–2, 85–6, 89–93, 136).[18] A woman who had been present at the Auschwitz uprising recalled that four chimneys had been blown up when, "in fact," only one had been. Given that her testimony could not be counted on to prove the facts of the uprising, historians felt it should be discounted entirely. One even went so far as to suggest that for her to grant importance to an event that did not change the course of the Final Solution proved that she was unreliable. The psychoanalysts, in comparison, argued that the historians improperly situated the testimony. Its importance lay not in its ability to coordinate with an emerging historical record, but in its revelation of the possibility of resistance (Oliver, *Witnessing* 1–2, 92, 136).

Oliver pulls two core principles of witnessing from this event, the first being that witnessing presents the impossible. To begin with, those that did not survive the Shoah cannot testify to it; they are its ultimate witnesses in the sense that their loss of life and the desecration of their bodies constituted the dominant action of the Shoah. The power of memorial speech and architecture comes from the ways they pull the impossible testimony of the murdered to new witnesses. Further, the Shoah, like all violence, rendered its targets objects. Oliver returns to the work of Felman and Laub, who describe the processes by which agents of the Shoah "annihilated the possibility of witness" not only through cruelty and violence, but also by refusing to refer to those they brutalized as "victims or people or even corpses," calling them instead "*figuren* (puppets) or *Schmattes* (rags)" (Oliver, *Witnessing* 89–90).[19] To survive these experiences does not in itself constitute a rejection of the objectification. For survivors of a violent objectification to address others, they must overcome the experience of being objectified—they cannot be objects while also emerging as subjects capable of witness. However, because an object cannot bear witness to its status as an object without transforming into a subject, the experience of violence will always be lost in its survivor's address to others. "It is impossible to bearing [sic] witness to becoming an object, since objects have nothing to say" (Oliver, *Witnessing* 99).[20]

Witnessing does not express an experience—it is a doing of the possibility of testimony. In a word, it is performative. It entangles the historically specific with the churn of present action in a repetition with difference (Oliver, *Witnessing* 105–6, 40–2). The experience of objectification "is not available for the witness or anyone else to access. Rather, the experience is constituted and reconstituted as such for the witness through testimony" (Oliver, *Witnessing* 143). Bearing impossible witness carries within it hope and transformation because what emerges in the doing of witnessing is the possibility of something better than the past. Similarly, witnessing reveals the tension between the necessity of witnessing an event and the impossibility of perceiving it in its entirety (Oliver, *Witnessing* 89). Not only can witnesses to the Shoah not address their own experiences of objectification to others, they cannot address the entire scope of the camps at the same time.

Although she does not explicitly appeal to Merleau-Ponty here, Oliver makes the same suggestion found at the core of his phenomenology of perception: as someone embodied by and in the world, I cannot perceive that world in its entirety. For Oliver, the work of witnessing "is not the finite task of comprehending [...] this is the infinite task of encountering" (*Witnessing* 87, 90). In the terms introduced in Chapter 2, witness transforms an experience of objectification into an experience that has sense, orientation, and the attention of others. An object might speak, but it has no sense—its meaning and direction are given to it. Witnesses embody the possibility of objecthood *and* subjecthood by collapsing pasts and presents in the actions of address and response. Witnessing one's own experience of violence embodies the never completed movement between object and subject that Merleau-Ponty considered foundational to bodily experience. However, while Oliver seeks to complete the transformation from objectification into subjecthood, Merleau-Ponty describes a movement that continues between two unreachable poles. In this world of perception I am never completely subject *or* object and there is no seeking either without harm to others. As someone participating in the world of perception, I am at all times capable of being seen, touched, heard, smelled, and tasted like an object. And I can also perceive these actions as my expression of others I see, touch, hear, smell, and taste.

The second principle that Oliver finds in the contested scene of witnessing described by Felman and Laub is that *everyone* must be witness/ed. If everyone depends on witnessing—on address-ability and response-ability—and if these are only possible through my affirmation of their doing by others, everyone requires witness; everyone requires it if they are to become subjects. The dual actions of witnessing ensure that I not only require address-ability, so does everyone else I encounter. They require it *by me and in order for me to remain a subject.* Such would seem to have been the case as described by the Edinburgh performers in *Exhibit B*: "In that moment when our eyes meet, we cease to be objectified and become human." Having set themselves up in the *role* of objects, the performers look *back*, provide their own witness; the attendants witness this in turn and attendant and performer emerge as subjects. It was not enough for the attendants to take in the scenes—the scenes took in the attendants. In this case it is difficult to say if it is the performers or the characters they portray who embody subjecthood in this encounter. The process described by Oliver would, all the same, locate either possibility in the dual witnessing of performer and attendant.

Witnessing is radically egalitarian in this way—every subject requires it and is obligated by it. Oliver aligns this obligation with bell hooks's commitment to love as care for others. For hooks, self-interest populates experience with blind spots where others may suffer and in which domination thrives. Love takes me to these blind spots and allows me to see beyond them (Oliver, *Witnessing* 218). Oliver takes up this call and claims that it is possible to "move beyond our blind spots" through a rigorous commitment to witnessing. The "loving eye is a critical eye in that it demands to see what cannot be seen," always moving beyond what is closest and known (Oliver, *Witnessing* 218, 219).[21] Once vision becomes a kind of circulation instead of distant domination, connections to others take precedence over a supposed gap that must be conquered. That which cannot be recognized or even seen at all can still be witnessed, responded to as an element of someone else's address to me. The goal is not to identify or comprehend, but to witness "the unseen in visions, the unsaid in language" in order to "reconstruct our relationships by imagining ourselves together" (Oliver, *Witnessing* 223).

The face of obligation

Witnessing and attending both address the intersubjective nature of being, and they both concern responses to the impenetrable depths of experience. They take root in different ground, however, and understanding their differences will further clarify the ethical import of attention. In particular, an ethics of witnessing requires obligations, it requires radical inclusion, and it begins as a defensive action; none of these can be said of a phenomenological ethics that remains committed to embodied experience.

Oliver's claim that, "without obligation, we do not have ethics"(*Witnessing* 57) eventually traces a path to Emmanuel Lévinas, the go-to philosopher of responsibility and compulsion.[22] Asbjørn Aarnes notes that the introduction of compulsion into ethics marked a break with "traditional humanism" that regarded the active, thinking agent as the highest expression of human dignity. Kant's autonomous thinker certainly offered this archetype. Aarnes tracks how Lévinas proposed an alternative:

what makes a man a human being is not what he does, but what happens to him. The *ego* has moved into the case of the sufferer, the accusative, *ego patiens*, where the *ego* has become the summoned, the prosecuted, the accused.

(61)

For Lévinas, the formative experience of being arrived through a face-to-face encounter with the Other. In this model, the Other's face expresses all that cannot be known and has not been experienced by the self, introducing an irreducible alterity. It is not a physical encounter and it is not something experienced. Rather, it forms the basis for all actions in the world of experience. Adjusting to this encounter with an incomprehensible Other and the nature of one's obligations to it formed the ongoing theme for much of Lévinas's work.[23] For Lévinas, the subject submits itself to a becoming achieved solely through responsibility to the Other. This responsibility is not founded on choice, but on an obligation that precedes all discursive, historical, and ontic contingency (Lévinas, *Otherwise than Being* 148). By establishing compulsion in the ethical encounter (going so far as to describe subjectivity as "persecution and martyrdom"), Lévinas not only removes agency from responsibility, he also excludes the ability to determine *to whom* I am obligated as a matter of ethics (*Otherwise than Being* 146–86).[24] Nicholas Ridout characterizes the result as "an ethics without content" because it is not only incapable of but also uninterested in distinguishing between faces (*Stage Fright* 30).[25] Making these distinctions is ultimately possible, but involves contingencies that may result in an "inversion" of the "primary" relationship, and they are a distortion brought about by the move into sociality (Lévinas, *Ethics and Infinity* 89). Lévinas ultimately turns to a supreme being as the source and analogue of responsibility to others, and Oliver gingerly suggests "taking a step away from Lévinas and leaving behind some of his religious language" in order to posit that our response to others "is obligated by our very subjectivity" (*Witnessing* 183).

Whether appealing to a supreme being or the constitution of subjectivities, this approach requires a defensive posture. It takes on a negative character in the sense of seeking to prevent something from happening. Refusing an ethics of abjection, Oliver nonetheless begins from the position of those excluded by dominant cultures. She explicitly aims to avoid objectification and to account for those left voiceless/unrecognized. In part, this makes her argument vulnerable to the is/ought fallacy—she describes the importance of witnessing to subjectivity but does not establish why everyone *ought* to be subjects. Further, she prioritizes one of the presuppositions of the "ethics of human rights" identified by Alain Badiou: "Evil is that from which the Good is derived, not the other way around" (9). This assertion follows from the understanding that the human subject is passive and suffering as well as capable of identifying and deciding to resist that suffering. This in turn produces an ethics that "defines man *as a victim*," or, more precisely, "man is *the being who is capable of recognizing himself as a victim*" (Badiou 10). Badiou draws a bold line from this conviction to the brutality of quote–unquote humanitarian interventions that hide both contempt for the supposed victims in need as well as the assumed superiority of those capable of offering aid.

Whatever might be made of Badiou's conclusions, he aptly describes the defensive nature of an ethics that begins from the position of a suffering subject. An ethics of aversion reflexively focuses on the negative in order to move away from it. It need not move towards foreign expeditionary forces "exporting" democracy abroad, but there is also no reason it wouldn't. Starting from victimhood—as Oliver does consistently—also risks encircling ethics in self-interest (Badiou 10).[26] Certainly Oliver's encouragement to bear witness *to* so that *I* can become a subject bears the imprint of this paradox. When a subject's "most fundamental obligation" turns out to be "its obligation to its founding possibility," then that subject will come to being in the grip of self-interest. This love recommended by witnessing winds up looking a lot like self-love. My obligations are given to me and are necessary for me to come into being as a "me" at all.

The appearance of obligation might not mitigate the self-interest of these ethics, but it does provide a link between the Aristotelian and Kantian traditions of ethics. For Oliver claims that whatever enables subjecthood—witnessing—must be pursued, and it must be pursued without regard for proximity or recognition. It must be pursued from love, which is an arresting conclusion: obligatory love. In its pursuit of what most fully expresses each being's subjectivity, Oliver's ethics echo Aristotle's virtue ethics; in its vision of a logical conclusion that applies to all beings capable of ethical thought—to all subjects—Oliver's ethics echo Kant's categorical imperative. All three of them express the same underlying conviction: ethics must be impartial. Everything and everyone is or will be included. All actions should follow categorical imperatives established beyond the contingencies of lived experience, and/or all things should pursue the embodiment of their true nature. The unethical is the partial, the incomplete. Anything that falls short is unethical because it will fail to allow subjects their subjectivity and fail to allow them their place among those included by categorical imperatives.

Although Oliver insists that "subjectivity itself [...] should not be conceived as a rigid binarism" (*Witnessing* 105), her debt to Lévinas and her model of witnessing that invokes pairs of witnesses does seem to suggest as much. There is dualism at the heart of Oliver's description of witnessing and it establishes its resulting ethics as bi-directional. Witnessing might require vigilant repetition and its effects can help establish a community, but it occurs, or first occurs, between two subjects, just like the face-to-face encounter (Oliver, *Witnessing* 143, 223). Even without the subject–object pair, Oliver maintains a binary—rigid or not—in the subject–subject relationship. Waldenfels—among others—notes: "Mere reversals never take us very far because they remain tied to that which they reverse" (*Phenomenology of the Alien* 36).

Oliver's witnessing binary produces other pairs, including these possibilities: that ethical obligation stems from a primordial pair, and that the pair stems from a primordial ethical obligation. In Rancière's critique of "the ethical turn," he notes that the excluded in politics can operate as a "conflictual actor" who precipitates the dissensus characterizing a robust political community. "But in the ethical community, this supplement is no longer supposed to arise, since everyone is included. As a result, there is no status for the excluded in the structuration of the community" (Rancière, "The Ethical Turn" 189). Including everyone requires a model of ethical behavior that originates and always ends in the pair. At the same time, the pair generates obligation—for if the two can only emerge through work done together, then each is bound to that work and must attend to it.

The pair, even free from a master–slave dialectic or a theory of vision as appropriation, might produce its enveloping obligation from an aversion to the violence of objectification. Oliver begins and ends with her interest in accounting for the coming into subjectivity of those living in conditions of oppression. Love can spare me and others—*must* spare us—but only from something that preexists it. Violence, or at least the threat of violence, births the attempts to prevent it. Working from even loving pairs this way produces ethics from conflict. For although I do not tear my subjectivity from another, I become a subject through an escape from objectification. Rancière further characterizes this kind of "ethical turn" as a turning away from a "revolution to come" and values that are drawn up from what has not yet been. Instead, these ethics look backwards to a "radical event that is no longer in front of us but already behind us" (Rancière, "The Ethical Turn" 201). The subject does not appear through a conflict with others but depends on evading it—perhaps through a Lévinasian submission to the face of the other or perhaps through shared witnessing. Merleau-Ponty describes what he finds to be the inevitable result of these pairs:

> The problem of the other is always explained by the philosophies of the negative in the form of a problem of *the* other. [...] This is significant: the other is here not *an* other, he is the non-I in general. [...] Perhaps it would be necessary to reverse the customary order of the philosophies of the negative, and say that the problem of *the* other is a particular problem of others, since the relation with someone is always mediated by the relationship of third parties.
>
> (*The Visible and the Invisible* 81/111–12)

By insisting on the specificity and sociality of encounters with others, Merleau-Ponty argues that if others are "the" other for me, then interactions will be reduced to opposition; the abstraction of others into the emblem of "the non-I" plunges me into a contest and relations of dominance. This includes Lévinas's obligatory ethics in which he places the Other outside of perception and offers an unrecognized face to whom I owe a primordial allegiance (*Totality and Infinity* 291). And it includes witnessing that exists between two in order to prevent each from objectifying the other. It would seem that *fear*, not love, drives the witness to witness the other. Merleau-Ponty finds that, even with one other, I encounter *an*other, one of *many others with whom I institute the world*. "What merits the name of being" consists of "the system of perspectives that open into it," and exists "at the intersection of my views and at the intersection of my views with those of the others, at the intersection of my acts with those of others" (Merleau-Ponty, *The Visible and the Invisible* 84/114).

Merleau-Ponty did not go on to describe in detail what an exit from the dual encounter would mean for ethics, leaving instead only the tease of a "good ambiguity." This ambiguity comfortably pervades the ethics of attention developing here. The implacable certainty of the obligation to another can instead be replaced with the rigors of the strange amongst many. When I attend I respond to a call, and in doing so I express a new way of being in the world: my transformation by an imaginative response to another, another who remains strange still. Instead of affirming each subject, ethical attention produces a different way of being. These responses open a third way of being which in turn produces a new attending to. Attention moves between *and beyond* each one included in the strange depth of perception. At least, until someone does not pay attention.

Whatever difficulties Oliver's ethics might encounter in the underlying dynamics of the pair, she nonetheless establishes the importance of witnessing others and having others witness. My involvement with the coming into being of others, our participation in the performance of the impossibility of complete witnessing, these may not yet deliver an *ought*, but they contribute to an ethics of attention. An ethics of attention stalls the obligations between pairs engaged either in domination or attempts to escape from the violence of objectification. I begin from a response to a shared participation in a strange, ambiguous encounter rather than from obligation or antagonism or fear. Within these awkward encounters lies the promise of responsibility based in the fundamentally inconclusive and open nature of attention. This is not to say that encounters with others cannot involve coercion, dominance, or violence. It is to say that these are neither necessary nor inevitable.

A peculiar paradox lurks outside the exit from the binary circuit posed by "negative philosophies" grounded in obligation: the foundational ethical encounter now includes multiples, but it also no longer includes everyone. Ethical imperatives are meant to include everyone, but the ambiguity of the strange will not. By leaving the defensive crouch of witnessing, the submission of the face-to-face, and the abstracted and disembodied perspective of "pure" reason, a phenomenological ethics of attention no longer protects the impartial.

Blind spots

If witnessing assists in the emergence of new subjects through address and response for everyone, why are witnesses so prized? If any moment could yield to the strange proximity of others, why does it feel like such a thrill? If I am to love everyone, why does some love move me more than others? If the motivating power of perception is wonder, why isn't everything astonishing? Why is there strangeness at all? Doesn't this experience presumably invest every encounter I have?

And yet it feels rare. More than rare, and more than a moment prized among others, the strange engenders a feeling of the extraordinary, something that undermines the very ground on which an ordinary order is founded (Waldenfels, "Strangeness, Hospitality, and Enmity" 90–1). Erika Fischer-Lichte addresses this experience with her "radical concept" of presence. This version of presence—an escalation from her "weak" and "strong" concepts of presence—is an analogue for more traditional descriptions of stage presence during which actors command "both space and the audience's attention" (Fischer-Lichte, *The Transformative Power of Performance* 98).[27] As she describes this mode of stage presence, it "marks the emergence of something ordinary and develops it into an event" (Fischer-Lichte, *The Transformative Power of Performance* 99; "Appearing as Embodied Mind" 116). For her, the "event" is a return to experiences paved over by mind–body dualism. It makes special something that would be experienced as common if it were not for the intervention and dominance of the Cartesian split between body and mind lived by "Western audiences." Only under this regime would the experience of embodied mind function as an event. Indeed, radical presence serves for Fischer-Lichte as the instantaneous achievement of the "promise of happiness" that concludes Norbert Elias' "civilizing process" whereby the body is completely abstracted and becomes one with the mind (*The Transformative Power of Performance* 99). When faced with performers with the radical concept of presence, "when the ordinary becomes conspicuous, when dichotomies collapse and things turn into their opposites, the spectators perceive the world as 'enchanted' [...] [P]erformance achieves the reenchantment of the world" (Fischer-Lichte, *The Transformative Power of Performance* 180–1).

To be sure, Fischer-Lichte's binary of compulsion does not fit with the world of perception described by this book. As she describes reenchantment, performers command attendants with a singular power, making things "turn into their opposites" as minds become bodied and bodies assume awareness. She also, like Oliver and Lévinas, concludes with a radical inclusion that forms the other side to obligation and separates it from embodied experience: "The reenchantment of the world is inclusive rather than exclusive" (Fischer-Lichte, *The Transformative Power of Performance* 207). However, her insistence that the everyday holds the extraordinary evokes a vibrant potential for an ethics of attention. In a phenomenological world of perception, it will not likely be the case that individual performers liberate me from a supposed post-Cartesian everyday. And yet it can be the case that the astonishment and wonder of perception finds expression in the phenomenon of stage presence. And not only can it be the case, it can be meaningful that experiences of the strange also await any encounter I have while also arising only with some of them.

The astonishment of encountering the strangeness of others begins with the inequality inherent to attention. In Waldenfels' melancholy, cautioning words, "The temptation of an absolutely inclusive community, to which nothing or nobody is exterior, belongs to ideas that fade as soon as one attempts to realize them" ("Strangeness, Hospitality, and Enmity" 91). Unlike reenchantment, strangeness is not evenly distributed or experienced. Through its dependence on attention, strangeness embodies the unequal allocation of care. I am intersubjectively involved with everyone but only concern myself with some. The phenomenological approach to stage presence produces an ethics based on reiterating that perception is not, fundamentally, egalitarian. Describing perception this way reifies the exclusion and inequality of attention *but it does not determine whom* I exclude. Some will be excluded. It isn't fair or avoidable. What *can* be avoided is habitually attending to particular classes or groups and excluding others. The stakes here can be seen in the term "political correctness" and the manically aggrieved straight white men horrified and offended that they might not be the center of attention. When attention moves, it leaves people out, and no matter where I am located in a system of privilege this can sting. An ethics of attention does not *provoke* inequality—it exposes the practice of inequality as an expression of a partial world of perception. So long as the perceived world requires openness to how things might or should be otherwise, foreclosing those possibilities does not remove them so much as it abridges their expression through me. The possibilities remain, unexpressed by me. I have not paid attention to them.

What lies furthest from attention is not inattention or ignorance but indifference. Indifference is the opposite of astonishment. I don't care about that to which I am indifferent. The indifferent falls from attention, does not express the depth of things through me. It does not participate in the vivid relations of the strange. I have not chosen to exclude, in which case it matters whom I exclude, and thus I pay some kind of attention to them. Those kept on the outside very much occupy my attention—they are the exterior that affirms the privileged interior. Exclusion takes *work*. Not so with indifference. With indifference I slip into laziness. I have simply failed to concern myself with any distinction between what has my attention and what does not, what concerns me and what does not. Everyone and everything *can* move me if I let them. To choose not to let someone do so is already to be moved into action, the action of exclusion, of making sure to attend elsewhere. Even ignorance of others allows for the possibility of their coming to attention in the future. But indifference eludes all movement. Indifference does not allow others the place to be actively ignored or responded to. They just don't matter. These are the people on whom the greatest potential violence may be inflicted.

Oliver and hooks seek to protect such people—by extension, everyone at some point or another—through the eradication of blind spots, through "working through" them (Oliver, *Witnessing* 218).[28] Blind spots can only house domination; within them subjects transform into objects through the loss of their ability to express their subjectivity. The work of revealing blind spots is unending and exhausting, and no less necessary for it. For phenomenology, however, blind spots take on a very different meaning. They cannot hide experiences of violence because blind spots are the very arrangement of experience. Merleau-Ponty described the eye's *punctum caecum*, the point where the optic nerves meet the retina and where the eye does not see, as the organizing principle of vision: the visible is founded on the non-seeing, which is nonetheless *of* the visible (Merleau-Ponty, *The Visible and the Invisible* 247/295).[29] He then extrapolated this biological function to claim that perception itself requires a blind spot where the threads of the world are knit into the fabric of experience. In terms of touch, this phenomenon arrives through the *écart* between the touching and touched hands: their circuit of feeling contains a gap in which the two sensations do not coincide but by which they are bound.

Blind spots, then, cannot be abolished without radically reducing perception of the world. No one and nothing can be completely seen. Eradicating blind spots undoes the possibility of perceiving others because it insists on a totalizing vision no one can possess. Alia Al-Saji notes that "ethical vision does not seek to bring invisibility to sight," not least because "the totalization of vision is a forgetting, or more accurately, a refusal to remember, the remainder of invisibility" (56, 53). Blind spots are not what I do not see, they are the unseeable that makes vision possible. They do not adhere to particular people or even to vision, but to perception itself. In this sense, blind spots do not hide the experiences of other people, and domination does not depend on them to do its work. Instead blind spots secure experiences as strange—accessible through a particularized creative response rather than through bringing them to light.

This does not mean of course that I can attend to all people in the fullest sense (just as it does not determine what or who falls within my blind spots). The strange requires an engagement that is not possible with everyone or everything all the time. I could not make it through the day if I remained totally open to the strange depth of experience. My daily acts of translation and classification allow me passage through the world precisely by shielding me from its depth. Merleau-Ponty notes that by allowing closure to the simple question of where I am, "the answer satisfies us because we do not attend to it [...] [T]he question would arise again and indeed would be inexhaustible, almost insane, if we wished to situate our levels, measure our standards in their turn" (Merleau-Ponty, *The Visible and the Invisible* 104/138–9). And so even though I *could* be astonished by everything all of the time, I am not—not even most of the time.

I cannot pay attention to everyone or to everything. Attention is egalitarian in principle—anyone *could* be paid attention to and anyone *could* pay attention. Attention is anti-egalitarian in practice. It is inescapably and unjustly and lovingly and dangerously unequal. And yet surely everyone deserves attention, needs it, and cracks into the greatest despair of all when feeling that no attention can be had. And surely ethics of any sort *begin* with attention.

And surely this is a truism. It goes without saying that without attention there would be nothing to be ethical about. Virtually all ethics concerns what I do *after* I have paid attention to something, and still yet after I have understood another person or thing as a possible partner in ethical behavior. At the same time this *should* go with saying. There are different kinds of attention that institute different kinds of relationships with others, and it seems fair to say that most of them do not address themselves to the unknowable possibilities imaginable between others and myself. Even further, I can pay attention to others in a way that objectifies them, either with their consent or without it. Attention "itself" is neither ethical nor unethical, but a means of playing out many kinds of relationships with others. The grounding of ethics in attention needs to be said because it establishes *partiality* at the basis of ethics. Attention is an embodied action, which means it is irreducibly constrained and imperfect and incomplete. It inhabits a world of possibility and transformation that can be astonishing. That *should* be ever more astonishing.

The wonder of expression

In the unpublished fragment that promised "the principle of an ethics," Merleau-Ponty described a movement from the "bad ambiguity" of perception to the "good ambiguity" of expression. In contrast to an understanding of perception that posited a consciousness paired with the world, Merleau-Ponty imagined endless expressions of the world through each thing's style of being. These would generate "a spontaneity which gathers together the plurality of monads, the past and the present, nature and culture" (Merleau-Ponty, "Unpublished Text" 11). Scholars seeking this principle of an ethics tend to frequent two paths: the intersubjectivity of the *chiasm* and the development of expression in Merleau-Ponty's thought. As I have argued above, intersubjectivity can indeed offer a principle of multiplicity that describes my experience of and dependence on others. And yet to extrapolate an ethics from the principle of intersubjectivity is to skip a step—describing how I relate to others does not yet establish that this is a *good* way of relating to them. As Greg Johnson notes, the nature of perception formulated by Merleau-Ponty does not *guarantee* ethical responses to others; it is, rather, what makes ethical responses *possible* (183).[30] Simply because I am irreducibly involved with others does not endorse any particular way of being involved with them. In any event, Merleau-Ponty does not suggest searching for a principle of ethics in the maintenance of plurality alone.

Working more directly from the fragment, some authors have sought in *expression* a key to unlocking Merleau-Ponty's mysterious principle of ethics. For example, Al-Saji describes a multi-dimensional ethical vision characterized by its expressivity (54–8). And Gary Madison works up his understanding of Merleau-Ponty's ethics by following the latter's later theory of language (166–73). Madison concludes that "a Merleau-Pontyan ethics would focus on the communicative process [...] I would be tempted to label an ethics such as this an ethics of communicative rationality" (162, 163).[31]

To truly extrapolate ethics from this fragment means taking Merleau-Ponty at his word, and that word is *wonder*. Merleau-Ponty wrote of expression that "*to establish this wonder* would be metaphysics itself and *would at the same time give us the principle of an ethics*" ("Unpublished Text" 11).[32] Rather than expression, it is the *wonder* of expression that will give the ground of ethics. Madison's ethics of communicative rationality may or may not be compelling in its own right, but it will surely not be ethics derived from Merleau-Ponty's glance at the promise of expression. Furnishing such an ethics would mean focusing on the wonder of expressing the unfathomable depth of each person and thing encountered. This is the kind of wonder I am locating in stage presence, which not only embodies the phenomenon of astonishment but also stages it and presents it to me by inviting reflection on itself.

Iris Marion Young cautions that not all wonder is benign and that some forms of it are dangerous. In "Asymmetrical Reciprocity: On Moral Respect, Wonder, and Enlarged Thought" (1997), Young thinks through the possibilities of ethical relationships outside of the imperative to consider things from another person's point of view. The idea of symmetry suggests fairness—no side is more weighted than another, and both may be compared to each other as equals. But as Young points out, an equalized exchange subsumes others into my experience and erases their abilities to destabilize me because I am granted the power to grasp the world as they do. This fictional model also reifies institutional injustice by proposing that all subject formations are equally legitimate and possible, which obscures the dominance of some agents over others: "When privileged people put themselves in the position of those who are less privileged, the assumptions derived from their privilege often allow them unknowingly to misrepresent the other's situation" (I.M. Young, "Asymmetrical Reciprocity" 346–53, 349). She argues that accommodating the experience of another as a surprise, as something unknown and unknowable except through indirection, requires imagining that exchanges with others are asymmetrical. Each subject has its own time and position, and these can be expressed but never known by others (I.M. Young, "Asymmetrical Reciprocity" 352–3). All mutual understanding derived from asymmetrical reciprocity will involve "a moment of *wonder*, of an openness to the newness and mystery of the other person" (I.M. Young, "Asymmetrical Reciprocity" 357).

Young's approach to wonder comes from René Descartes by way of Luce Irigaray. In *The Passions of the Soul* (1649) Descartes considered wonder to be the "first of all passions; and it has no opposite, because if the object which presents itself has nothing in it that surprises us, we are in no wise moved regarding it, and we consider it without passion" (Descartes, art. 53, qtd in Irigaray, *An Ethics of Sexual Difference* 73). For Irigaray, wonder was the basis of ethics because it was the portal through which one encountered difference. It provokes attention to others, and "its force derives from the fact that the appearance of something or someone new modifies the movement of spirits in an unexpected manner" (Irigaray, *An Ethics of Sexual Difference* 78). And yet, the wonderful does not serve me in particular: "Wonder goes beyond that which is or is not suitable for us. The other never suits us simply. We should in some way have reduced the other to ourselves if he or she suited us completely. An *excess* resists" (Irigaray, *An Ethics of Sexual Difference* 74).

This is where Young finds danger. She understands that attention can also be prurient or based in curiosity rather than opening. "It would not be difficult to use it [wonder] to imagine the other person as exotic. One can interpret wonder as a kind of distant awe before the Other that turns their transcendence into an inhuman inscrutability" (I.M. Young, "Asymmetrical Reciprocity" 357). This touches on the risk written about in the last chapter—what kind of assumptions are at work when a straightish white man finds an experience of the strange through an encounter with an African American man in drag persona wearing a Reagan mask? In order for this astonishment to avoid a probing prospect, in order for it to eschew a basis in privilege, it must instead involve my accepting the experience of a creative response to what I did not know. Far from an *inhuman* inscrutability attached to a person, I found a deeply human and a very particular strangeness between Williams and myself during his solo. Following the concept of centrifugal space, Williams "himself" does not become strange to me. Instead, an astonishing possibility opens in the space of play between Williams, the other performers and attendants, and myself. An "exotic" Reagan would indeed have demeaned Williams by using him as a prop. The centrifugal space of the performance evaded objectification and instead spoke to the strange depth of others.

Young finds possibilities in a "respectful stance of wonder" that does not impose on people or things but allows them to participate in the work of opening the perceiving subject further and further: "Wonder also means being able to see one's own position, assumptions, perspective as strange" (I.M. Young, "Asymmetrical Reciprocity" 358). This kind of wonder is rigorous, interrogatory, and moving. It embodies Merleau-Ponty's "hyper-reflection," which addressed not only perceived phenomena, but also the terms of perception and of reflection. Wonder does not stupefy or gape. It reorients. It does work. As mentioned in Chapter 1, Laura Cull also writes of an "attentive respect" that involves an opening onto a world composed itself of a continual opening (237). Similarly, Al-Saji writes of Merleau-Ponty's expressive vision that it allows a response to others such that "one's response to the other then comes not through habitual and ready-made formulas, but with attention and nuance," ultimately engaging another as "a singular and unrepeatable event, and expressing and sustaining the difference" (57). What makes others singular events is not a unique identity I pin to them but the provocation of a singular expression that emerges from constraints and possibilities unique to me.

I cannot know completely what differences describe the distance between another and myself, but I can know they exist. And I can grasp how I express through them a committed action of attention that opens me to an astonishing series of possibilities. Wonder does not seek to join me to the wonderful as desire seeks to bring me to the desired. Instead it opens me to the movement another provokes for and within me, movement that pushes me away from what I know. It is an experience of shared, uneven alteration that promotes continued opening to others and my surroundings.

Waldenfels wrote about the attention involved with the strange that "the originary attention waits for something that will never be fully there. It not only extends experience but also increases it" (*Phenomenology of the Alien* 65). As I have argued, *what* experience is being increased deserves careful consideration. If it is a given that I am inescapably involved with others, then simply paying attention to and increasing this state is not enough. Embodied relationships are the means by which I experience the world and they are just as capable of brightening the world as of darkening it. The violent are also involved with those they abuse. These kinds of relationships aggressively decrease the astonishment in and of the world by denying others the possibility of expanding it. An ethics of attention requires more and will involve the generosity Rosalyn Diprose finds in Merleau-Ponty's account of intercorporeality, "an openness to others that not only precedes and establishes communal relations but constitutes the self as open to otherness," and a "being-given to others" (5). Like witnessing and attention, generosity as Diprose describes it expresses an unceasing movement among others. Although generosity might advance towards justice, should this end ever be met "by passing final judgment, this effects a violence towards, and closure to, the other" (Diprose 193).[33]

When I deny my openness to others and myself, I insist on identity based in positive materiality and on difference as a proof of selfhood. Annemie Halsema claims that ethics "means first and foremost a call for self-limitation. Respect for others starts namely with acknowledging one's own finiteness. And there is nothing that makes us aware of that more pervasively than our embodiment" (77). This kind of respect recalls the strictures of obligation, but it translates very quickly into fear and closure to others. It also turns Merleau-Ponty's understanding of embodiment upside down. Beginning from embodiment points to the most profound acknowledgment of each body's porousness, of our strange inability to contain ourselves completely. It is true that I may and do impose limits on others and myself, but these are precisely the denials of shared embodiment. These withdrawals will not likely form the basis of an ethics, but neither will they express the *un*ethical. Closure can be sought as protection from *unwelcome* shared embodiment and thus cannot be categorized as "unethical." Not everyone wants to be perceived.

For example, Erving Goffman coined the term "civil inattention" to describe the performance of not acknowledging someone. Civil inattention addresses a tacit expectation that people I do not know deserve to be free from my attention; when it is inevitable that they fall within it, I act as if they haven't in order to offer them anonymity (385). Now, in order for the inattention to be civil, it has to take account of the other person, which means they have been attended to in the first place. Goffman's term acknowledges that, notwithstanding whatever role attention might play in my formation as a subject, I do not always want it. Not only that, but others will perform their withholding of attention in order to grant me the safe passage I have asked for. To use Oliver's terms, witnessing might allow me to emerge as a subject, but I don't want everything I do to be witnessed. The person shrinking from involvement with others may do so for endless reasons, and these may include retreat from harm or from the sense that one has not been perceived the way one would like. It could be that at times and for myriad reasons I want to feel alone, to feel free from both the judgmental gaze and the loving eye. This might constitute its own failure on my part, an attempt to deny my bonds to those that can or would perceive me. All the same, withholding this failure from me by insisting that I remain "visible" would pose no smaller a problem. This suggests another reason why Waldenfels' observation about attention increasing the experience of the world cannot support an ethics on its own: even if this experience could be imagined as always positive, I would still have to ask for whom.

As a phenomenon of centrifugal space, astonishment does not belong to the astonished person, nor does it belong to the astonishing thing.

Astonishment belongs to the world of perception, and ethical attention increases the wonder of that world.

"Philosophy is not a hospital"

The experience of stage presence I have described heightens the sense of disorientation at the root of embodied encounters with others. In doing so it does not loosen responsibility to others but enacts and strengthens it because this responsibility is itself a function of the inability to draw limits to ourselves. It is thus an affirmation of phenomenology's central premise and an embodiment of its ethics without being their *result*. Between attendants and performers stage presence prompts transformations involving the public work of attention and a heightened experience of possibility brought about as a reorganization of space. Relationships to others and the responsibilities to them arise from the continual and incomplete movement between each other in an embodied world of perception.

To suggest that there is an ethical basis for performance relationships is not to suggest that there is only a single kind of relationship that embodies it. Stage presence can simply serve to foreground how this kind of ethical relationship works when, for example, a generous performer meets with the ethical attention of an attendant. When performers are generous as Diprose proposes generosity they are committed to what happens around them rather than to making themselves objects of excitement. I might still thrill to performance relationships removed from this ethical basis. In fact, removal from the ethical could provide its own excitement. All the same, performer–attendant relationships that decrease the wonder of the world and the strange possibilities borne of perception live outside of the ethical. The generous performer and the ethically attentive theatre-goer, however, generate stage presence between them and experience the dizzying relationship of astonishment.

Uneven, compromised, and forever contingent, perception frames and defines ethical possibilities. The goal is not perceptibility for all, but more astonishment. The aim of an ethics of attention will not be attending to everyone, will not be increasing the "visibility" of the world. Blind spots will continue, people and things will go unattended. The chief responsibility of a phenomenological ethics of attention will thus be to seek out the astonishment at the co-existence and interdependence of being.

The choice about when and with whom wonder arrives constitutes the central task, problem, failure, and privilege of an ethics of attention. *Everyone* needs attention. And we all live without it. The questions prompted by an ethics of attention will revolve around to whom we deny our involvement in their becoming astonishing. Astonishment is unequal—unequally lived and unequally afforded. This does not mean that those without *should* be without, but rather that, in any ethical calculation about how to live strange encounters with others, I will consider these advantages. Different kinds of privilege can attach to astonishment, as discussed in Chapter 4. It may be considered the province of the young, the career artist, the economically comfortable, the physically secure. If ethical attention concerns enlarging the wonder of the world, it will involve engaging with the constraints and possibilities of anyone else to experience wonder. An ethical attention considers these kinds of privilege in the pursuit of making *more* wonder rather than simply solidifying the status of those that already experience it.

Ethical attention rests on the failure of impartiality. There is no completely ethical attention. Wonder can be found anywhere, but finding it somewhere requires my absence from it elsewhere. And so each act of ethical attention partners with a failure to attend ethically to others. The ethical will still be found in the possibility of increasing the wonder of the world. While people will always fall outside attention, the wonder of the world can always be increased. Who falls outside attention matters. And it won't always be a simple question of attending to the hunger of the poor instead of the profit margins of corporations. It will involve, for example, how to attend to vulnerability without requiring it, and how to increase strength without subjecting others to it. The question is not how I avoid failing to attend to everyone. I will fail, and that failure produces the fraught terrain of ethical decision-making. The question is, how do I bend that failure toward increasing the wonder of the world? Not *my* wonder or experience of it, but the wonder that comes to being between others and me. This might diminish my political or economic power, it might increase it, or it might gain me advantage or someone else, but it will increase the strangeness and wonder of the world rather than decrease it.

Ethical attention encourages the expansion of the strange encounter with others that displaces me from the center of action and concern. It moves me towards the possibilities of space rather than towards its conclusions. Even further, rooting astonishment in an experience of space provides an exit from the is/ought fallacy plaguing phenomenology's attempts at ethics. Space concerns the virtual—past constraint and the present possibility aim at a future unfettered by either. My inability to comprehend the strangeness of an encounter with another suggests how an ethics of attention grounds itself in *both* the "is" and in the "ought" because astonishment is a horizon. It "is" only a thing insofar as I imagine its continuous opening into an experience I cannot understand. The horizon is always where I cannot be *and* where I begin. It cannot be crossed, cannot even be approached. As opposed to the distance I can travel towards what I desire or what I do not know, the distance between me and the unknowable is always the same. The "ought" of an ethics of attention finds ground not in the "is" of perceptual failure, but in the future tense of astonishment. Attention fails me every day, but wonder can always transform me into something beyond what I knew.

This principle invests my experience of the contingencies of ethical decision-making. An ethics of attention recommends actively choosing to share in astonishing, asymmetrical relationships of perception. These relationships with the strange participate in an asymmetry that, Waldenfels writes, "is not explained by the fact that the roles established in a dialogue are unequally distributed. It pertains rather to the fact that the call of the stranger and the response never converge" ("Réponse à l'autre" 373). Determining the nature and course of these asymmetries can only happen in the fluidity of each encounter and accounts for the enmeshment of ethics and Merleau-Ponty's "good ambiguity." What is kept from perceptibility? Who doesn't want to be perceived? Whose imperceptibility increases wonder and whose decreases it? From one situation to another, what it means to enlarge wonder will vary. Each time I participate in the growth of wonder I will turn from other people and other things, all of whom possess the capacity for a strange rapport with me.

Exhibit B and the photographs from Abu Ghraib can be taken to further suggest that while circumstances might constrain the possibility of ethical attention they may not be able to entirely foreclose it. If performances and images cannot determine but only propose ethical value, if they serve as a ground for ethical decision-making by attendants, I could attend to almost anything. Ethical attention could involve attending *Exhibit B* in a way that refuses the possible objectifications that arise from the installations. This is presumably the kind of attention its detractors imagined to be impossible. An ethics of attention also acknowledges that some attendants might be able to work their way through *Exhibit B* while others may not. The challenge, however, rests with the attendants, not the artwork. If Kehinde Andrews believes himself incapable of *not* objectifying the performers, then his act of ethical attention will indeed consist of not attending. These ethics admit that one person's failure cannot guarantee everyone else's. Even the vilest representation of violence might help secure ethical attention to its subjects. At the same time, turning one's attention elsewhere might also constitute an act of ethical attention. Turning from others does not mean ceasing to care for them.

It may yet be that turning away from someone can constitute an expression of care for them if I do not believe myself capable of attending to them ethically. For example, walking out of Socìetas Raffaello Sanzio's *Giulio Cesare* (1997) might be the highest expression of care for the anorexic women cast as Cassius and Brutus in the second part of the performance. Helena Grehan proposes that the director Romeo Castelluci "casts a range of performers who sit outside traditional ideas of the 'actor,' thus *exposing* spectators to a range of bodily forms that are themselves at times exposed, vulnerable, innocent, and provocative" (40).[34] She goes on to note that in *Giulio Cesare* "many performers were chosen because of their bodily characteristics," among whom were a man whose larynx had been surgically removed, another morbidly obese, and the two anorexic women (Grehan 41).[35] But anorexia is not a bodily characteristic, it is a disease that can be fatal as well as cured. The production not only incorporated the illness, it demanded that the actresses be ill: if they were healed of anorexia they would not have belonged in the production. The production did not work with the specific cases of these two women's sicknesses, but inserted their sick bodies into Castelluci's interpretation of *Julius Caesar*. Confronted with this "use" of an ill person, do I stay put and attend to her as best I can? Do I try to move beyond the sick joke of an anorexic playing the famously "lean and hungry" Cassius and embrace the possibilities of representing illness on stage, to the possibilities of the actresses' interest in making their illness meaningful in the performance of a Shakespeare play? Or do I leave, rejecting the spectacle while also depriving the actresses of a pair of loving eyes, albeit a pair of eyes likely unfelt amidst hundreds of others? Which action allows the fullest experience of the strange between the actresses and myself? Such a question may or may not find an answer in the report that during the German tour of the production in 1998 one of the actresses died (Fischer-Lichte, *The Transformative Power of Performance* 86).

Faced with these kinds of quandaries, the promise of an ethics of attention rests in its capacity to direct the work of losing and then finding my orientation in relationships to others. The responsibility found in these relationships takes root in the contingency of perception—its formation by locale and history, its modification by habit—but also in how to perform this responsibility. What it *means* to be responsible to the wonder of the world, what other values this enacts and protects, will be difficult to establish locally and impossible to apply universally. The actions after astonishment matter tremendously but cannot be dictated in advance. And yet, far from an "ethics without content," or a descent into formless relativism, this kind of responsibility makes its own stringent demands—to vigilance, adaptability, and to humility before the experience of wonder and astonishment.

This responsibility will not be defensive and will not seek to protect—actions which contain altruism, selfishness, and self-aggrandizement. This kind of responsibility *listens*, attends, and expands—it adds to the world rather than seeking to protect each corner of it. The commitment to enlarging the wonder of the world might result in defensive actions—turning away from images or performances instead of objectifying the people represented in them, or helping people shield themselves from harm. And yet it will not in itself seek to preserve astonishment but to enlarge it. An ethics of attention is additive—it moves, transforms, invents. Ethical attention expresses an imagining of how the world should be, not an endorsement of how it is.

After his lecture "Man and Adversity" in 1951, Merleau-Ponty was asked if his proposed "rejection of all explanations" was a legitimate approach for philosophy. He responded with the line quoted in Chapter 4: "Philosophy is *thaumazein* [wonder], the consciousness of strangeness. It does away with 'philosophical' explanations in systems." His interlocutor, Protestant theologian Charles Westphal, pushed back:

> Westphal: But in saying that you refuse all explanation, in compelling man to remain in this ambiguity, don't you offer him only the call to invention? You leave him in a situation that you yourself call vertiginous, but can we live in a vertiginous situation?
>
> Merleau-Ponty: Philosophy is not a hospital. If people are vertiginous and want to take medication against it, I don't stop them, but I say: this is medication.
>
> (Merleau-Ponty, "Man and Adversity—Discussion" 236)

The strange *is* vertiginous, the astonishing *is* disorienting. I steady myself by pretending to wade in shallows instead of swimming in depths. I do this to avoid living every moment in the insane questioning Merleau-Ponty identified as the fate of anyone who pays incessant attention. An ethics of attention will recognize the quotidian utility of not paying attention while also holding fast to the good of increasing wonder. As Westphal feared and as I have argued, this involves "invention," the active, creative response to a world that, attended to ethically, forever eludes my grasp.

Traditionally, this role has belonged to performance-makers and other artists, and more than one manifesto throughout history has extolled the virtues of disordering habitual perspectives. Confining this work to artists and philosophers, however, misplaces both the privilege and the responsibility of astonishment. Phenomenology in Merleau-Ponty's tradition insists that the world is a work that requires the perceiver's participation. Attendants who go to the theatre and await an appearance of the wonderful have abdicated responsibility. As Robert Switzer puts it in his description of Merleau-Ponty's ontology, "My looking and feeling are thus not, in a sense, my 'own'; I engage in vision, and even more in touch, as at once undertaken and undergone, as both toward and from the things and the others" (271). Switzer, after Merleau-Ponty, describes how what I perceive is neither mine nor the world's. This applies with particular force to the experience of art, in which an expression of the world has been brought to and sought by others.

In the First Prologue of *The Bite of the Night*, one of English playwright Howard Barker's manifestos, he writes, "If that's art, I think it is hard work" (1). The voice here is not an artist's, but an attendant's. For all the joy to be found in astonishment, for all the humor in the strange, for all the thrills of disorientation, there is also work. And it belongs properly to everyone who makes meaning during performance. Just as it would be absurd to indemnify art from all consequences of its presentation, it is absurd to believe attendants are absolved of all responsibility for the meanings they make from performance. Art is not simply whatever one makes of it, but it is nothing without what one makes of it. Instead of asking whether or not art is ethical, I can ask whether I have attended to it, can attend to it, ethically. If I cannot, the impediment will lie between the artwork and myself, not in either one of us.

William S. Hamrick explicitly places Merleau-Ponty's fragmented thoughts about ethics in an artistic context, claiming that, "for Merleau-Ponty, moral decision-making is much closer to artistic expression" (296–7).[36] This kind of expression describes formalized art as well as the "attempt to institute values within the limitations of a given situation (the 'medium')" (Hamrick 297). Ethical attention does not require conjuring meaning from nothing; it requires inventing a response to the strange inspired by the particular situation of each different encounter with others. Each of these encounters, though invoking the unknowable in general, harbors an unknowable very specific to a current situation. I can only experience it through the world's expression through me; anyone else's encounter will reflect other expressions of the world. What the principle of increased astonishment looks like in any given situation cannot be predicted without attending to its constraints and its possibilities. This is the work of artists and it is the work of attendants. It is hard work.

Westphal also feared that we cannot continuously live in a vertiginous situation. This seems right. In my terms, doing so would entail ethically attending to everything. This is impossible, and so I fail to be ethical every day. I *depend* on being unethical in order to make it from one end of the day to the other. I make generalizations, I take shortcuts, I take medication. André Gide, in a frequently quoted line from his poem Les Nourritures Terrestres (1897), writes: "The wise man is astonished by everything" (27).[37] But this would be less a wise person than an immobilized one. This person would resemble the parody of the neutral mask transfixed by each blade of grass, unable to move. In the phenomenological world of perception, the ethical person is astonished by *anything*, not everything. The ground of ethical attention consists in my failure to attend to all the world, while still being able to cultivate astonishing encounters with others. We all, every single one of us, *should* be part of an astonishing world. None of us can claim that membership without attending ethically to and being ethically attended to by others. And others—which means all of us—will never attend to everyone. This leave-taking, this absenting from the continuing work of attention, characterizes an inevitable and foundational ethical failure. When I cease attending, I deny someone else a place in an astonishing world. When I care for enlarging the wonder of the world, I am virtuous. This will not reduce my failures with those to whom I do not attend. And yet each strange encounter makes the world more wonderful. An ethical life will be one dedicated to making the world more astonishing. I know that each day will bring more failures of attention. And I know that each day can bring more wonder if I only allow myself to be transformed by others caught up, as I am, in the strangeness of being.

Notes

1 The piece was a response to a prompt in my Devising New Work course at Beloit College to create a work based on their answers to self-created questionnaires. The students were Jon Chamberlin, Emily Evans, Melinda Kraus-Perrotta, Michael Kreiser, and Mira Treatman. The other students in the class were Dana Bye, Blaize D'Angelo, Caitlyn de Araujo, Carolyn Ellis, Patrick Firme, Al Kemp, Alen Kerić, Joey Long, Casey Perkins, and Turner Smith.

2 Presented at festivals throughout Europe. Performers: Locally cast, the performers for *Exhibit B* number more than 150 over the length of its tour so far. In order to protect the performers, some of whom have been abused on social media, Third World Bunfight does not release their names. The four singers from Namibia have appeared in all productions. They are Melvin Dupont, William Mouers, Chris Nekongo, and Avril Nuuyoma. Direction: Brett Bailey.

3 All were silent except for four, whose bodies were encased in boxes and from whose "decapitated" heads arose a succession of hymns. This tableau was related to the work of German eugenicist Eugen Fischer, who used stuffed and skewered heads to bolster his theory of "racial hygiene" later endorsed by the Nazis.

4 During the writing of this chapter, Third World Bunfight updated their website to include four images of recent productions in which attendants are pictured. These attendants, all but one of them white, appear in attitudes of shock, curiosity, and discomfort. These are the only images I am aware of that depict attendants (Third World Bunfight).

5 An analysis of local habits concerning what and whom performance image captions identify deserves its own study. Although he does not address this particular issue, Matthew Reason examines the use of publicity images in Part III of *Documentation, Disappearance and the Representation of Live Performance* (2006).

6 For a critique of how *Exhibit B* used its specific performance sites to speak directly to local histories and current practices of racist violence while also failing to engage local discourses on that violence, see Chikha and Arnaut 675.

7 My translation.

8 See, for example, Krueger; Ebony.

9 This specific question was raised in Timothy Mooney's touring "educational" solo show *Molière Than Thou*. When he performs the scenes in which Tartuffe accosts Elmire, he uses an audience member to play the wife of Tartuffe's host. The second scene is famous for its depiction of Elmire playing along with Tartuffe's increasingly aggressive advances in order to expose him as dishonest while Orgon, Elmire's husband, cowers under a table refusing to believe in his guest's perfidy. In the performance I attended at Franklin & Marshall College in 2011, Mooney relentlessly bullied and slathered over a physically recoiling and nervously laughing student with no acting experience. (When no one volunteered to play the role, Mooney asked the audience members if they weren't eager to see this particular student on stage. Once she acceded to the public pleading and joined Mooney, he asked if she had ever acted before. She said no, and he turned

to the audience and leered, "So this is your first time.") In a heated conversation with me after the show, Mooney asserted this scene taught attendants that people in seventeenth-century France are just like us today. Whether or not one finds this a compelling analysis of the scene, without an Orgon, and without an actress familiar with the play and capable of portraying Elmire's formidable strength and wiliness, the scene became solely about Tartuffe's assault of Elmire. Most of my fellow attendants at Franklin & Marshall College, faculty and students alike, found this hilarious. As I left the performance I overheard the accosted student's male companion say to her, "Oh, but you know you liked it."

10 See, for example, Memela.
11 Young is citing Trachtenberg 59.
12 *Stillness*, however, might signal something more than itself. For Young, the stillness required of the subjects depicts a kind of movement—back to the Middle Passage and forward to the inspecting eyes of the Harvard professor and contemporary viewers of the images (39).
13 Her book does not reproduce the images.
14 See also Oliver, *Subjectivity Without Subjects* 173–8.
15 Oliver draws most explicitly from his "master–slave" dialectic, first through Fanon's reading of it in *Black Skin, White Masks*, and then directly. See Oliver, *Witnessing* 27–9, 95–9; Fanon 218–22; Hegel 113–18.
16 Oliver presents *Cheryl Hopwood v. the State of Texas*—in which four rejected white applicants sued the state for admitting students of color with similar academic credentials—as an example of how false witness distorts both history and the present emergence of subjecthood. The circuit court decided on appeal that Hopwood had been unfairly denied admission to the University of Texas at Austin's law school on the basis of an affirmative action policy that considered race alongside other factors in a candidate's portfolio. Precedent had been set at the Supreme Court for considering race in admissions policies so long as previous discriminatory practices could be proven to have a negative effect on present-day situations. Nonetheless, the Texas court decided that proof of historical racism was not justification for considering race in the present-day process of selecting candidates for the law school. Further, the court held that considering race was discriminatory in the same way that previous racist and segregationist practices had been.

In Oliver's formulation, reaching these conclusions required ignoring the connection between the past and the present, between groups historically and presently disadvantaged and those more advantaged (*Witnessing* 125–31). The court's conclusions, while explicitly including witnesses, denied the response-ability of students of color and of people of color in Texas in general. The decision bore false witness to the address of students of color in Texas whose struggle to gain admittance to law school carried the burden of institutionally racist policies across housing, banking, and educational terrains. Equating the fate of Hopwood and her co-plaintiffs with the situation of those students of color admitted under the affirmative action policy of the school acknowledged the white students' claims of discrimination, to be sure. But these claims required equating all considerations of race, which in turn requires suppressing the history and present fact of institutional racism against people of color. Centuries of considering race in order to further the advantage of a ruling majority does not compare to the recent consideration of race in order to adjust for the unfair treatment of a minority. The claim that it is racist to *pay attention* to how white people experience race differently than people of color serves the needs of a structurally racist system by obscuring its governing principles. This claim closes down the address of those most wounded by racism while also stifling responses that might include the rejection of objectification. Both history and the future are denied.

17 Quoting Kittay 131.

18 The work cited is Felman and Laub.

19 Oliver here cites Felman and Laub 210.

20 As her own analysis of Hegel makes clear, however, objects have nothing to say *as witnesses* (Oliver, *Witnessing* 95–8). The bondsman *does* have something to say to the lord, but the manner and content of that speech do not allow the bondsman to push very far beyond the objecthood assigned him by the lord. Objects have something to say, but only as objects.

21 Oliver is working from hooks 243–8.

22 Lévinas produced a corpus of confounding and moving work that resists easy summation. As much as his work maintains an interest in the intimate ethical encounter between one and the face of the other, many points he argued during his lifetime can find their rejoinder elsewhere in his work. This peek at his work aims only to suggest the ways it informs Oliver's account of subjectivity and the ethics she derives from witnessing.

23 For the beginning of this trajectory see Lévinas, *Totality and Infinity* 187–220.

24 Such a determination remains, for Lévinas, a function of "justice," the post-social grasp of the Other's relation to others (*Ethics and Infinity* 99).

25 This is so despite the point made by Arne Vetlesen that "to be responsible for the Other is to be so uniquely" (14). How I am unique remains insignificant to the ethics borne of an ultimate responsibility for the Other, even if it is significant to *me.*

26 Further, it produces art that, according to Rancière, "interminably bears witness to catastrophe" ("The Ethical Turn" 193). Hence *Soulographie*, as discussed in Chapter 3.

27 Despite the dominance of the performer during the "radical concept" of presence, Fischer-Lichte argues that attendants generate meanings and experiences alongside performers in an "autopoietic" feedback loop (*The Transformative Power of Performance* 38–74).

28 Oliver deploys "working through" in its explicitly Freudian sense. To "work through" a past trauma means to act it out without knowing that one is repeating it and to have the performance interpreted by the therapist (*Witnessing* 76–7). Oliver cites Freud, "Remembering, Repeating, Working-Through" 150.

29 "*Punctum caecum*" is Latin for "blind spot."

30 Hamrick also discusses how loving and cruel touches both express intersubjectivity (307).

31 Madison also considers this "an ethics of reciprocity or an ethics of recognition" (171). The problems of the latter have already been addressed above in Oliver's description of recognition. The problems with the former will be addressed later in the chapter.

32 My emphasis.

33 M.C. Dillon expresses exasperation with the linkage of discourse and violence. In his example, a storm can be called a storm by the weather report without undue concern. "Not all acts of discourse are violent [...] in violating the ipseity of these events [hurricanes, moonrises] it [the weather report] benignly helps us to dress appropriately" (150). But, of course, confining global weather and astronomical events to suggestions for outerwear precisely reduces their capacity to astonish me.

34 Original emphasis.

35 Grehan here and throughout her book positions performance and performance-makers as the source of ethical instruction and conflict to which audiences can subject themselves, a model of attendance fundamentally at odds with a phenomenological account of attention.

36 Hamrick came up empty in his search for Merleau-Ponty's ethics. He considered Merleau-Ponty's "principle of an ethics" equivalent to the concept of the "flesh" described in Chapter 2—an "element" through which I move as a perceiving and a perceived being. Hamrick notes that, as a medium that secures my intersubjectivity, the "flesh" cannot transition from a descriptive to a normative phenomenon.

37 My translation of "Le sage est celui qui s'étonne de tout."

Bibliography

Aarnes, Asbjørn. "End of Fulfilment of Phenomenology? On the Philosophy of Levinas." *Closeness: An Ethics*. Eds Harald Jodalen and Arne Johan Vetlesen. Oslo: Scandinavian University Press, 1997.

Agnew, John. "Space: Place." *Spaces of Geographical Thought: Deconstructing Human Geography's Boundaries*. Ed. Paul J. Cloke. London: Sage, 2005: 81–95.

Ahmed, Sara. *Queer Phenomenology: Orientations, Objects, Others*. Durham: Duke University Press, 2006.

Al-Saji, Alia. "Vision, Mirror, and Expression: The Genesis of the Ethical Body in Merleau-Ponty's Later Works." *Interrogating Ethics: Embodying the Good in Merleau-Ponty*. Eds James Hatley, Janice McLane, and Christian Diehm. Pittsburgh: Duquesne University Press, 2006: 39–64.

Andrews, Kehinde. "Exhibit B, the Human Zoo, is a Grotesque Parody—Boycott it." *Comment is Free*. www.theguardian.com/commentisfree/2014/sep/12/exhibit-b-human-zoo-boycott-exhibition-racial-abuse, September 12, 2014. Accessed December 14, 2015.

Andrews, Kehinde and Stella Odunlami. "Is Art Installation Exhibit B Racist?" *Comment is Free*. www.theguardian.com/commentisfree/2014/sep/27/is-art-installation-exhibit-b-racist, September 27, 2014. Accessed December 14, 2015.

Aristotle. *On Poetry and Style*. Trans. G.M.A. Grube. Indianapolis: Hackett, 1989.

Arvidson, P. Sven. "A Lexicon of Attention: From Cognitive Science to Phenomenology." *Phenomenology and the Cognitive Sciences*, 2 (2003): 99–132.

Auslander, Philip. "Humanoid Boogie: Reflections of Robotic Performance." *Staging Philosophy: Intersections of Theater, Performance, and Philosophy*. Eds David Krasner and David Z. Saltz. Theater: Theory/Text/Performance. Ann Arbor: University of Michigan Press, 2006: 87–103.

—— "Live from Cyberspace, or, I Was Sitting at My Computer This Guy Appeared He Thought I Was a Bot." *Critical Theory and Performance*. Eds Janelle G. Reinelt and Joseph R. Roach. 2nd edn. Theater: Theory/Text/Performance. Ann Arbor: University of Michigan Press, 2007: 526–31.

—— *Liveness: Performance in a Mediatized Culture*. 1999, 2nd edn. London: Routledge, 2008.

Bachelard, Gaston. *The Poetics of Space*. 1957. Trans. Maria Jolas. Boston: Beacon, 1969.

Badiou, Alain. *Ethics: An Essay on the Understanding of Evil*. 1993. Trans. Peter Hallward. Radical Thinkers. 2nd edn. London: Verso, 2012.

Bailes, Sara Jane. *Performance Theatre and the Poetics of Failure: Forced Entertainment, Goat Island, Elevator Repair Service.* New York: Routledge, 2011.

Barba, Eugenio. *Beyond the Floating Islands.* 1st edn. New York: PAJ, 1986.

—— *The Paper Canoe: A Guide to Theatre Anthropology.* London: Routledge, 1995.

Barba, Eugenio and Nicola Savarese. *A Dictionary of Theatre Anthropology: The Secret Art of the Performer.* 1991. Trans. Richard Fowler. 2nd edn. London: Routledge, 2006.

Barbaras, Renaud. *Desire and Distance: Introduction to a Phenomenology of Perception.* 1996. Cultural Memory in the Present. Stanford: Stanford University Press, 2006.

—— *Merleau-Ponty.* Philo-Philosophes. Ed. Jean-Pierre Zarader. Paris: Ellipses, 1997.

—— "Perception and Movement: The End of the Metaphysical Approach." *Chiasms: Merleau-Ponty's Notion of Flesh.* Eds Fred Evans and Leonard Lawlor. SUNY Series in Contemporary Continental Philosophy. Albany: State University of New York Press, 2000: 77–87.

Barker, Howard. *The Bite of the Night: An Education.* Playscript. Vol. 115. London: John Calder, 1988.

Barker, Sarah A. "The Alexander Technique: An Acting Approach." *Theatre Topics,* 12.1 (2002): 35–48.

Barrault, Jean-Louis. *Reflections on the Theatre.* London: Rockliff, 1951.

Bassnett, Susan. "Perceptions of the Female Role: The ISTA Congress." *New Theatre Quarterly,* 3.11 (1987): 234–6.

Becker, Jonathan Kipp. "The Actor Architect of the Empty Space: A Study of the Pedagogical Approach of Jacques Lecoq." Master's Thesis. University of Akron, 1997.

Benjamin, Walter. "Little History of Photography." 1931. Trans. E.F.N. Jephcott and Kingsley Shorter. *The Work of Art in the Age of its Mechanical Reproducibility, and Other Writings on Media.* Eds Michael William Jennings, Brigid Doherty, and Thomas Y. Levin. Cambridge: Belknap Press of Harvard University Press, 2008: 274–98.

—— "The Work of Art in the Age of Its Mechanical Reproducibility." 1935. Trans. E.F.N. Jephcott and Harry Zohn. *The Work of Art in the Age of its Mechanical Reproducibility, and Other Writings on Media.* Eds Michael William Jennings, Brigid Doherty, and Thomas Y. Levin. Cambridge: Belknap Press of Harvard University Press, 2008: 19–55.

—— "The Work of Art in the Age of Mechanical Reproduction." 1936. Trans. Harry Zohn. *Illuminations.* Ed. Hannah Arendt. New York: Schocken, 1968: 217–51.

Bhabha, Homi. "Of Mimicry and Man: The Ambivalence of Colonial Discourse." *The Location of Culture.* London: Routledge, 1994: 85–92.

Bharucha, Rustom. "A Collision of Cultures: Some Western Interpretations of the Indian Theatre." *Asian Theatre Journal,* 1.1 (1984): 1–20.

—— *Theatre and the World: Essays on Performance and Politics of Culture.* New Delhi: Manohar, 1990.

Birch, Anna and Joanne Tompkins, eds, *Performing Site-Specific Theatre: Politics, Place, Practice*. Basingstoke: Palgrave Macmillan, 2012.

Bishop, Claire. "Antagonism and Relational Aesthetics." *October*, 110. Fall (2004): 51–79.

—— *Artificial Hells: Participatory Art and the Politics of Spectatorship*. London: Verso, 2012.

—— "The Social Turn: Collaboration and its Discontents." *Artforum*, 44. February (2006): 178–83.

Blair, Rhonda and John Lutterbie. "Introduction: Journal of Dramatic Theory and Criticism's Special Section on Cognitive Studies, Theatre, and Performance." *Journal of Dramatic Theory and Criticism*, XXV.2 (2011): 63–70.

Blanchard, Pascal. "Exhibit B: Ce spectacle n'est pas raciste, c'est l'inverse." http://tempsreel.nouvelobs.com/culture/20141128.OBS6468/exhibit-b-ce-spectacle-n-est-pas-raciste-c-est-l-inverse.html, November 29, 2014. Accessed December 14, 2015.

Blau, Herbert. "Universals of Performance: Or, Amortizing Play." *SubStance*, 11.4 (1983): 140–61.

Bleeker, Maaike, Jon Foley Sherman, and Eirini Nedelkopoulou, eds, *Performance and Phenomenology: Traditions and Transformations*. London: Routledge, 2015.

Blom, Barend. "Colonial Aphasia in Museums in the Netherlands." University of Amsterdam, 2014. Unpublished thesis.

Bogart, Anne and Tina Landau. *The Viewpoints Book: A Practical Guide to Viewpoints and Composition*. 1st edn. New York: TCG, 2005.

Boucris, Luc. *L'espace En Scène*. Paris: Librairie Théâtrale, 1993.

Bourhis, Morgane. "Jacques Lecoq, Les Lois Du Mouvement." *Registres*, 4 (1999): 21–32.

Brandl-Risi, Bettina. "The New Virtuosity: Outperforming and Imperfection on the German Stage." *Theater*, 37.1 (2007): 9–37.

Brandon, James R. "A New World: Asian Theatre in the West Today." *TDR: The Drama Review*, 33.2 (1989): 25–50.

Brantley, Ben. "Brother, Can You Spare My Sanity?" Review. *New York Times*, June 22, 2013. www.nytimes.com/2013/06/22/theater/reviews/amanda-plummer-and-brad-dourif-in-tennessee-williams-rarity.html. Accessed December 14, 2015.

—— "London Theater Journal: Memory Plays." *ArtsBeat*. http://artsbeat.blogs.nytimes.com/2013/03/05/london-theater-journal-memory-plays, March 5, 2013. Accessed December 14, 2015.

Briginshaw, Valerie A. *Dance, Space, and Subjectivity*. New York; Basingstoke: Palgrave, 2001.

Burke, J. Patrick. "Listening at the Abyss." *Ontology and Alterity in Merleau-Ponty*. Eds Galen A. Johnson and Michael B. Smith. Northwestern University Studies in Phenomenology and Existential Philosophy. Evanston: Northwestern University Press, 1990: 81–97.

—— "The Moral Power of the Face of the Child." *Merleau-Ponty's Later Works and Their Practical Implications*. Ed. Duane H. Davis. New York: Humanity, 2001: 289–308.

Burton, Tara Isabella. "Immersive Theatre and the Anxiety of Choice." Review. *The New Statesman*, March 16, 2013: 10–12. www.newstatesman.com/culture/2013/03/immersive-theatre-and-anxiety-choice. Accessed December 14, 2015.

—— "What Fourth Wall? On 'Sleep No More,' Punchdrunk Theatre Company's Reimagining of 'Macbeth.'" *Los Angeles Review of Books* (2013). http://lareviewofbooks.org/essay/what-fourth-wall. Accessed December 14, 2015.

Butler, Judith. *Gender Trouble: Feminism and the Subversion of Identity.* 10th anniversary edn. London: Routledge, 1999.

—— "Sexual Ideology and Phenomenological Description: A Feminist Critique of Merleau-Ponty's *Phenomenology of Perception.*" *The Thinking Muse: Feminism and Modern French Philosophy.* Eds Jeffner Allen and Iris Marion Young. Bloomington: Indiana University Press, 1989: 85–99.

Caillois, Roger. *Le Mimétisme Animal.* Aventure de la Vie, 1. Paris: Hachette, 1963.

—— *Le Mythe et L'homme.* 1938. Collection Folio/Essais. Vol. 56. Paris: Gallimard, 1987.

—— *Les Jeux et Les Hommes: Le Masque et Le Vertige.* 1958. Éd revue et augm. Paris: Gallimard, 1967.

—— *Man, Play, and Games.* 1958. New York: Free Press of Glencoe, 1961.

—— "Mimicry and Legendary Psychasthenia." *October,* 31. Winter (1984): 16–32.

Camp, Pannill. "The Stage Struck out of the World: Theatricality and Husserl's Phenomenology of Theatre, 1905–1918." *Performance and Phenomenology: Traditions and Transformations.* Eds Maaike Bleeker, Jon Foley Sherman, and Eirini Nedelkopoulou. London: Routledge, 2015: 20–34.

Carlson, Marvin A. *Places of Performance: The Semiotics of Theatre Architecture.* Ithaca: Cornell University Press, 1989.

Carvajal, Doreen. "On Display, and on a Hot Seat." *New York Times,* November 26, 2014. www.nytimes.com/2014/11/26/arts/exhibit-b-a-work-about-human-zoos-stirs-protests.html#. Accessed December 14, 2015.

Casey, Edward S. *The Fate of Place: A Philosophical History.* Berkeley: University of California Press, 1997.

Caygill, Howard. *The Kant Dictionary.* Oxford: Blackwell, 1995.

Chamberlain, Franc. "Foreword." *Negotiating Cultures: Eugenio Barba and the Intercultural Debate.* Ed. Ian Watson. Manchester: Manchester University Press, 2002: xi–xix.

—— "Theatre Anthropology: Definitions and Doubts." *Theatre Theories from Plato to Virtual Reality.* Ed. Anthony Frost. Norwich: Pen & Inc, 2000: 171–94.

Charbonnier, Georges, ed. *Le Monologue Du Peintre.* 2 vols. Paris: René Juillard, 1959.

Chatzichristodoulou, Maria and Rachel Zerihan. "Introduction." *Intimacy Across Visceral and Digital Performance.* Eds Maria Chatzichristodoulou and Rachel Zerihan. Basingstoke: Palgrave Macmillan, 2012: 1–11.

Chikha, Chokri Ben and Karel Arnaut. "Staging/Caging 'Otherness' in the Postcolony: Spectres of the Human Zoo." *Critical Arts: South-North Cultural and Media Studies,* 27.6 (2013): 661–83.

Chin, Daryl. "Interculturalism, Postmodernism, Pluralism." *Performing Arts Journal,* 11.3 (1989): 163–75.

Cook, Amy. "Interplay: The Method and Potential of a Cognitive Scientific Approach to Theatre." *Theatre Journal,* 59.4 (2007): 579–94.

Crary, Jonathan. *Suspensions of Perception: Attention, Spectacle, and Modern Culture.* Cambridge: MIT Press, 1999.

Creative, Rob Bliss. "10 Hours of Walking in NYC as a Woman." YouTube, October 28, 2014. www.youtube.com/watch?v=b1XGPvbWn0A. Accessed December 14, 2015.

Cull, Laura. *Theatres of Immanence: Deleuze and the Ethics of Performance.* Basingstoke: Palgrave Macmillan, 2012.

de Certeau, Michel. *The Practice of Everyday Life.* 1980. Trans. Steven Rendall. Berkeley: University of California Press, 1988.

Descartes, René. *The Philosophical Works of Descartes.* Trans. Elizabeth Sanderson Haldane and G.R.T. Ross. 2nd edn. Vol. 1. Mineola: Dover, 1955.

Dillon, M.C. "The Ethics of Particularity." *The Ontology of Becoming and the Ethics of Particularity.* Ed. Lawrence Hass. Series in Continental Thought. Athens: Ohio University Press, 2012: 99–200.

Diprose, Rosalyn. *Corporeal Generosity: On Giving with Nietzsche, Merleau-Ponty, and Levinas.* SUNY Series in Gender Theory. Albany: State University of New York Press, 2002.

DiSanto, Dody. Personal Interview, October 27, 2007.

Druick, Douglas W., Peter Zegers, Britt Salvesen, Kristin Hoermann Lister, and Mary C. Weaver. *Van Gogh and Gauguin: The Studio of the South.* New York: Thames & Hudson, 2001.

Ebony, David. "Protests Turn Violent over Controversial *Exhibit B* Performance in Paris." http://news.artnet.com/in-brief/protests-turn-violent-over-controversial-exhibit-b-performance-in-paris-184990, December 1, 2014. Accessed December 14, 2015.

Eldredge, Sears A. *Mask Improvisation for Actor Training and Performance.* Evanston: Northwestern University Press, 1996.

Erickson, Jon. "The Body as the Object of Modern Performance." *Journal of Dramatic Theory and Criticism,* 5.1 (1990): 231–45.

—— "Presence." *Staging Philosophy: Intersections of Theater, Performance, and Philosophy.* Eds David Krasner and David Z. Saltz. Theater: Theory/Text/Performance. Ann Arbor: University of Michigan Press, 2006: 142–59.

—— "Tension/Release and the Production of Time in Performance." *Archaeologies of Presence: Art, Performance and the Persistence of Being.* Eds Gabriella Giannachi, Nick Kaye, and Michael Shanks. London: Routledge, 2012: 82–99.

Fanon, Frantz. *Black Skin, White Masks.* 1952. Trans. Charles Lam Markmann. New York: Grove, 1967.

Farcy, Gérard-Denis and René Prédal, eds, *Brûler les planches, Crever l'écran: La présence de l'acteur.* Saint-Jean-de-Védas: Éditions L'Entretemps, 2001.

Felman, Shoshana and Dori Laub. *Testimony: Crises of Witnessing in Literature, Psychoanalysis, and History.* New York: Routledge, 1991.

Felner, Mira. *Apostles of Silence: The Modern French Mimes.* Rutherford: Fairleigh Dickinson University Press, 1985.

Féral, Josette. "Performance and Theatricality: The Subject Demystified." *Modern Drama,* 25 (1982): 170–91.

—— "Theatricality: The Specificity of Theatrical Language." *SubStance,* 31.2 & 3 (2002): 94–108.

Fischer-Lichte, Erika. "Appearing as Embodied Mind: Defining a Weak, a Strong and a Radical Concept of Presence." *Archaeologies of Presence: Art, Performance and the Persistence of Being*. Eds Gabriella Giannachi, Nick Kaye, and Michael Shanks. London: Routledge, 2012: 103–18.

—— *The Transformative Power of Performance: A New Aesthetics*. 2004. Trans. Saskya Iris Jain. London: Routledge, 2008.

Foley Sherman, Jon. "Space and Mimesis." *The Routledge Companion to Jacques Lecoq*. Eds Mark Evans and Rick Kemp. London: Routledge, 2016.

Foster, Susan Leigh. "Choreographing Empathy." *Topoi*, 24 (2005): 81–91.

—— *Choreographing Empathy: Kinesthesia in Performance*. London: Routledge, 2011.

—— "The Earth Shaken Twice Wonderfully." *Considering Calamity: Methods for Performance Research*. Eds Linda Ben-Zvi and Tracy C. Davis. Tel Aviv: Assaph Books; Faculty of the Arts, Tel Aviv University, 2007.

—— "Kinesthetic Empathies and the Politics of Compassion." *Critical Theory and Performance*. Eds Janelle G. Reinelt and Joseph R. Roach. 2nd edn. Theater: Theory/Text/Performance. Ann Arbor: University of Michigan Press, 2007: 245–58.

—— "Movement's Contagion: The Kinesthetic Impact of Performance." *The Cambridge Companion to Performance Studies*. Ed. Tracy C. Davis. Cambridge: Cambridge University Press, 2008: 46–59.

French, Alex. "The Impresario of Smut." *New York Magazine*, November 23, 2008. http://nymag.com/nightlife/features/52453. Accessed December 14, 2015.

Freud, Sigmund. "Remembering, Repeating, Working-Through." *The Complete Works of Sigmund Freud*. Ed. James Strachey. Vol. 12. London: Hogarth, 1914.

Fried, Michael. "Art and Objecthood." 1967. *Minimal Art: A Critical Anthology*. Ed. Gregory Battock. New York: Dutton, 1968: 116–47.

Frost, Anthony and Ralph Yarrow. *Improvisation in Drama*. 1990, 2nd edn. Basingstoke: Palgrave Macmillan, 2007.

Gallagher, Shaun. "Bodily Self-Awareness and Object Perception." *International Journal of Interdisciplinary Studies*, 7 (2003): 53–68.

Gallese, Vittorio, Christian Keysers, and Giacomo Rizzolatti. "A Unifying View of the Basis of Social Cognition." *Trends in Cognitive Science*, 8.9 (2004): 396–403.

Gardner, Lyn. "Exhibit B—Facing the Appalling Reality of Europe's Colonial Past." Review. www.theguardian.com/stage/2014/aug/12/exhibit-b-edinburgh-festival-2014-review, August 12, 2014. Accessed December 14, 2015.

Garner, Stanton B. *Bodied Spaces: Phenomenology and Performance in Contemporary Drama*. Ithaca: Cornell University Press, 1994.

—— "Theater and Phenomenology." *Dégres: Revue de synthèse à orientation sémiologiques*, 107–8 (2001): B1–17.

Geertz, Clifford. *Interpretation of Cultures: Selected Essays*. New York: Basic Books, 1977.

Giannachi, Gabriella. "Environmental Presence." *Archaeologies of Presence: Art, Performance and the Persistence of Being*. Eds Gabriella Giannachi, Nick Kaye, and Michael Shanks. London: Routledge, 2012: 50–63.

Giannachi, Gabriella and Nick Kaye. *Performing Presence: Between the Live and the Simulated*. Manchester: Manchester University Press, 2011.

—— "Presence." *Performance Research*, 11.3 (2006): 103–5. http://dx.doi.org/10.1080/13528160701276691. Accessed December 14, 2015.

Giannachi, Gabriella, Nick Kaye, and Michael Shanks, eds, *Archaeologies of Presence: Art, Performance, and the Persistence of Being*. London: Routledge, 2012.

Gibson, James Jerome. *The Ecological Approach to Visual Perception*. 1979. Hillsdale: Lawrence Erlbaum Associates, 1986.

Gide, André. *Les Nourritures Terrestres*. 1897, 31st edn. Paris: Gallimard, 1921.

Gilligan, Carol. *In a Different Voice: Psychological Theory and Women's Development*. Cambridge: Harvard University Press, 1982.

Goffman, Erving. *Relations in Public: Microstudies of the Public Order*. New York: Basic Books, 1971.

Goodall, Jane. *Stage Presence*. London: Routledge, 2008.

Grehan, Helena. *Performance, Ethics and Spectatorship in a Global Age*. Studies in International Performance. Basingstoke: Palgrave Macmillan, 2009.

Grau, Oliver. *Virtual Art: From Illusion to Immersion*. Trans. Gloria Custance. Leonardo Book Series. Cambridge: MIT Press, 2003.

Grene, Marjorie. "Merleau-Ponty and the Renewal of Ontology." *Review of Metaphysics*, 29.4 (1976): 605–25.

Grosz, Elizabeth. *Architecture from the Outside: Essays on Virtual and Real Space*. Cambridge: MIT Press, 2001.

—— "Merleau-Ponty and Irigaray in the Flesh." *Thesis Eleven*, 36 (1993): 37–59.

—— *Space, Time, and Perversion: Essays on the Politics of Bodies*. New York: Routledge, 1995.

—— *Volatile Bodies: Toward a Corporeal Feminism*. Theories of Representation and Difference. Bloomington: Indiana University Press, 1994.

Halberstam, Judith. *The Queer Art of Failure*. Durham: Duke University Press, 2011.

Hall, Edward T. *The Hidden Dimension*, Anchor Books edn. Garden City: Doubleday & Co., 1969.

Hallward, Peter. "Staging Equality." *Jacques Rancière: History, Politics, Aesthetics*. Eds Gabriel Rockhill and Philip Watts. Durham: Duke University Press, 2009: 140–57.

Halsema, Annemie. "Phenomenology in the Feminine: Irigaray's Relationship to Merleau-Ponty." *Intertwinings: Interdisciplinary Encounters with Merleau-Ponty*. Ed. Gail Weiss. Albany: State University of New York Press, 2008: 63–84.

Hamington, Maurice. *Embodied Care: Jane Addams, Maurice Merleau-Ponty, and Feminist Ethics*. Urbana: University of Illinois Press, 2004.

—— "Resources for Feminist Care Ethics in Merleau-Ponty's Phenomenology of the Body." *Intertwinings: Interdisciplinary Encounters with Merleau-Ponty*. Ed. Gail Weiss. Albany: State University of New York Press, 2008: 203–20.

Hamrick, William S. "Maurice Merleau-Ponty: 'Ethics' as an Ambiguous, Embodied Logos." *Phenomenological Approaches to Moral Philosophy*. Eds John J. Drummond and Lester E. Embree. Dodrecht: Kluwer, 2002: 289–310.

Hegel, Georg Wilhelm Friedrich. *Phenomenology of Spirit*. 1807. Trans. Arnold V. Miller. Oxford: Clarendon Press, 1977.

Held, Virginia. *The Ethics of Care: Personal, Political, and Global*. Oxford: Oxford University Press, 2006.

—— "Liberalism and the Ethics of Care." *On Feminist Ethics and Politics*. Ed. Claudia Card. Lawrence: University Press of Kansas, 1999: 288–309.

Hertz, Erich. "Rethinking Aura through Temporality: Benjamin and 'Industrial' Otherness." *Benjamin's Blindspot: Walter Benjamin and the Premature Death of Aura*. Ed. Lise Patt. Vol. 5. Santa Monica: Institute of Cultural Inquiry, 2001: 100–8.

Hill, Leslie and Helen Paris, eds, *Performance and Place*. Basingstoke: Palgrave Macmillan, 2006.

—— *Performing Proximity: Curious Intimacies*. Basingstoke: Palgrave Macmillan, 2014.

Holland, Nancy J. "In a Different Ch[i]asm: A Feminist Rereading of Merleau-Ponty on Sexuality." *Rereading Merleau-Ponty: Essays Beyond the Continental-Analytic Divide*. Eds Lawrence Hass and Dorothea Olkowski. Amherst: Humanity, 2000: 315–37.

hooks, bell. *Outlaw Culture: Resisting Representations*. New York: Routledge, 1994.

Husserl, Edmund. *Analyses Concerning Passive and Active Synthesis: Lectures on Transcendental Logic*. Trans. Anthony J. Steinbock. Dordrecht: Kluwer, 2001.

—— *Ideas Pertaining to a Pure Phenomenology and to a Phenomenological Philosophy*. 1913. Collected Works/Edmund Husserl. Ed. Edmund Husserl. Vol. 3. 3 vols. The Hague: M. Nijhoff, 1982.

Irigaray, Luce. *An Ethics of Sexual Difference*. 1984. Ithaca: Cornell University Press, 1993.

—— *This Sex Which Is Not One*. Ithaca: Cornell University Press, 1985.

Issacharoff, Michael. "Space and Reference in Drama." *Poetics Today*, 2.3 (1981): 211–24.

Jaeger, Suzanne M. "Embodiment and Presence: The Ontology of Presence Reconsidered." *Staging Philosophy: Intersections of Theater, Performance, and Philosophy*. Eds David Krasner and David Z. Saltz. Theater: Theory/Text/Performance. Ann Arbor: University of Michigan Press, 2006: 122–41.

Jammer, Max. *Concepts of Space: The History of Theories of Space in Physics*. 3rd enlarged edn. New York: Dover, 1993.

Jenkins, Tiffany. *Contesting Human Remains in Museum Collections: The Crisis of Cultural Authority*. London: Routledge, 2011.

—— "Exhibit B: A Guilty Pleasure." www.spiked-online.com/newsite/article/iexhibit-b-i-a-guilty-pleasure/15717#.VTLXUWZJuYl, September 2, 2014. Accessed December 14, 2015.

Johnson, Greg. "Merleau-Ponty, Reciprocity, and the Reversibility of Perspectives." *Intertwinings: Interdisciplinary Encounters with Merleau-Ponty*. Ed. Gail Weiss. Albany: State University of New York Press, 2008: 169–88.

Jones, Amelia. *Body Art/Performing the Subject*. Minneapolis: University of Minnesota Press, 1998.

Jousse, Marcel. *L'Anthropologie du Geste*. Vol. 1. Paris: Gallimard, 1974.

Kaprow, Allan. *Essays on the Blurring of Art and Life*. Expanded pbk edn. Berkeley: University of California Press, 2003.

Kaye, Nick. *Multi-Media: Video–Installation–Performance*. London: Routledge, 2007.

—— *Site-Specific Art: Performance, Place and Documentation*. London: Routledge, 2000.

Kennedy, Mark. "UK Theater Company Finds Success in Jaded New York." www. backstage.com/news/uk-theater-company-finds-success-in-jaded-new-york, July 15, 2011. Accessed December 14, 2015.

Kern, Stephen. *The Culture of Time and Space, 1880–1918: With a New Preface.* Cambridge: Harvard University Press, 2003.

Kissel, Howard. "Superstar Doesn't Shine in Show." Review. *Daily News,* April 20, 1999. www.nydailynews.com/archives/news/superstar-doesn-shine-show-article-1.645080. Accessed December 14, 2015.

Kittay, Eva. "Welfare, Dependency, and a Public Ethic of Care." *Social Justice,* 25.1 (1998): 123–45.

Knowles, Ric. *Reading the Material Theatre.* Theatre and Performance Theory. Cambridge: Cambridge University Press, 2004.

Koss, Juliet. "On the Limits of Empathy." *The Art Bulletin,* 88.1 (2006): 139–58.

Kozel, Susan. *Closer: Performance, Technologies, Phenomenology.* Cambridge: MIT Press, 2007.

Krasner, David. "Empathy and Theater." *Staging Philosophy: Intersections of Theater, Performance, and Philosophy.* Eds David Krasner and David Z. Saltz. Theater: Theory/Text/Performance. Ann Arbor: University of Michigan Press, 2006: 255–77.

Krueger, Anton. "Gazing at Exhibit A: Interview with Brett Bailey." *Liminalities: A Journal of Performance Studies,* 9.1 (2013): 1–13.

Lakoff, George and Mark Johnson. *Philosophy in the Flesh: The Embodied Mind and its Challenge to Western Thought.* New York: Basic Books, 1999.

Lecoq, Jacques. "Le corps et son espace." *Notes méthodologiques en architecture et urbanisme,* 3/4 (1974): 273–81.

—— Ed. *Le théâtre du geste: mimes et acteurs.* Bordas Spectacles. Paris: Bordas, 1987.

—— *Theatre of Movement and Gesture.* 1987. Ed. and trans. David Bradby. London: Routledge, 2006.

Lecoq, Jacques and Jean Perret. "Le geste sous le geste." *Marcel Jousse: du geste à la parole.* Travaux et Conférences du Centre de Sèvres, 1986.

Lecoq, Jacques, Jean-Gabriel Carasso, and Jean-Claude Lallias. *Le corps poétique: un enseignement de la création théâtrale.* Les Cahiers Théâtre/Education. Vol. 10. Arles: Actes Sud, 1997.

—— *The Moving Body: Teaching Creative Theatre.* 1997. Trans. David Bradby. London: Methuen Publishing, 2000.

Lecoq, Jacques, Jean-Noël Roy, Jean-Gabriel Carasso, and Jean-Claude Lallias. *Les deux voyages de Jacques Lecoq.* OnLine Productions, Scérén CNDP, 1999. Video.

Lefebvre, Henri. *The Production of Space.* 1974. Trans. Donald Nicholson-Smith. Oxford: Blackwell, 1991.

Letts, Quentin. "Why is Hollywood's sexiest man Bradley Cooper slumming it as a West End monster in *The Elephant Man*—just to prove he can act?" www. dailymail.co.uk/tvshowbiz/article-3106492/Why-Hollywood-s-sexiest-man-Bradley-Cooper-slumming-West-End-monster-Elephant-Man-just-prove-act-QUENTIN-LETTS.html, June 1, 2015. Accessed December 14, 2015.

Lévinas, Emmanuel. *Ethics and Infinity: Conversations with Philippe Nemo*. 1982. Trans. Richard a. Cohen. Pittsburgh: Duquesne University Press, 1985.

—— *Otherwise than Being, or Beyond Essence*. 1974. Trans. Alphonso Lingis. Pittsburgh: Duquesne University Press, 1998.

—— *Totality and Infinity: An Essay on Exteriority*. 1961. Trans. Alphonso Lingis. Pittsburgh: Duquesne University Press, 1998.

Lo, Jacqueline and Helen Gilbert. "Toward a Topology of Cross-Cultural Theatre Praxis." *TDR: The Drama Review*, 46.3 (2002): 31–53.

Love, Lauren. "Resisting the 'Organic': A Feminist Actor's Approach." *Acting (Re)Considered: Theories and Practices*. 1995. Ed. Phillip Zarrilli. 2nd edn. London: Routledge, 2002: 277–90.

Low, Setha M. and Denise Lawrence-Zúñiga. *The Anthropology of Space and Place: Locating Culture*. Blackwell Readers in Anthropology. Malden: Blackwell, 2003.

Lutterbie, John. "Phenomenology and the Dramaturgy of Space and Place." *Journal of Dramatic Theory and Criticism*, 16.1 (2001): 123–30.

Machon, Josephine. *Immersive Theatres: Intimacy and Immediacy in Contemporary Performance*. Basingstoke: Palgrave Macmillan, 2013.

Madison, Gary B. "The Ethics and Politics of the Flesh." *Merleau-Ponty's Later Works and Their Practical Implications: The Dehiscence of Responsibility*. Ed. Duane H. Davis. Amherst: Humanity, 2001: 161–85.

Mallgrave, Harry Francis and Eleftherios Ikonomou. "Introduction." *Empathy, Form, and Space: Problems in German Aesthetics, 1873–1893*. Eds Harry Francis Mallgrave and Eleftherios Ikonomou. Texts & Documents. Santa Monica: Getty Center for the History of Art and the Humanities, 1994: 1–85.

Manning, Susan. "Looking from a Different Place: Gay Spectatorship of American Modern Dance." *Dancing Desires: Choreographing Sexualities On and Off the Stage*. Ed. Jane C. Desmond. Madison: University of Wisconsin Press, 2001: 403–13.

—— *Modern Dance, Negro Dance: Race in Motion*. Minneapolis: University of Minnesota Press, 2004.

Massey, Doreen. *For Space*. London; Thousand Oaks: Sage, 2005.

Mauss, Marcel. "Techniques of the Body." 1935. *Economy and Society*, 2.1 (1973): 70–88.

McAuley, Gay. *Space in Performance: Making Meaning in the Theatre*. Ann Arbor: University of Michigan Press, 1999.

McConachie, Bruce. "Falsifiable Theories for Theatre and Performance Studies." *Theatre Journal*, 59.4 (2007): 553–77.

McLane, Janice. "The Boundaries of a Victim-Life." *Interrogating Ethics: Embodying the Good in Merleau-Ponty*. Eds James Hatley, Janice McLane, and Christian Diehm. Pittsburgh: Duquesne University Press, 2006: 135–48.

McNutt, Marcia. "Editorial Retraction." *Science*, 348.6239 (2015): 1100. www.sciencemag.org/content/348/6239/1100.2. Accessed December 14, 2015.

Memela, Sandile. "Brett Bailey Must Choose—Respect Africa or Be Damned!" *thought leader*. www.thoughtleader.co.za/sandilememela/2014/09/26/brett-bailey-must-choose-respect-africa-or-be-damned, September 26, 2014. Accessed December 14, 2015.

Merleau-Ponty, Maurice. "The Child's Relation with Others." 1960. Trans. William Cobb. *The Primacy of Perception, and Other Essays on Phenomenological Psychology, the Philosophy of Art, History, and Politics*. Ed. James M. Edie. Northwestern University Studies in Phenomenology & Existential Philosophy. Evanston: Northwestern University Press, 1964: 96–155.

—— "The Concept of Nature, II." 1968. Trans. John Daniel Wild and James M. Edie. *In Praise of Philosophy and Other Essays*. Northwestern University Studies in Phenomenology & Existential Philosophy. Evanston: Northwestern University Press, 1988: 156–66.

—— "The Experience of Others." 1951–2. Trans. Fred Evans and Hugh J. Silverman. *Review of Existential Psychology*, 18 (1982): 33–63.

—— "Eye and Mind." 1961. Trans. Carleton Dallery. *The Primacy of Perception, and Other Essays on Phenomenological Psychology, the Philosophy of Art, History, and Politics*. Ed. James M. Edie. Northwestern University Studies in Phenomenology & Existential Philosophy. Evanston: Northwestern University Press, 1964.

—— *Le visible et l'invisible; Suivi de notes de travail*. 1964. Paris: Gallimard, 1979.

—— *Les relations avec autrui chez l'enfant*.1960. Paris: Centre de Documentation Universitaire, 1975.

—— *L'œil et l'esprit*. 1961. Paris: Gallimard, 1985.

—— "Man and Adversity—Discussion." 1952. Trans. Ted Toadvine. *The Merleau-Ponty Reader*. Eds Ted Toadvine and Leonard Lawlor. Evanston: Northwestern University Press, 2007.

—— *Merleau-Ponty à la Sorbonne: Résumé de cours 1949–1952*. Paris: Cynara, 1988.

—— *Phénoménologie de la perception*. 1945. Paris: Gallimard, 2006.

—— *Phenomenology of Perception*. 1945. Trans. Donald A. Landes. London: Routledge, 2012.

—— *The Prose of the World*. 1969. Trans. John O'Neill. Evanston: Northwestern University Press, 1973.

—— *Signes*. 1960. Folio/Essais. Paris: Gallimard, 2003.

—— *Signs*. 1960. Trans. Richard C. McCleary. Northwestern University Studies in Phenomenology & Existential Philosophy. Evanston: Northwestern University Press, 1964.

—— "An Unpublished Text by Maurice Merleau-Ponty: A Prospectus of His Work." 1962. Trans. Arleen B. Dallery. *The Primacy of Perception, and Other Essays on Phenomenological Psychology, the Philosophy of Art, History, and Politics*. Ed. James M. Edie. Northwestern University Studies in Phenomenology & Existential Philosophy. Evanston: Northwestern University Press, 1964: 3–11.

—— "Un inédit de Maurice Merleau-Ponty." *Revue de métaphysiques et de morale*, 4 (1962): 401–9.

—— *The Visible and the Invisible; Followed by Working Notes*. 1964. Trans. Alphonso Lingis. Northwestern University Studies in Phenomenology & Existential Philosophy. Evanston: Northwestern University Press, 1968.

—— *The World of Perception*. 1948. Trans. Oliver Davis. London: Routledge, 2008.

Molzahn, Laura. "Reagan Revisited." Review. *The Reader*, October 19, 2009, Performing Arts section.

Moran, Dermot. *Introduction to Phenomenology*. London: Routledge, 2000.

—— "The Problem of Empathy: Lipps, Scheler, Husserl and Stein." *Amor Amicitiae: On the Love That Is Friendship. Essays in Medieval Thought and Beyond in Honor of the Rev. Professor James McEvoy*. Eds Thomas A. Kelly and Phillip W. Rosemann. Leuven: Peeters, 2004: 269–312.

Morris, David. *The Sense of Space*. Albany: State University of New York Press, 2004.

Murray, Simon. *Jacques Lecoq*. Routledge Performance Practitioners. Ed. Franc Chamberlain. London: Routledge, 2003.

Myers, Sara. "Withdraw the Racist Exhibition 'Exhibit B—the Human Zoo' from Showing at the Barbican from 23rd–27th September." www.change.org/p/withdraw-the-racist-exhibition-exhibition-b-the-human-zoo, 2014. Online petition. Accessed December 14, 2015.

Noë, Alva. *Action in Perception*. Representation and Mind. Cambridge: MIT Press, 2004.

—— *Varieties of Presence*. Cambridge: Harvard University Press, 2012.

Nyirenda, Tamara, Rania Modi, Anne Moraa, Jay C. Shingirai Musunhe, Anna Modi, and Stephen Mwiya Simonde. "Exhibit B: Is the 'Human Zoo' Racist? The Performers Respond." www.theguardian.com/culture/2014/sep/05/exhibit-b-is-the-human-zoo-racist-the-performers-respond, September 5, 2014. Accessed December 14, 2015.

O'Mahony, John. "Edinburgh's Most Controversial Show: Exhibit B, a Human Zoo." www.theguardian.com/stage/2014/aug/11/-sp-exhibit-b-human-zoo-edinburgh-festivals-most-controversial, August 11, 2014. Accessed December 14, 2015.

Oliver, Kelly. *Subjectivity Without Subjects: From Abject Fathers to Desiring Mothers*. Lanham: Rowman & Littlefield, 1998.

—— *Witnessing: Beyond Recognition*. Minneapolis: University of Minnesota Press, 2001.

Oxford English Dictionary. 2nd edn. Oxford: Oxford University Press, 1992.

Paris, Helen. "Too Close for Comfort: One-to-One Performance." *Performance and Place*. Eds Leslie Hill and Helen Paris. Basingstoke: Palgrave Macmillan, 2006: 179–91.

Passow, Wilfried and R. Strauss. "The Analysis of Theatrical Performance: The State of the Art." *Poetics Today*, 2.3 (1981): 237–54.

Pavis, Patrice. "Underscore: The Shape of Things to Come." *Contemporary Theatre Review*, 6, pt 4 (1997): 37–61.

Pearson, Mike. *Site-Specific Performance*. Basingstoke: Palgrave Macmillan, 2010.

Pearson, Mike and Michael Shanks. *Theatre/Archaeology*. London: Routledge, 2001.

Perpich, Diane. "Moral Blind Spots and Ethical Appeals: A Response to Bernhard Waldenfels." *Interrogating Ethics: Embodying the Good in Merleau-Ponty*. Eds James Hatley, Janice McLane, and Christian Diehm. Pittsburgh: Duquesne University Press, 2006: 107–31.

Phelan, Peggy. *Unmarked: The Politics of Performance*. London: Routledge, 1993.

Piff, Paul K., Pia Dietza, Matthew Feinberg, Daniel M. Stancato, and Dacher Keltner. "Awe, the Small Self, and Prosocial Behavior." *Journal of Personality and Social Psychology*, 108.6 (2015): 883–99. www.apa.org/pubs/journals/releases/psp-pspi0000018.pdf. Accessed December 14, 2015.

Power, Cormac. *Presence in Play: A Critique of Theories of Presence in the Theatre.* Consciousness Literature & the Arts. Ed. Daniel Meyer-Dinkgräfe. Vol. 12. Amsterdam: Rodopi, 2008.

Pradier, Jean-Marie. "The Pre-Expressive Level: A Mechanist-Alchemist Concept." Trans. Sally Jane Norman. *Contemporary Theatre Review*, 6, pt 4 (1997): 7–23.

Prattki, Thomas. Personal Interview, 2008.

Rancière, Jacques. "Aesthetic Separation, Aesthetic Community." Trans. Gregory Elliott. *The Emancipated Spectator.* 2008. London: Verso, 2009: 51–82.

—— "The Emancipated Spectator." Trans. Gregory Elliott. *The Emancipated Spectator.* 2008. London: Verso, 2009: 1–24.

—— "The Ethical Turn of Aesthetics and Politics." Trans. Steven Corcoran. *Dissensus: On Politics and Aesthetics.* 2010. Ed. Steven Corcoran. London: Bloomsbury, 2014: 184–202.

—— "The Paradoxes of Political Art." Trans. Steven Corcoran. *Dissensus: On Politics and Aesthetics.* 2010. Ed. Steven Corcoran. London: Bloomsbury, 2014: 134–51.

—— *The Politics of Aesthetics.* 2000. Trans. Gabriel Rockhill. Revelations. London: Bloomsbury, 2013.

Rawlinson, Mary C. "The Contingency of Goodness." *Interrogating Ethics: Embodying the Good in Merleau-Ponty.* Eds James Hatley, Janice McLane, and Christian Diehm. Pittsburgh: Duquesne University Press, 2006: 65–90.

Raynova, Yvanka. "Maurice Merleau-Ponty's Turning Point and the Ethics of Responsibility." Trans. William Leon McBride. *Merleau-Ponty's Later Works and Their Practical Implications: The Dehiscence of Responsibility.* Ed. Duane H. Davis. Amherst: Humanity, 2001: 225–51.

Reason, Matthew. *Documentation, Disappearance and the Representation of Live Performance.* Basingstoke: Palgrave Macmillan, 2006.

Rehm, Rush. *The Play of Space: Spatial Transformation in Greek Tragedy.* Princeton: Princeton University Press, 2002.

Reynolds, Jack. *Merleau-Ponty and Derrida: Intertwining Embodiment and Alterity.* Series in Continental Thought. Vol. 32. Athens: Ohio University Press, 2004.

Richir, Marc. "The Meaning of Phenomenology in *The Visible and the Invisible.*" *Thesis Eleven*, 36 (1993): 60–81.

Richter, Gerhard. "Adorno and the Excessive Politics of Aura." *Benjamin's Blindspot: Walter Benjamin and the Premature Death of Aura.* Ed. Lise Patt. Vol. 5. Santa Monica: Institute of Cultural Inquiry, 2001: 25–36.

Ridout, Nicholas. "Mis-Spectatorship, or 'Redistributing the Sensible.'" *Archaeologies of Presence: Art, Performance and the Persistence of Being.* Eds Gabriella Giannachi, Nick Kaye, and Michael Shanks. London: Routledge, 2012: 172–82.

—— *Stage Fright, Animals, and Other Theatrical Problems.* Theatre and Performance Theory. Cambridge: Cambridge University Press, 2006.

Roach, Joseph R. "It." *Theatre Journal*, 56.4 (2004): 555–68.

—— *It.* Ann Arbor: University of Michigan Press, 2007.

Rothfield, Philipa. "Differentiating Phenomenology and Dance." *Topoi*, 24.1 (2005): 43–53.

Russon, John. "Embodiment and Responsibility: Merleau-Ponty and the Ontology of Nature." *Man and World*, 27 (1994): 291–308.

Sack, Robert David. *Conceptions of Space in Social Thought: A Geographic Perspective*. Minneapolis: University of Minnesota Press, 1980.

Savarese, Nicola. "Antonin Artaud Sees Balinese Theatre at the Paris Colonial Exposition." *TDR: The Drama Review*, 45.3 (2001): 51–77.

Schneider, Rebecca. "Archives: Performance Remains." *Performance Research*, 6.2 (2001): 100–8.

—— *Performing Remains: Art and War in Times of Theatrical Reenactment*. London: Routledge, 2011.

Scolnicov, Hanna. "Theatre Space, Theatrical Space, and the Theatrical Space Without." *The Theatrical Space*. Ed. James Redmond. Themes in Drama. Vol. 9. Cambridge: Cambridge University Press, 1987: 11–26.

Sheets-Johnstone, Maxine. *The Primacy of Movement*. Advances in Consciousness Research. Vol. 14. Amsterdam: John Benjamins, 1999.

Shevtsova, Maria. "Interculturalism, Aestheticism, Orientalism: Starting from Peter Brook's *Mahabarata*." *Theatre Research International*, 22.2 (1997): 98–104.

—— *Theatre and Cultural Interaction*. Sydney: Sydney Studies, 1993.

Shrubsall, Anthony. "Jos Houben: Understanding the Neutral Mask." *Jacques Lecoq and the British Theatre*. Eds Ralph Yarrow and Franc Chamberlain. Vol. 42. Routledge Harwood Contemporary Theatre Studies. London: Routledge, 2002: 99–111.

Silvestre, Agnès. "Punchdrunk and the Politics of Spectatorship." www.culturebot.org/2012/11/14997/punchdrunk-and-the-politics-of-spectatorship, November 14, 2012. Accessed December 14, 2015.

Slade, Hollie. "Meet Emursive, the Company Behind 'Sleep No More,' The Off-Broadway Production that's Been Sold out for Three Years." www.forbes.com/sites/hollieslade/2014/03/19/meet-emursive-the-company-behind-sleep-no-more-the-off-broadway-production-thats-been-sold-out-for-three-years, March 19, 2014. Accessed December 14, 2015.

Slote, Michael. *The Ethics of Care and Empathy*. London: Routledge, 2007.

Smith, Sid. "'Dance Better' Keeps Growing as it Goes Along." Review. *Chicago Tribune*, March 3, 2007.

States, Bert O. *Great Reckonings in Little Rooms: On the Phenomenology of Theater*. Berkeley: University of California Press, 1985.

—— "The Phenomenological Attitude." *Critical Theory and Performance*. Eds Janelle G. Reinelt and Joseph R. Roach. 2nd edn. Theater: Theory/Text/Performance. Ann Arbor: University of Michigan Press, 2007: 26–36.

Steinbock, Anthony J. "Merleau-Ponty's Concept of Depth." *Philosophy Today*, 31.4 (1987): 336–49.

Stewart, Nigel. "Actor as *Refusenik*: Theatre Anthropology, Semiotics and the Paradoxical Work of the Body." *Negotiating Cultures: Eugenio Barba and the Intercultural Debate*. Ed. Ian Watson. Manchester: Manchester University Press, 2002: 46–58.

Ströker, Elisabeth. *Investigations in Philosophy of Space*. Series in Continental Thought. Vol. 11. Athens: Ohio University Press, 1987.

Sulcas, Roslyn. "Suffering for Her Art, and Beckett." *New York Times*, September 28, 2014, sec. Arts: AR6. www.nytimes.com/2014/09/28/theater/lisa-dwan-performs-solo-at-bam-in-3-beckett-plays.html?_r=0. Accessed December 14, 2015.

Suvin, Darko. "Approach to Topoanalysis and to the Paradigmatics of Dramaturgic Space." *Poetics Today*, 8.2 (1987): 311–34.

Switzer, Robert. "Together in the Flesh: Ethics and Attunement in Hume and Merleau-Ponty." Trans. William Leon McBride. *Merleau-Ponty's Later Works and Their Practical Implications: The Dehiscence of Responsibility.* Ed. Duane H. Davis. Amherst: Humanity, 2001: 253–88.

Taussig, Michael T. *Mimesis and Alterity: A Particular History of the Senses.* New York: Routledge, 1993.

Taylor, Val. "Body in Mind: Exploring Pre-Expressivity." *Contemporary Theatre Review*, 7, pt 1 (1997): 1–10.

Third World Bunfight. *Third World Bunfight.* http://thirdworldbunfight.co.za/exhibit-b. Accessed December 14, 2015.

Tian, Min. "'Alienation-Effect' for Whom? Brecht's (Mis)Interpretation of the Classical Chinese Theatre." *Asian Theatre Journal*, 14.2 (1997): 200–22.

Tillis, Steve. "East, West, and World Theatre." *Asian Theatre Journal*, 20.1 (2003): 71–87.

Tompkins, Joanne. *Unsettling Space: Contestations in Contemporary Australian Theatre.* Studies in International Performance. Basingstoke: Palgrave Macmillan, 2006.

Trachtenberg, Alan. *Reading American Photographs: Images as History. Mathew Brady to Walker Evans.* 1st edn. New York: Hill and Wang, 1989.

Tronto, Joan. "An Ethic of Care." *Feminist Theory: A Philosophical Anthology.* 1993. Eds Ann E. Cudd and Robin O. Andreasen. Oxford: Blackwell, 2005: 251–63.

Tuan, Yi-fu. *Space and Place: The Perspective of Experience.* Minneapolis: University of Minnesota Press, 1977.

Turner, Fred. "The Universal Solvent: Meditations on the Marriage of World Cultures." *Interculturalism and Performance.* Eds Bonnie Marranca and Gautim Dasgupta. New York: PAJ, 1991.

Ubersfeld, Anne. *Lire le Théâtre II: l'École du Spectateur.* Paris: Belin Sup Lettres, 1981.

Vetlesen, Arne Johan. "Introducing an Ethics of Proximity." *Closeness: An Ethics.* Eds Harald Jodalen and Arne Johan Vetlesen. Oslo: Scandinavian University Press, 1997: 1–19.

Vischer, Robert. "On the Optical Sense of Form: A Contribution to Aesthetics." 1873. Trans. Harry Francis Mallgrave and Eleftherios Ikonomou. *Empathy, Form, and Space: Problems in German Aesthetics, 1873–1893.* Eds Harry Francis Mallgrave and Eleftherios Ikonomou. Texts & Documents. Santa Monica: Getty Center for the History of Art and the Humanities, 1994: 89–123.

Waldenfels, Bernhard. *Order in the Twilight.* 1987. Trans. Alexander Kozin and Tanja Stahler. Series in Continental Thought. Athens: Ohio University Press, 1996.

—— "The Paradox of Expression." Trans. Chris Nagel. *Chiasms: Merleau-Ponty's Notion of Flesh.* 1995. Eds Fred Evans and Leonard Lawlor. SUNY Series in Contemporary Continental Philosophy. Albany: State University of New York Press, 2000: 89–102.

—— *Phenomenology of the Alien: Basic Concepts*. 2006. Trans. Alexander Kozin and Tanja Stahler. Northwestern University Studies in Phenomenology & Existential Philosophy. Evanston: Northwestern University Press, 2011.

—— *The Question of the Other*. Hong Kong: The Chinese University Press, 2007.

—— "Réponse à l'autre: Éléments d'une phénoménologie responsive." Trans. Pascale Delhom. *Phénoménologie Française et Phénoménologie Allemande*. Eds Bernhard Waldenfels and Éliane Escoubas. Vol. 4. Cahiers de philosophie de Paris XII Val de Marne. Paris: L'Harmattan, 2000: 358–74.

—— "Responsivity of the Body: Traces of the Other in Merleau-Ponty's Theory of Body and Flesh." *Interrogating Ethics: Embodying the Good in Merleau-Ponty*. Eds James Hatley, Janice McLane, and Christian Diehm. Pittsburgh: Duquesne University Press, 2006: 91–106.

—— "Strangeness, Hospitality, and Enmity." Trans. Mark Gedney. *Philosophy and the Return of Violence: Studies from the Widening Gyre*. Eds Nathan Eckstrand and Christopher Yates. London: Continuum, 2011: 89–100.

Walsh, Talia. "The Developing Body: A Reading of Merleau-Ponty's Conception of Women in the Sorbonne Lectures." *Intertwinings: Interdisciplinary Encounters with Merleau-Ponty*. Ed. Gail Weiss. Albany: State University of New York Press, 2008: 45–59.

Watson, Ian. "Eastern and Western Influences on Performer Training at Eugenio Barba's Odin Teatret." *Asian Theatre Journal*, 5.1 (1988): 49–60.

—— "Introduction." *Negotiating Cultures: Eugenio Barba and the Intercultural Debate*. Ed. Ian Watson. Manchester: Manchester University Press, 2002: 1–17.

—— "Staging Theatre Anthropology." *Negotiating Cultures: Eugenio Barba and the Intercultural Debate*. Ed. Ian Watson. Manchester: Manchester University Press, 2002: 20–35.

—— "Training with Eugenio Barba: Acting Principles, the Pre-Expressive and 'Personal Temperature.'" *Twentieth Century Actor Training*. Ed. Alison Hodge. London: Routledge, 2000: 209–23.

Weber, Max. *The Theory of Social and Economic Organization*. 1922. Trans. Alexander Morell Henderson and Talcott Parsons. 1st American edn. New York: Oxford University Press, 1947.

Weber, Samuel and Alan Cholodenko. *Mass Mediauras: Form, Technics, Media*. Stanford: Stanford University Press, 1996.

White, Gareth. *Audience Participation in Theatre: Aesthetics of the Invitation*. Basingstoke: Palgrave Macmillan, 2013.

Wilcox, Dean. "Ambient Space in Twentieth-Century Theatre: The Space of Silence." *Modern Drama*, 46.4 (2003): 542–57.

Wiles, David. *A Short History of Western Performance Space*. New York: Cambridge University Press, 2003.

Willis, Emma. "Emancipated Spectatorship and Subjective Drift: Understanding the Work of the Spectator in Erik Ehn's *Soulographie*." *Theatre Journal*, 66.3 (2014): 385–403. https://muse.jhu.edu/login?auth=0&type=summary&url=/journals/theatre_journal/v066/66.3.willis.pdf. Accessed December 14, 2015.

Worthen, W.B. "'The Written Troubles of the Brain': *Sleep No More* and the Space of Character." *Theatre Journal*, 64.1 (2012): 79–97.

Wright, John. "The Masks of Jacques Lecoq." *Jacques Lecoq and the British Theatre*. Eds Ralph Yarrow and Franc Chamberlain. Vol. 42. Routledge Harwood Contemporary Theatre Studies. London; New York: Routledge, 2002: 71–85.

Wylie, John. "Depths and Folds: On Landscape and the Gazing Subject." *Environment and Planning D: Society and Space*, 24.4 (2006): 519–35.

Young, Harvey. *Embodying Black Experience: Stillness, Critical Memory, and the Black Body*. Ann Arbor: University of Michigan Press, 2010.

Young, Iris Marion. "Asymmetrical Reciprocity: On Moral Respect, Wonder, and Enlarged Thought." *Constellations*, 3.3 (1997): 340–63.

—— "Throwing Like a Girl: A Phenomenology of Feminine Body Comportment, Motility, and Spatiality." *The Thinking Muse: Feminism and Modern French Philosophy*. 1980. Eds Jeffner Allen and Iris Marion Young. Bloomington: Indiana University Press, 1989: 51–71.

—— "'Throwing Like a Girl': Twenty Years Later." *Body and Flesh: A Philosophical Reader*. Ed. Donn Welton. Malden: Blackwell, 1998: 286–90.

Zarrilli, Phillip B. "The Actor's Work on Attention, Awareness and Active Imagination: Between Phenomenology, Cognitive Science and Practices of Acting." *Performance and Phenomenology: Traditions and Transformations*. Eds Maaike Bleeker, Jon Foley Sherman, and Eirini Nedelkopoulou. London: Routledge, 2015.

—— "An Enactive Approach to Understanding Acting." *Theatre Journal*, 59.4 (2008): 635–47.

—— "For Whom Is the 'Invisible' Not Visible? Reflections on Representation in the Work of Eugenio Barba." *TDR: The Drama Review*, 32.1 (1988): 95–106.

—— "' ... Presence ...' as a Question and Emergent Possibility: A Case Study from the Performer's Perspective." *Archaeologies of Presence: Art, Performance and the Persistence of Being*. Eds Gabriella Giannachi, Nick Kaye, and Michael Shanks. London: Routledge, 2012: 119–52.

—— *Psychophysical Acting: An Intercultural Approach after Stanislavski*. London: Routledge, 2009.

—— "Senses and Silence in Actor Training and Performance." *The Senses in Performance*. Eds Sally Banes and André Lepecki. Worlds of Performance. New York; London: Routledge, 2007: xi, 216.

—— "Towards a Phenomenological Model of the Actor's Embodied Modes of Experience." *Theatre Journal*, 56.4 (2004): 653–66.

Zerihan, Rachel. *One to One Performance: Live Art Development Agency*, 2009. www.thisisliveart.co.uk/uploads/documents/SRG_Zerihan_reducedsize.pdf. Accessed December 14, 2015.

Index